RedHat and Centos

Precise

Version 7

Shiv Kumar Goyal

Preface

This book is my second attempt of writing book. This book is for system administrators or Linux enthusiast, who wants to learn or deploy Redhat/Centos but do not have time to read tons of books. This is book is excellent choice for preparing interview. I tried my level best to keep the text as precise as possible.

This book is specially prepared for practical implementation of Redhat. I hope it will help the administrators in deploying Redhat in the production environment.

Thanks

Shiv Kumar Goyal

Contents

Chapter 1

Introduction

Linux is UNIX like Operating system. Linux is an open source project started by Linus Torvalds in 1991. There are thousands of Linux distributions in the market, but broadly can be classified on their root distribution for example Centos, Oracle and Scientific Linux based on Redhat, Debian based distributions like Ubuntu, Mint etc. The prominent player in free Linux are Ubuntu, Debian, Fedora, Opensuse etc. Redhat and SUSE is major player in non- free enterprise Linux distribution. Redhat and SUSE is RPM package based distribution where as Debian based distribution are of DEB packaging.

Fedora and Redhat

Fedora is free distribution and community project sponsored by Redhat. Fedora is upstream for Redhat enterprise Linux. Fedora is test bed for new features, which may get incorporate in upcoming Redhat Linux version. Main difference between the Fedora Linux and Redhat Enterprise Linux is support and life cycle of the product. Redhat is commercially supported product whereas Fedora is community supported. Redhat Enterprise Linux has life cycle of few years and supported up to 10 years but in case of Fedora new release come out after every 6 months and gets update for 13 months only. Redhat provides service level agreements, certification of hardware and software, which is important for enterprise organization.

Oracle Linux, Centos Linux and Scientific Linux distributions are derived from the sources of Red Hat Enterprise Linux. Provides same software as Redhat but without support from Redhat.

Chapter 2

New Features in Redhat Enterprise Linux 7 Version

Redhat 7 has many new features compare to its predecessor version following are some of the main new features:-

1. Grub2
2. New installation GUI
3. Automatic partitioning gives more choices like LVM, BRTFS and standard partitioning.
4. **LVM Cache** provides option to use small fast block device such as SSD as cache device for large slower block device.
5. **Parallel NFS** pNFS is part of NFSv4.1 standard that allows clients access storage devices directly and in parallel.
6. XFS file system.
7. Kernel version 3.10
8. **Dynamic kernel patching** which empowers you to patch the kernel without rebooting
9. Swap memory compression
10. Non uniform memory access NUMA
11. Hardware Error Reporting Mechanism.
12. Linux containers with Docker format
13. **Systemd** is system and service manager for Linux and replaces **sysv** and **upstart**.
14. Pacemaker cluster manager
15. **Keepalived** as load balancer
16. **HAproxy** as reverse proxy

17. Precision time protocol
18. New firewalld dynamic firewall daemon
19. New Gnome 3 Desktop
20. ABRT - Automatic Bug Reporting Tool

Chapter 3

Installation

The common two ways to install Redhat are:-

1. Interactive
2. Automated i.e. Kickstart

Interactive method

Interactive method can be either Text based or GUI.

Kickstart

For Kickstart installation, we have to create a single file containing the answers to all the questions Redhat installation normally asks during interactive installation. Once the installation starts, no user intervention is required.

Steps to do Interactive installation

1. To start installation first download media from https://access.redhat.com/downloads.
2. Burn the downloaded ISO image file. Start the system with first boot device as DVDROM.
3. Once Installation menu comes, Select **Install Redhat Enterprise Linux 7.0**

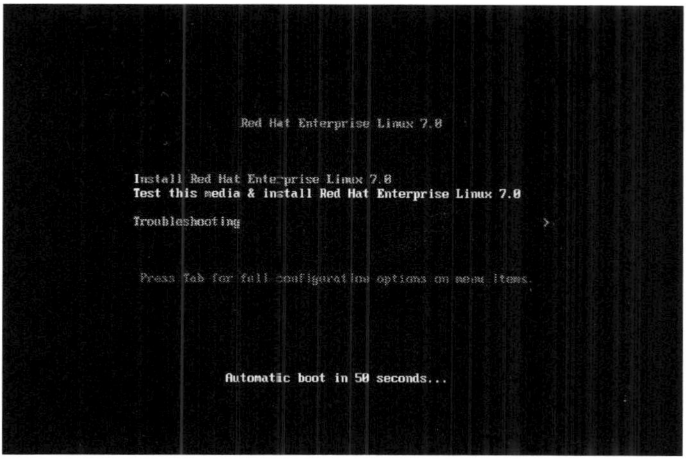

4. Select Language and press **continue**

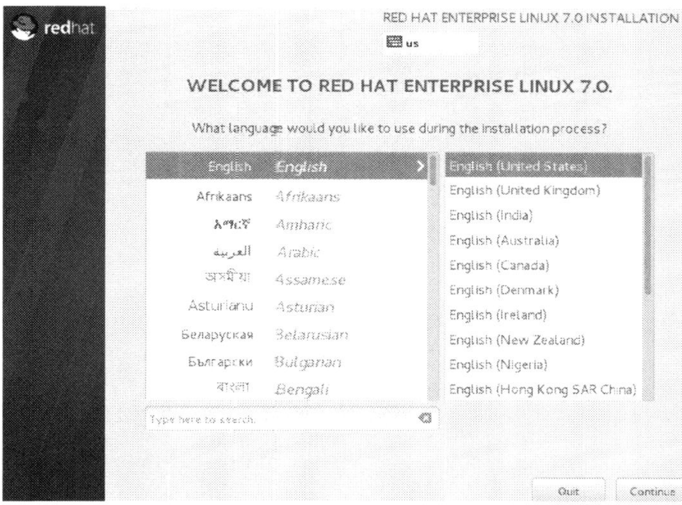

5. Select **Date and time**

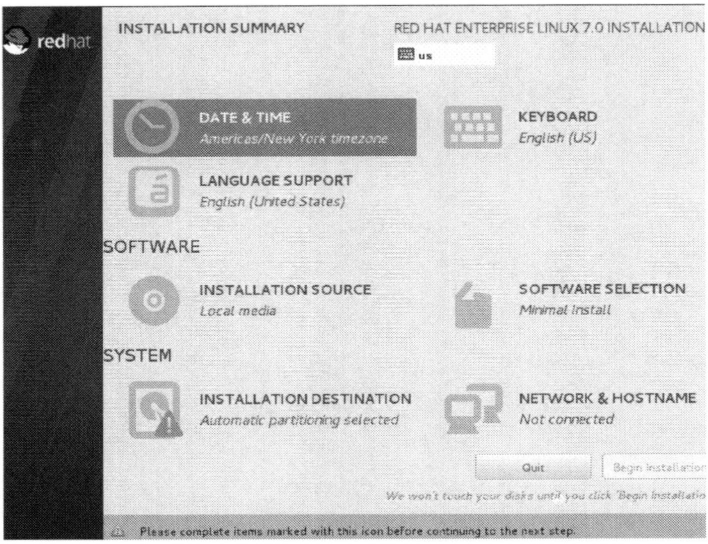

6. Select Time zone you are in and press **Done**

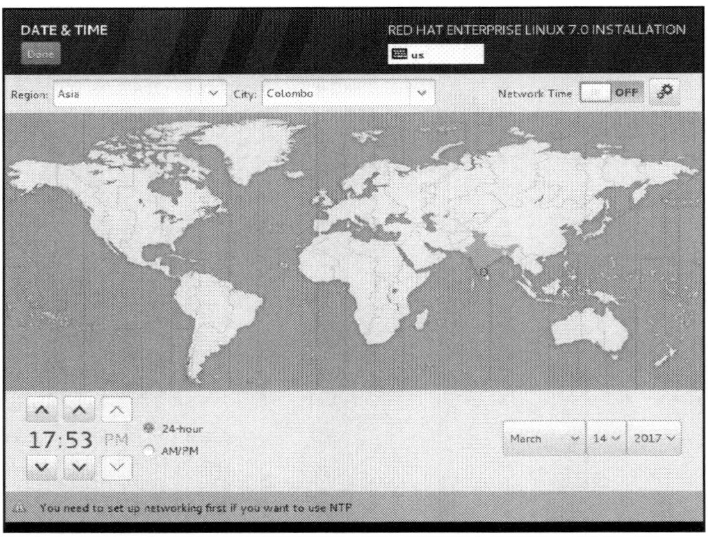

7. If required select and change the **Keyboard**.

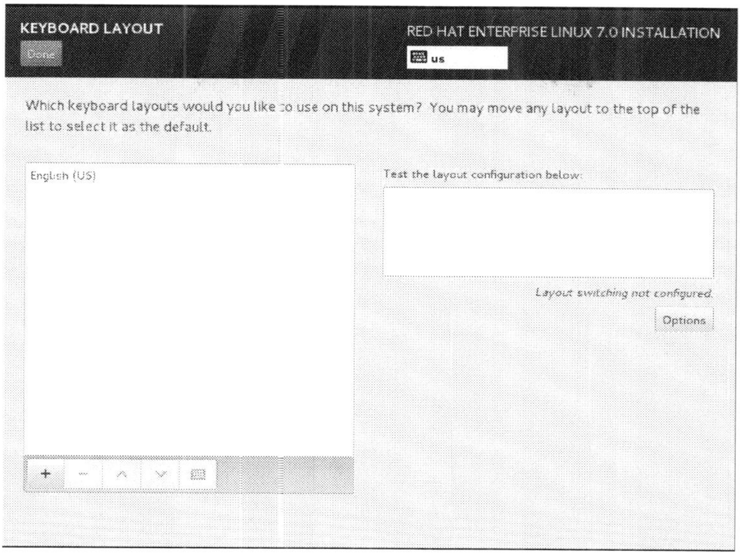

8. Select software selection and select required base environment. In my case, I selected server with GUI.

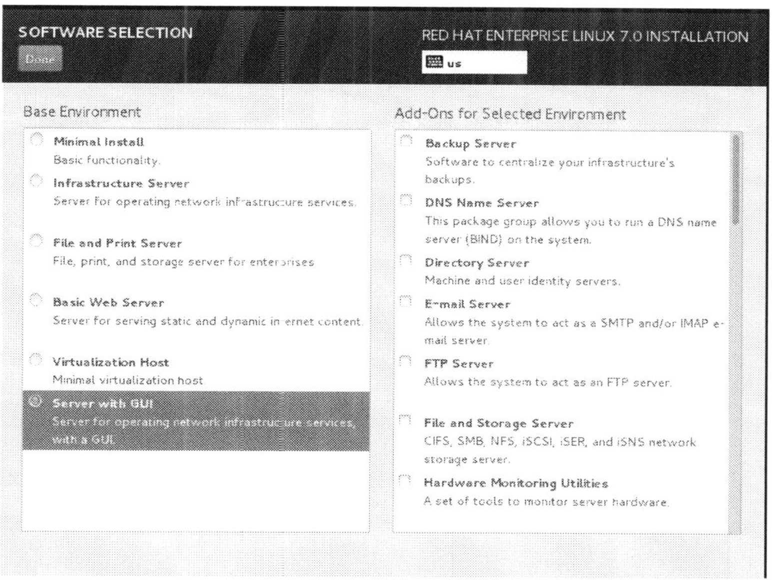

9. Click on configure network and hostname. First change Hostname

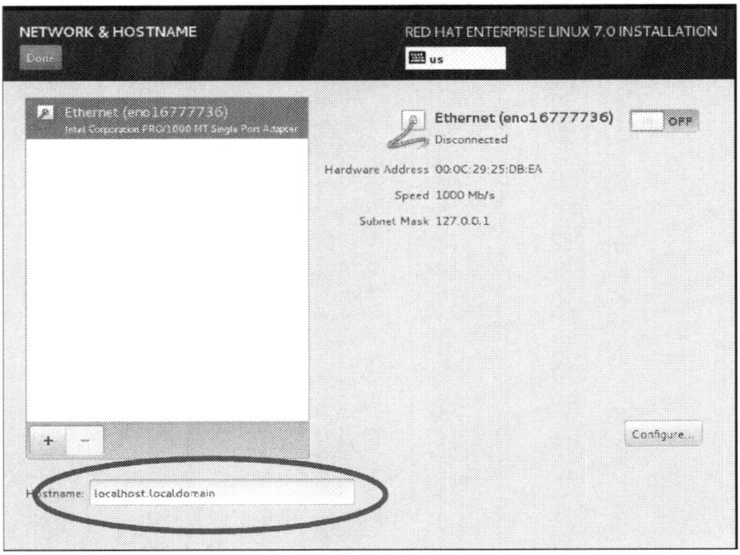

10. Select the network card and press **configure**

11. Select **IPv4 setting** tab > Select method as manual from drop down menu if you have static IP address otherwise select Automatic.

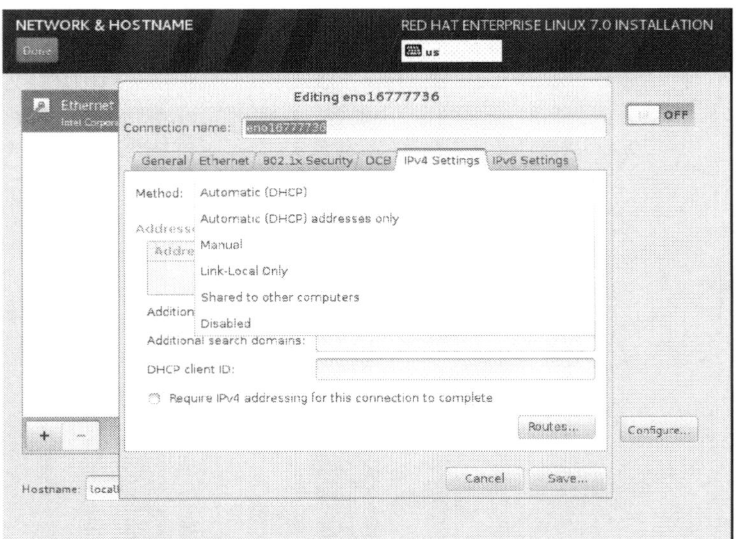

12. In case of static IP address, select add and provide IP address, Netmask, gateway and DNS server setting after that press **Save**. Now press General tab click **automatically connect to network when it is available**. After finishing press save and **done**

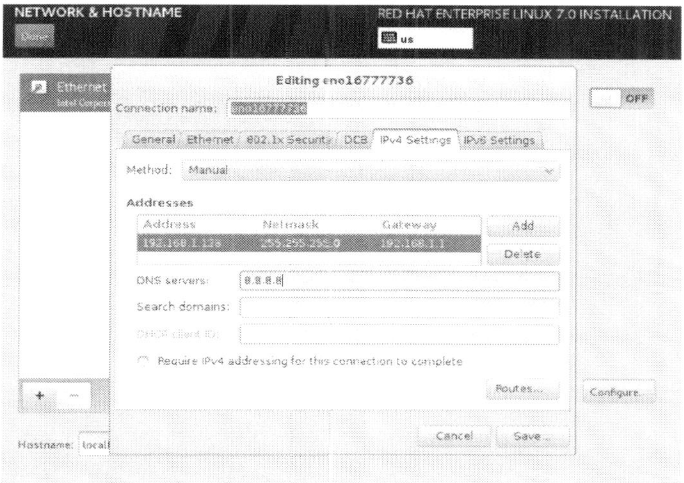

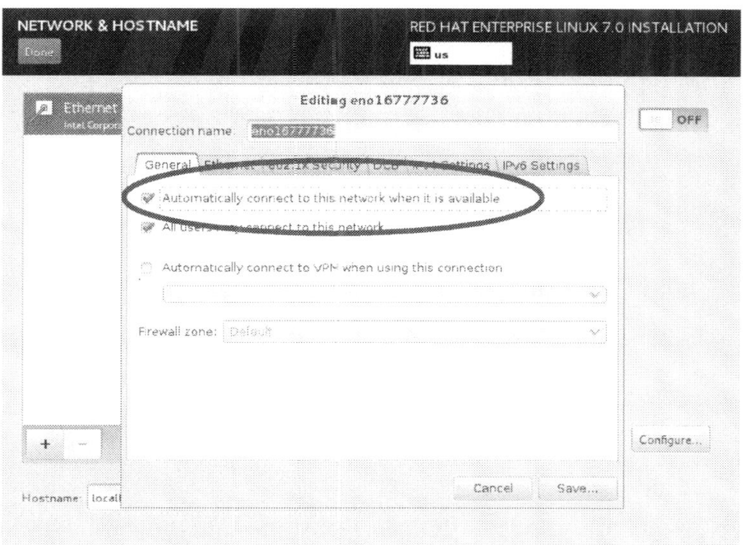

13. From main menu, select Installation destination. Either leave it to Automatic Configure partitioning or you can select **I will configure partitioning**, after finishing press **Begin Installation**

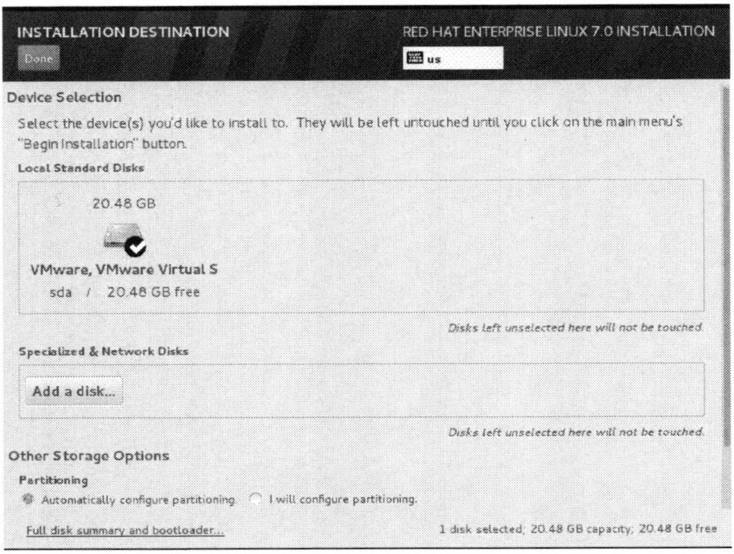

14. Select Root password and set root password.

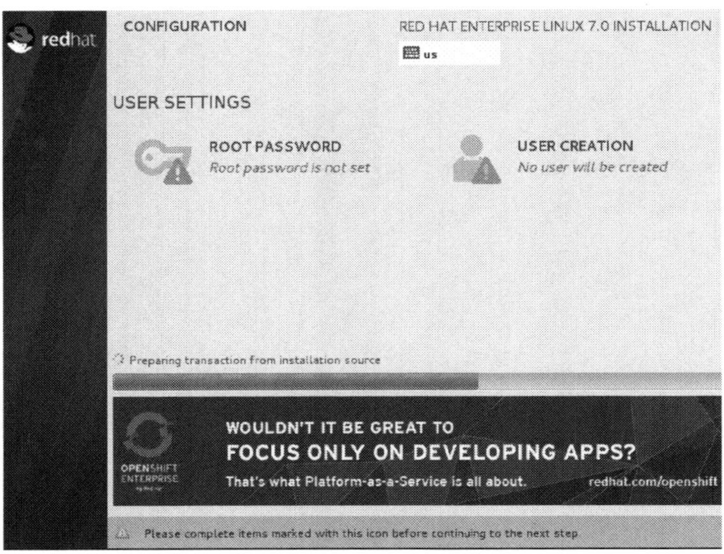

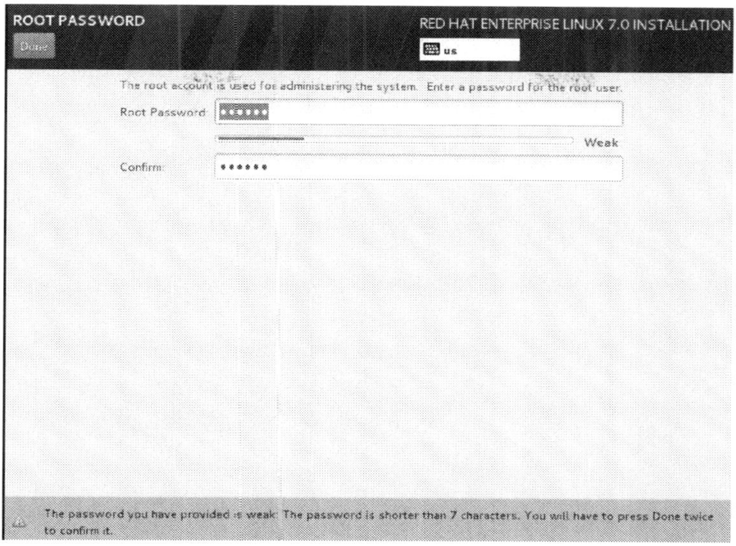

15. Once coping is finished. following screen will come

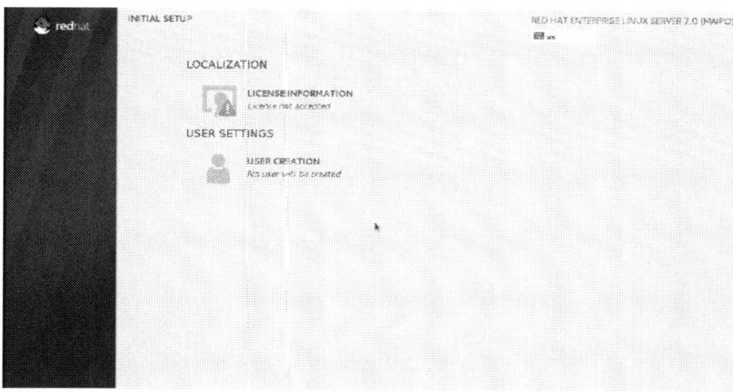

16. Press License information. Select I accept the license agreement and press **Done**

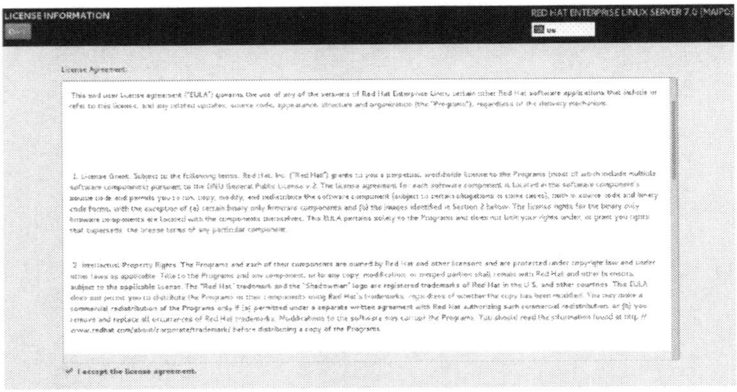

17. If you want, you can create additional user by pressing **User creation.**
18. On **kdump** screen press forward.

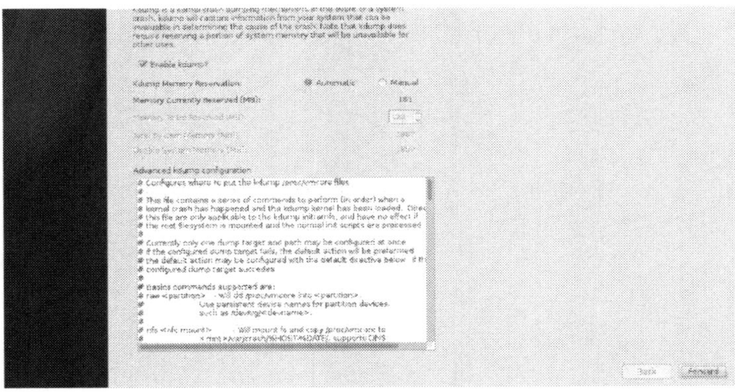

19. If you want to register to **Redhat network** (for updates and support) now, you can select **yes I'd like to register now**. Or you can select **No I prefer to register at later time**. For moment we will select **No I prefer to register at later time** and press **finish**

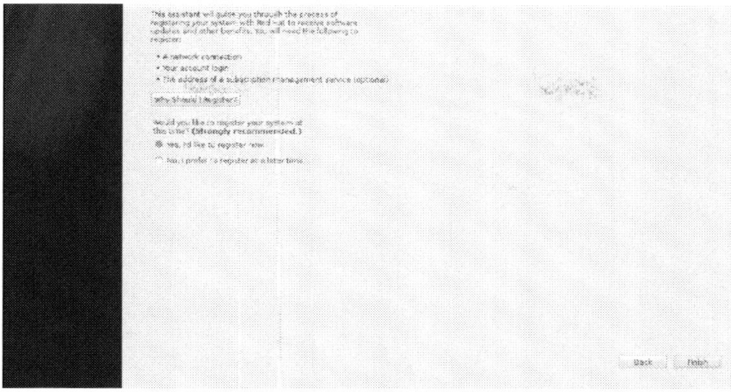

20. Select language and press next

21. Now create **local account**

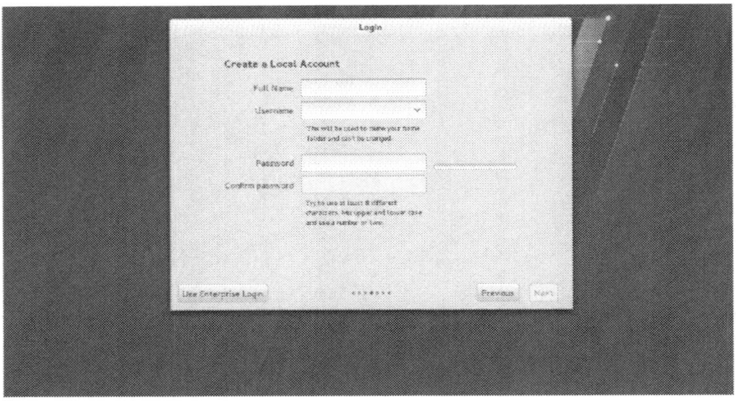

22. Select Location .

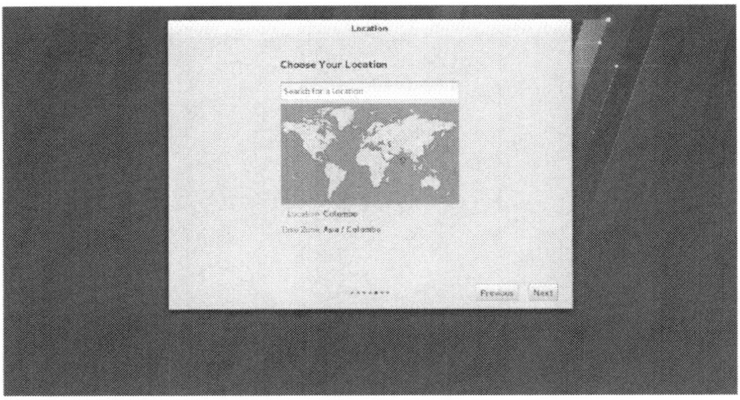

23. Press **next**.

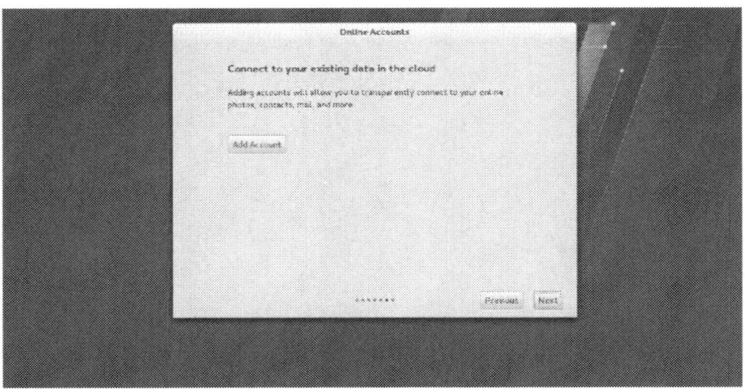

24. Press start using **Redhat Enterprise Linux.**

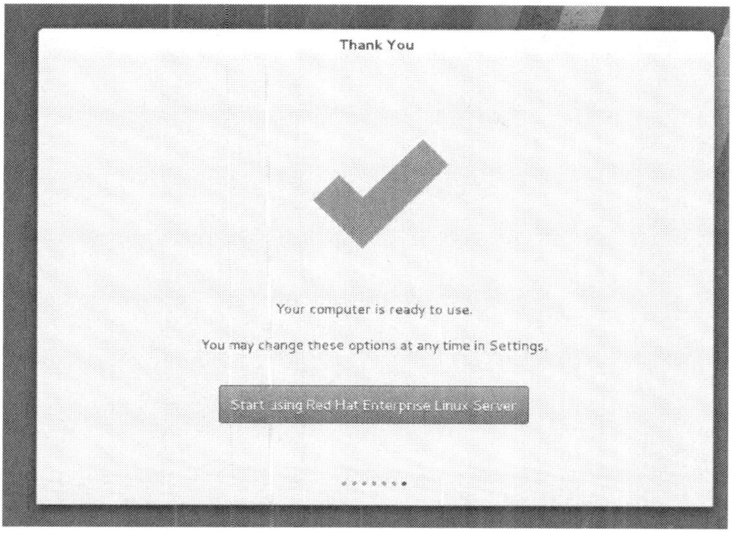

Connecting MS windows PC to Linux machine

1. Download putty from http://www.chiark.greenend.org.uk/~sgtatham/putty/latest.html
2. Install putty on windows PC
3. After installation start putty

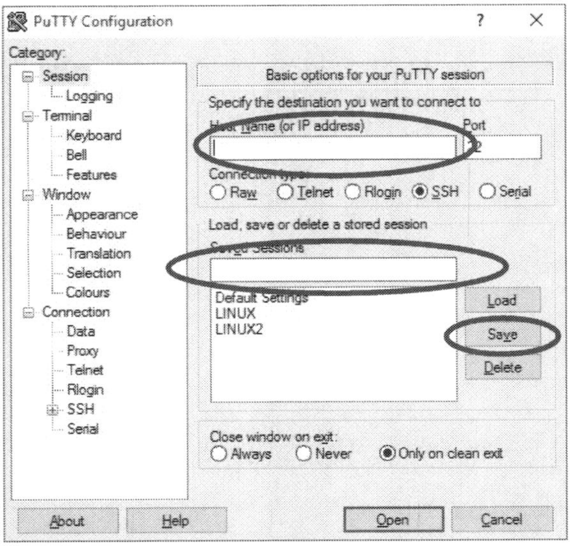

4. Wite the IPaddress of the linux machine and name of session and save
5. Double click the session name to connect to the Linux Machine.

Network

Network allows to inter connect different machine. You require network card on computer to connect. Every network card has physical address called as media access control address (MAC address). MAC address works on layer 2 of OSI model. Manufacturer of network interface card assigns MAC addresses. To access the network card we assign IP address to network card, which works on layer 3 of OSI model. Hosts on different network can connect using layer3. As IP address are still numeric value it is difficult to remember more over there is possibility of IP address may change. To make life easy we use **hostname**.

Seven layer of OSI and TCP Mapping

OSI Model	TCP Model	Application	Address	Devices
7:Application layer	Application Layer	HTTP / Telnet / SSH	Applications DNS, DHCP.ntp,HTTP,	
6:Presentation layer		SSL / MIME		
5: Session layer		Sockets and Remote Procedure Call (RPC)		
4: Transport layer	Transport layer	Transmission Control Protocol (TCP)	TCP/UDP	Gateway

3: Network layer	Internet layer	Internet Protocol (IP)	IP4, IP6, IPX, ICMP	Router, firewall Layer 3 switch
2: Data link layer	Network Access Layer	Ethernet / Frame Relay	MAC address, ARP	Bridge Layer 2 switch
1: Physical layer		IEEE 802.x	Ethernet	HUB

Check IP address and routing table

Show IP address

```
# ip addr show
```

Or

```
# ifconfig -a
```

Show Link status

```
# ip link show
```

Show routing table

```
# ip route
```

Or

```
# netstat -rn
```

Check and change hostname

Show hostname

```
# hostname
```

Change hostname

Whenever you want to change hostname, you have to change it by

1. Using command **hostnamectl**
2. And change it in /etc/hosts

Method 1

1. Give hostnamectl command status to check the current

```
# hostnamectl status
   Static hostname: rhl-one
         Icon name: computer
           Chassis: n/a
        Machine ID: 98c0429d893c48b88fba101f95aa70ca
           Boot ID: 864f0f4e99cd4442b4f388a15a7fc132
```

Or

```
# hostname
```

2. Change the hostname

```
# hostnamectl set-hostname redhat1
```

3. Next step is to change **/etc/hosts** file

```
127.0.0.1 redhat1 localhost.localdomain localhost
```

Method #2: nmtui command

1. You can set host name using **nmtui** command which has text user interface for new users:

```
# nmtui
```

2. Select set System hostname >> Press the “Ok” button:

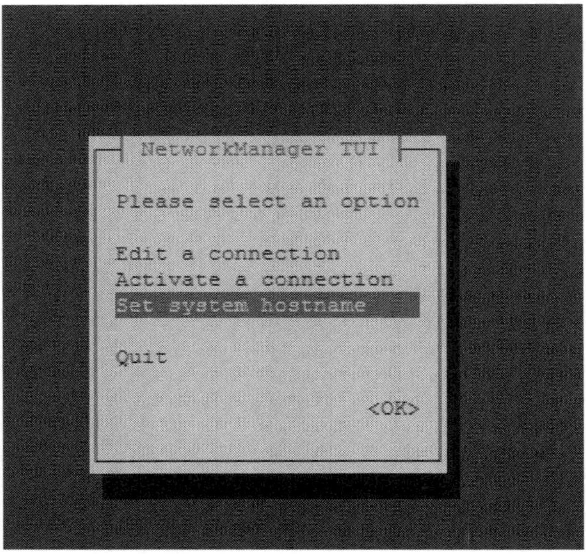

3. Change the hostname > Press Ok

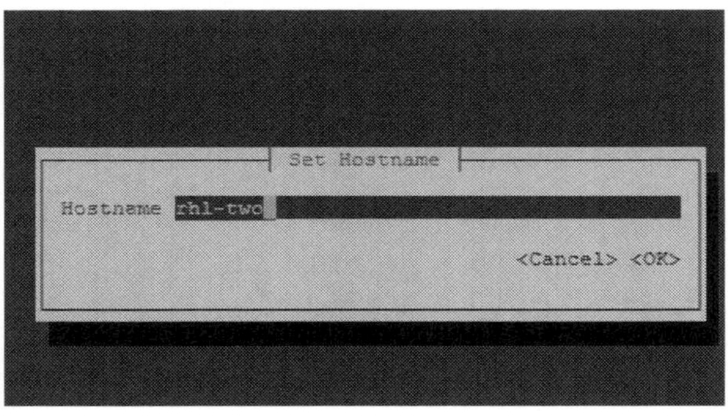

Setting Up the DNS Name Resolution

Whenever you write hostname instead of IP address to ping or to connect Linux host. You have multiple option to resolve hostname to IP address.

- Local file i.e. /etc/hosts
- DNS server
- NIS

/etc/hosts

Using local file **/etc/hosts** for hostname to IP address mapping provides ability to store list of hostname to their respective IP address you don't require to look for DNS server. It is also useful if you are connecting to limited servers due scope or security reason you do not have to depend on DNS server.

Format

```
IP_address       hostname aliases
```

Example

```
127.0.0.1              redhat1 localhost
::1                    redhat1 localhost
192.168.228.129        redhat2
```

Using Domain Name Server for name resolution

/etc/resolv.conf

To resolve hostnames to IP addresses system reads a file called **resolv.conf**. You need to put your DNS server IP addresses in this file. Generally, you need one name server, but you can include up to three if you want redundancy.

If the first one on the list is not responding, system tries to resolve against the next one on the list, and so on.

Edit **/etc/resolv.conf** to add list of name servers, like this:

```
nameserver 8.8.8.8
```

```
nameserver 8.8.8.9
nameserver 1.2.3.6
```

Changing order for hostname resolution

/etc/nsswitch.conf

If hosts file and DNS configuration is there in **resolv.conf** in your server, Whenever you do hostname resolution the system looks for local file **(/etc/hosts)** for entry of hostname and respective IP address. If there is no entry, it looks for **/etc/resolv.conf** file for DNS configuration. If there is no DNS configuration also then it will check for NIS configuration. However, you can change this behavior by changing **/etc/nsswitch.conf**

```
vi /etc/nsswitch.conf
```

```
#hosts:      db files nisplus nis dns
hosts:       files dns
```

In this example search sequence is first files means **/etc/hosts** then DNS server.

Modifying network configuration with GUI

1. click network manager icon and select network settings

2. Select click setting icon

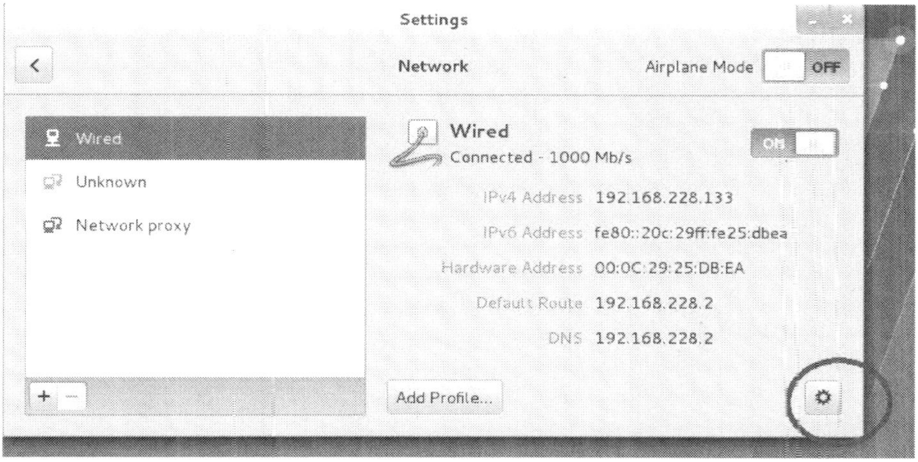

3. Select IP4 settings

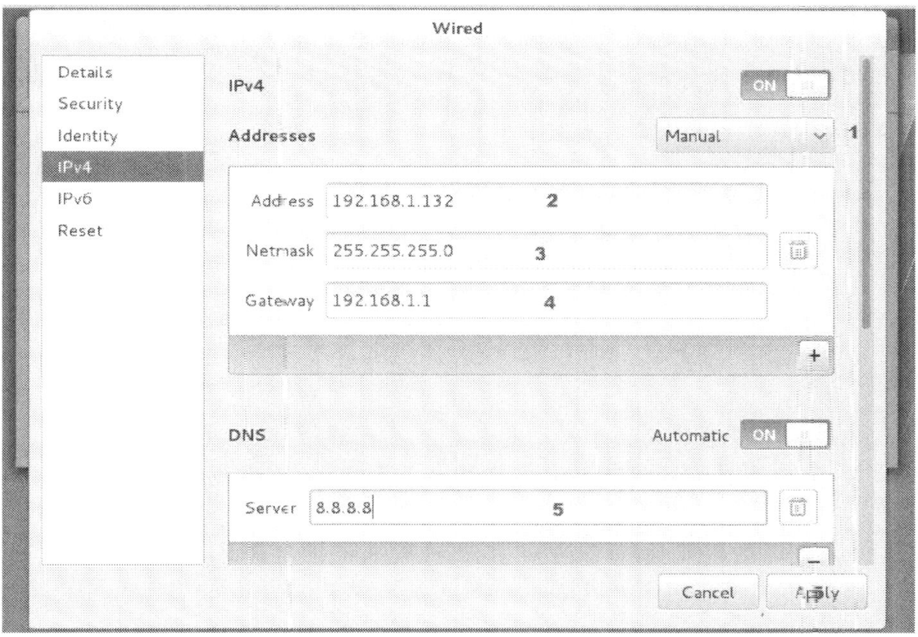

4. On method drop down menu change DHCP to manual, Give IP address, Netmask , Gateway and DNS > Apply

Modifying network configuration with TUI

1. Type this command "nmtui" to open Network manager and press enter after choosing " Edit a connection" (Use TAB for choosing options)

2. It will open Network manager and press enter after choosing **Edit a connection**.

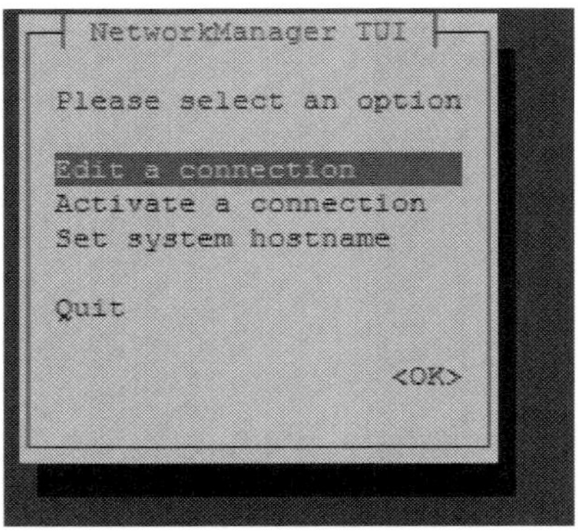

3. It will show all network interfaces, choose one and click **Edit.**(you can navigate using **TAB** key)

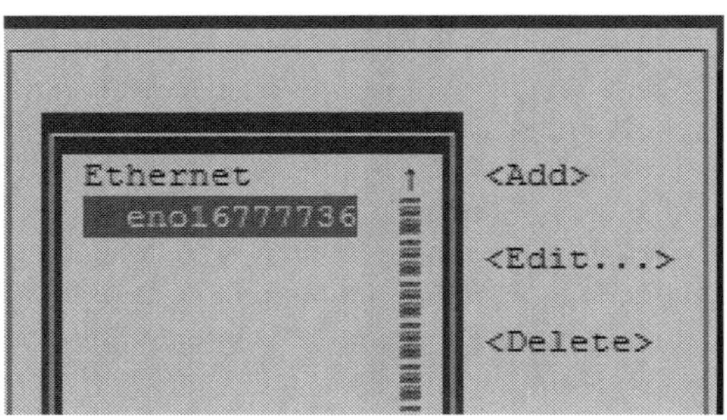

4. For **DHCP Configuration**

    1. Choose “Automatic” in IPv4 CONFIGURATION.

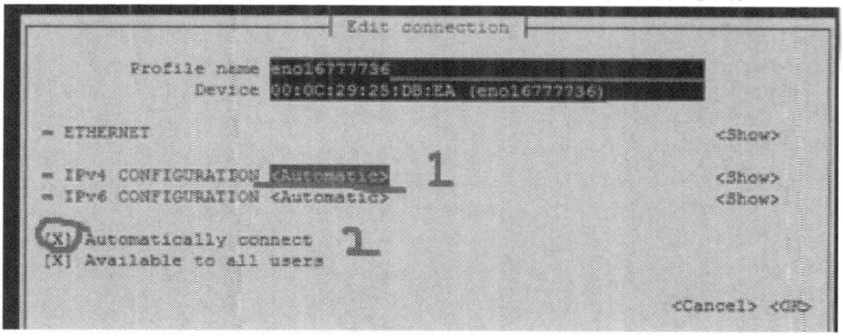

    2. Choose Automatic Connect check box.

    3. Press OK and quit Network manager.

    4. `systemctl restart network`

5. For **Static IP configuration**

    1. Select “**Manual**” in IPv4 CONFIGURATION. By pressing space bar at automatic

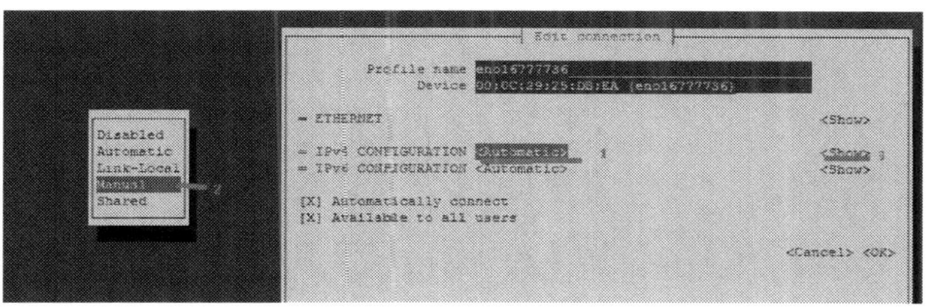

    2. Press **Show then** press **add in addresses**

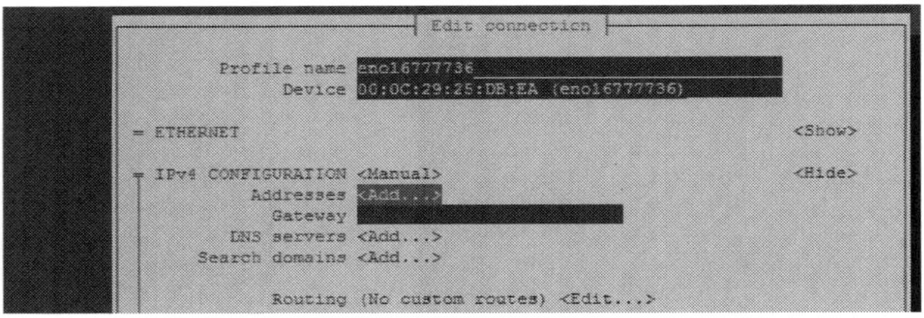

3. Give IP Address with Subnet , Gateway and DNS

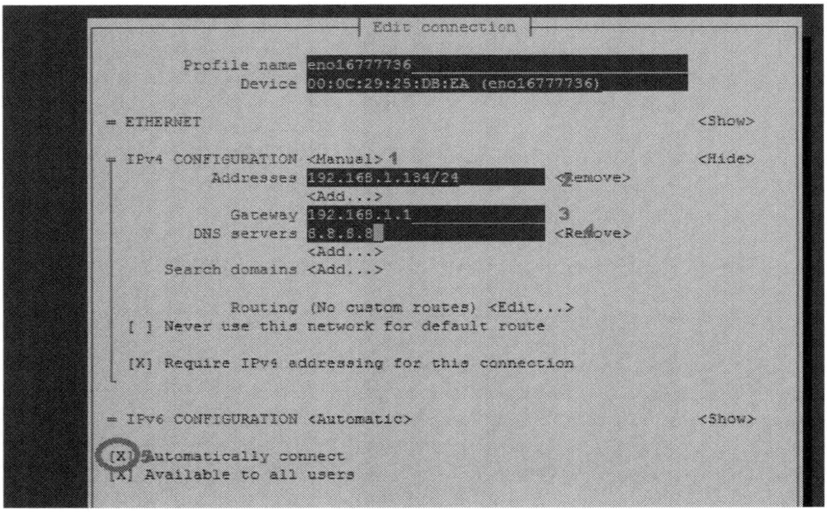

4. Choose Automatic Connect check box.
5. Press OK and quit Network manager.
6. Restart the network service

```
systemctl restart network
```

Modifying network configuration manually

If you don't have Graphical desktop on the host and want to change the IP address or network is not working.

1. Check current setting

```
# ip addr show
```

2. Check current devices

```
# nmcli d
DEVICE       TYPE      STATE      CONNECTION
eno16777736  ethernet  connected  eno16777736
lo           loopback  unmanaged  --
```

3. Edit **/etc/sysconfig/network-scripts/ifcfg-***. Where **ifcfg-*** file is device file you just checked in last command like **ifcfg-eno16777736**

```
# vi /etc/sysconfig/network-scripts/ifcfg-eno16777736
```

4. Change **/etc/sysconfig/network-scripts/ifcfg-*** file depending on where you have static IP address or you are using DHCP

Static	DHCP
DEVICE=eth0 BOOTPROTO=static IPADDR =192.168.0.132 NETMASK=255.255.255.0 GATEWAY=192.168.0.1 ONBOOT=yes	DEVICE=eth0 BOOTPROTO=dhcp

5. Restart network services

```
# systemctl restart network
```

Adding static route

To change static routes do the following

1. Check current routing table

```
# netstat -rn
```

or

```
# route -n
```

or

```
# ip route show
```

2. Edit /etc/sysconfig/network-scripts/route-interfacefile and add X.X.X.X/X via Y.Y.Y.Y dev interface Where X.X.X.X is IP address or network and Y.Y.Y.Y is gateway used by X.X.X.X

```
# vi /etc/sysconfig/network-scripts/route-eth0- eno16777736
```

```
10.0.0.0/8 via 192.168.1.1
```

3. Restart network services

```
# systemctl restart network
```

4. Check the route table again

```
# route -n
```

5. Ping the destination address

```
# ping 10.0.0.2
```

Changing DNS server

Edit **/etc/resolv.conf**

search example.com // give own FQDN

nameserver 8.8.8.8 // IPaddress of first DNS

nameserver 8.8.4.4 // IPaddress of Second DNS

Managing network interface

Bring down Ethernet interface etho

```
# ifdown eth0
```

Bring up Ethernet interface etho

```
# ifup eth0
```

Important Network Commands

Task	Command
Check connectivity between two system	ping *IP_address* Example ping 10.1.1.2
Check IP address configuration	ifconfig –a or ip addr show
Check configuration of network card	cat /etc/sysconfig/network-scripts/ifcfg-*
Check routing table	ip route show
Querying Domain Name System	dig
Local file to resolve hosts to IP address	/etc/hosts

DNS server configuration file	/etc/resolv.conf

Chapter 5

Managing local users and groups

As Linux is a multi-user operating system, it allows multiple users on different computers to access a single system. As a system administrator you required to perform users and group management, which include add, modify remove users and groups according to policy of the organization the server belongs to.

User management

Add User

```
# useradd username
```

Or

```
# adduser username
```

Now set the password

```
# passwd username
```

Delete user

```
# userdel username
```

Modify user

```
# usermod -c "database user"  username
```

Display information about user

`# id`	show current user information
`# id username`	Show users information

Change password for other user

```
# passwd username
```

Change own password

```
# passwd
```

List password expiry information

```
# chage -l username
```

Disable password expiration for user

```
# chage -I -1 -m 0 -M 99999 -E -1 username
```

Force user to change password at next login

```
# chage -d 0 user1
```

Lock user

```
# usermod -L user1
```

Unlock user

```
# usermod -U user1
```

UID

Unique User ID called as UID is every user exist on system user it fixed for root and regular users

User	UID
root	0
System user	1 – 499
Regular users	500 +

Groups

Every user we create belongs to group and all groups have group ID. List all available groups can be found in /etc/groups and entry of all users member of these groups there are two type of groups

- primary group
- secondary group

Primary group

This is the group applied to you when you login and used by default when you create new files and directories. It is normally same name as username. Users primary group ID is written /etc/passwd file for respective users in the third field.

Secondary Group

These are the groups users are member other than primary group

/etc/group

```
groupname:shadow password:GID:list of users in group
```

Example

```
science:x:1003:class1,class2
```

Changing primary group

```
# usermod -g data1 user1
```

Changing secondary group

```
# usermod -G data2 user1
```

Add new group

```
# groupadd groupname
```

Delete group

```
# groupdel groupname
```

/etc/passwd

Stores user information

Format

```
username:x:UID:GID:Full_user_name:home_directory:shellaccount
```

Username up to 8 characters. Case-sensitive

x Passwords are stored in the ``/etc/shadow" file.

UID User ID

GID Group ID

shell account Often set to ``/bin/bash" to provide access to the bash shell but can other shell like c shell korn shell

Example

```
root:x:0:0:root:/root:/bin/bash
```

/etc/shadow

Stores actual password in encrypted format

Format

```
username:password:last_password_change:minimum
```

Username up to 8 characters. Case-sensitive, usually all lowercase. A direct match to the username in the /etc/passwd file.

Password 13 character encrypted. A blank entry (eg. ::) indicates a password is not required to log in (usually a bad idea), and a ``*'' entry (eg. :*:) indicates the account has been disabled.

last_password_change The number of days (since January 1, 1970) since the password was last changed.

Minimum: The number of days before password may be changed (0 indicates it may be changed at any time)

Maximum: The number of days after which password must be changed (99999 indicates user can keep his or her password unchanged for many, many years)

Warn : The number of days to warn user of an expiring password (7 for a full week)

Inactive: The number of days after password expires that account is disabled

Expire: The number of days since January 1, 1970 that an account has been disabled

Example

```
root:$6$YtTXd..cW9GYuWT9sNwX07B3i.:17201:0:99999:7:::
```

Chapter 6

NFS Network File System

NFS is file sharing file system, which works on server client basis. Server's shared file systems are mounted on client. Four version of NFS are there:-

1. NFS V1
2. NFS V2
3. NFS V3
4. NFS V4

Where NFS V3 and NFS V4 are more recent version of NFS, V3 is safer and asynchronous works on UDP protocol while V4 has added advantage of working through firewall and works on TCP.

/etc/exports

Configuration file used to export file system on server to clients

To export file system without /etc/exports manually.

```
# exportfs -i /user1
```

To unexport all exported file system

```
# exportfs -ua
```

Configure NFS on the server

1. Install packages

```
# yum install nfs-utils
```

```
# yum install rpcbind
```

2. Start the services

```
# systemctl start rpcbind
# systemctl start nfs-server
```

3. Make service start on next reboot

```
4. # systemctl enable rpcbind
5. # systemctl enable nfs-server
```

6. Edit /etc/exports file to add filesystem you want to share to clients format of that is :-

```
mountpoint    [host][permissions/options]
```

where

mountpoint is file systems you want export

host is optional the client you want to give access the file systems

permissions is optional it can be **ro** read only ,**rw** read write **insecure**, **sync** changes written before command finished.

7. Export file system

```
# exportfs -a
```

8. See the file system exported

```
# showmount -e
```

9. Configure firewall to allow NFS server to clients

```
firewall-cmd --permanent --zone public --add-service mountd
firewall-cmd --permanent --zone public --add-service rpc-bind
firewall-cmd --permanent --zone public --add-service nfs
firewall-cmd --reload
```

10. On client

```
# showmount -e server IP address / hostname
# mount -t nfs 192.168.0.1:/userfs /newmnt
```

Mounting DVD automatically

1. Make directory for mounting

```
# mkdir /cdrom
```

2. edit the /etc/fstab file

```
# vi /etc/fstab
```

3. add following line

```
/dev/cdrom          /cdrom          iso9660 ro          0 0
```

4. reboot the server
5. check mount

```
# mount
```

Chapter 7

Graphics User Interface

When you install Linux distribution, you have option to install GUI desktop environment, which makes administration easy.

There are many desktop environments are available from which prominent are:-

- GNOME
- KDE
- XFCE
- LXDE

GNOME 3 is the default desktop environment for RedHat.

Graphical Login

When you start the machine, you will get login window

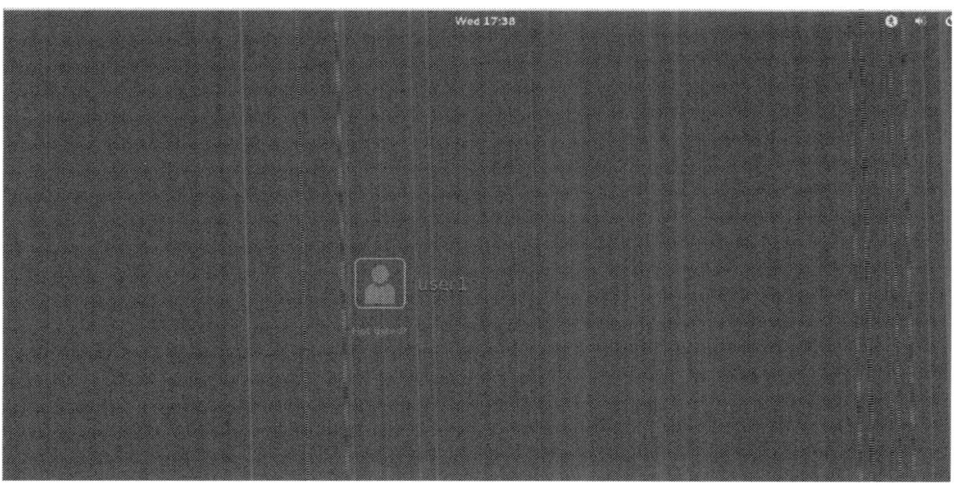

You select **not listed** to log in as root from the graphical login screen, type root at the login prompt, press **[Enter]**, type the root password that you selected during installation at the password prompt, and press **[Enter]**. To log in as a normal user, select username at the login prompt, press **[Enter]**, type your password that you selected when creating the user at the password prompt, and press **[Enter]**.

Virtual Console Login

When install Linux with Graphical desktop, usually you get six virtual consoles provide a text terminal with a login prompt to Linux shell. The graphical X Window System starts in the first virtual console. User switches between them with the key combination Alt plus a function key – for example Alt+F1 to access first virtual console. During installation, if you haven't selected graphical desktop you will see a login prompt similar to the following after booting your system

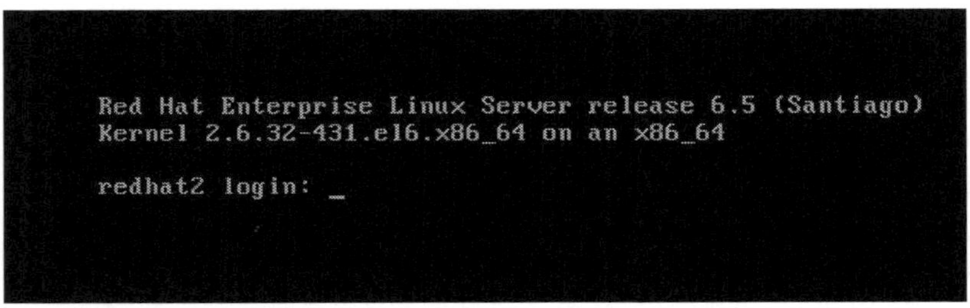

To log in from the console, type username at the login prompt, press Enter, then type the password and press Enter.

GNOME terminal

Gnome terminal is terminal emulator for gnome desktop environment. Terminal allows to you give command to your Redhat machine. By default you gets the **>** prompt if you login as normal user and **#** prompt if you login as root. To change to # prompt from > you use **su** command and password of root. To open Gnome Terminal Applications > Utilities > Terminal.

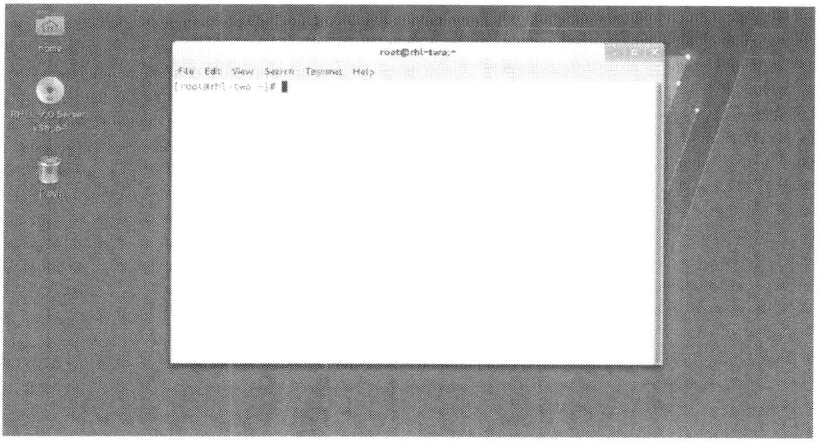

Commands

Ctrl +a	Moves the cursor to the beginning of the command prompt
Ctrl + e	Moves the cursor to the end of the command prompt
Ctrl + u	Clear the current line
Middle mouse button click	Paste the highlighted text
Tab	Completes the command
Up / Down Keys	Show history of commands
Ctrl +c	Terminate the current process
Ctrl + z	Suspends the foreground process

Disk Utility

With graphical disk utility you can

- Create / Delete / Edit partition
- Mount / Unmount file system
- Format volume to required File System Type
- Check File System
- Edit File system label
- Format drive
- Check benchmarks

From left pan select the required device then you can do operation on the device.

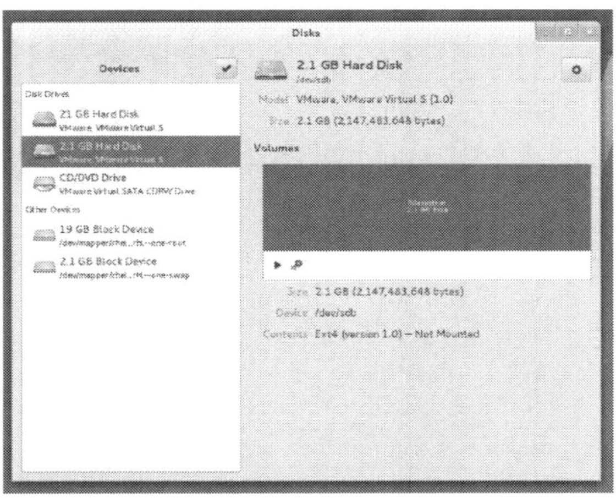

Chapter 8

Process and threads

Every task done by Linux OS has process associated with it. Process has priority based on the context switches on them.

Each process provide resources needed to execute the program

Each process starts with single thread known as primary thread. Process can have multiple threads.

Process runs in foreground and background

Commands

Command	Description
bg	Sends job to Background
fg	Bring job to foreground
jobs	Show current jobs
kill	Stops the process
ps	Show the process information
&	if command ends with the & the shell execute the command in background and shell will not wait for finish Example gcalctool &

Bring command to foreground

```
# fg
ctrl + c
```

Check the running jobs

```
# jobs
```

List the current running process

```
# ps -ef |grep gcalctool
```

or

```
# ps aux
```

Kill the process forcefully

First check the process ID with `ps -ef` command then

```
# kill -9 <process -id >
```

Monitoring the process with ps command

ps command show the percentage of CPU & memory utilization of the process it is very useful if your machine is under performing. **ps** command gives you indication which process is hogging memory/CPU.

Process scheduling

Scheduler is part of kernel, which select process to run next. The purpose is to run the processes according to priorities. To set the priority of running process nice and renice command is used which decide how longer or smaller CPU time is given to process.

nice set the priority or niceness of new process.

renice adjust nice value of running process

niceness of -20 is highest priority and 19 is lowest priority. The default priority is 0

Example

```
# nice -n 19 cp -r /as /map
```

Commands show priorities of running processes

```
# ps -al
```

or

```
# top
```

To change the priority

```
# renice -n 10 <pid>
```

Note: You need root privilege to change to higher priority.

Chapter 9

Automating tasks

Redhat has utilities to automate the task which system administrator do regularly or at specified time. Following are the main utilities

- cron
- at
- batch

Cron

cron is daemon that can be used to schedule the execution of recurring tasks according to time, day of month, day of week .

Configuration file

/etc/crontab

Command

Command	Description
crontab –l	List crontab entries
crontab –e	Edit crontab
crontab –r	Remove crontab

Format

```
minutes hours Day_of_month Month Day_of_week  Command
```

Where

Minutes (from 0 to 59)

hours (from 0 to 23)

day of month (from 1 to 31)

month (from 1 to 12)

day of week (from 0 to 6) (0=Sunday)

To schedule a recurring task

1. Edit crontab by giving command **crontab -e**

2. Add entries at bottom of file press **i**

Suppose you want to run backup script every night at 11:30

```
30 23 * * *       /myscripts/backup.sh
```

3. Press [escape] and press : write **x** after that press [enter] to save the entry

at and batch

crontab is used for recurring task but for one time tasks at specified time **at** and **batch** commands are used.

To run at command rpm must be installed and **atd** service must be running

Check Installation

```
# rpm -q at
```

Install at package

```
# yum install at
```

Start service

```
# service start atd
```

Start command

```
# at 4:00
at > ls
ctrl + d
```

Batch command executes one time task when system average load decreases bellow 0.8

```
# at
at > ls
ctrl + d
```

Display list of pending jobs

```
atq
```

Chapter 10

Log management

Log files are very useful in troubleshooting and auditing system for unauthorized system access. In Redhat 7 some logs are controlled by rsyslogd daemon. It is enhanced replacement of **sysklogd**. It offers high-performance, great security features, modular design and support for transportation via the TCP or UDP protocols.

rsyslogd reads the file **/etc/rsyslog.conf. rsyslogd** can be configured vai **rsyslog.conf** file. List of log files maintained by **rsyslogd** can be found in the rsyslog.conf configuration file. Log files are usually located in the /var/log/ directory.

install

```
# yum install rsyslog
```

Configuration file

/etc/rsyslog.conf

Sample rsyslog.conf

```
[root@redhat1 etc]# cat rsyslog.conf
# rsyslog v5 configuration file

# For more information see /usr/share/doc/rsyslog-*/rsyslog_conf.html
# If you experience problems, see
http://www.rsyslog.com/doc/troubleshoot.html

#### MODULES ####
```

```
$ModLoad imuxsock # provides support for local system logging (e.g. via
logger command)
$ModLoad imklog   # provides kernel logging support (previously done by
rklogd)
#$ModLoad immark  # provides --MARK-- message capability

# Provides UDP syslog reception
#$ModLoad imudp
#$UDPServerRun 514

# Provides TCP syslog reception
#$ModLoad imtcp
#$InputTCPServerRun 514


#### GLOBAL DIRECTIVES ####

# Use default timestamp format
$ActionFileDefaultTemplate RSYSLOG_TraditionalFileFormat

# File syncing capability is disabled by default. This feature is
usually not required,
# not useful and an extreme performance hit
#$ActionFileEnableSync on

# Include all config files in /etc/rsyslog.d/
$IncludeConfig /etc/rsyslog.d/*.conf


#### RULES ####

# Log all kernel messages to the console.
# Logging much else clutters up the screen.
#kern.*                                                 /dev/console

# Log anything (except mail) of level info or higher.
# Don't log private authentication messages!
*.info;mail.none;authpriv.none;cron.none
/var/log/messages
```

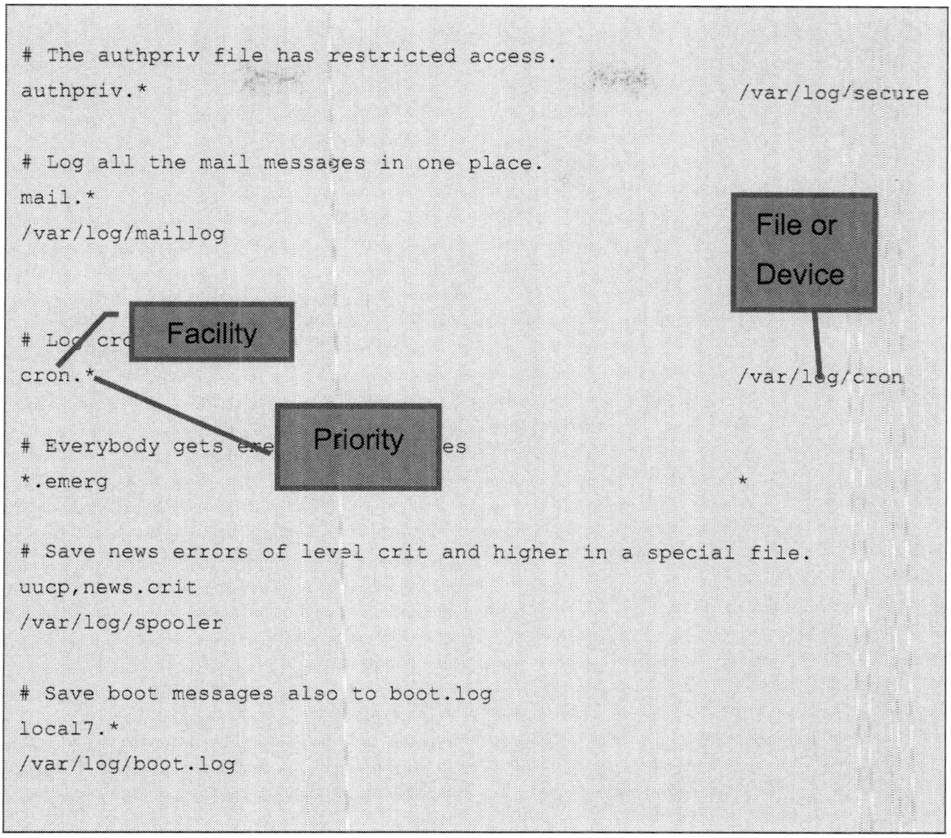

```
# The authpriv file has restricted access.
authpriv.*                                              /var/log/secure

# Log all the mail messages in one place.
mail.*
/var/log/maillog


# Log cr
cron.*                                                  /var/log/cron

# Everybody gets eme                    es
*.emerg                                                 *

# Save news errors of level crit and higher in a special file.
uucp,news.crit
/var/log/spooler

# Save boot messages also to boot.log
local7.*
/var/log/boot.log
```


Log filtering

There is too much logging happens in the system if it is not filtered it become almost impossible to use logs. To filter the logs we use **/etc/rsyslog.conf** file. It has two parameter facility and priority separated with dot(.). Facility is name of process for which you want to log and priority specify level of log like debug, info, notice, warning, err, crit , alert, emerg you want to keep.

Example

```
# The authpriv file has restricted access.
```

```
authpriv.*
/var/log/secure

# Log all the mail messages in one place.
mail.*                                                              -
/var/log/maillog
```

In the example where **authpriv** and **mail** is facility and * is priority mean all logs.

journald

Logs can also be managed by the **journald** daemon – a component of systemd. It's a centralized location for all messages logged by different components in a systemd-enabled Linux system. This includes kernel and boot messages, initial RAM disk, messages coming from syslog or different services, it indexes them and makes this available to the user. The native journal file format, improves searching it stores Meta data with time stamp and user's ID. Log files produced by journald are not persistent, log files are stored only in memory or a small ring-buffer in the **/run/log/journal/** directory. The amount of logged data depends on free memory, logs gets rotated periodically.

Viewing log with journalctl

To view log

```
# journalctl
```

To view full meta data about all entries

```
# journalctl -o verbose
```

Live view of logs

```
# journalctl -f
```

Filtering by Priority

```
# journalctl -p priority
```

Filtering by error

```
# journalctl -p err
```

To view log entries only form the current boot

```
# journalctl -b
```

To make logs persistent

```
# mkdir -p /var/log/journal
```

Then, restart journald to apply the change:

```
# systemctl restart systemd-journald
```

Viewing logs in GUI

Install gnome system log package

```
# yum install gnome-system-log
```

View logs graphically

To view log Applications > System Tools > System Log

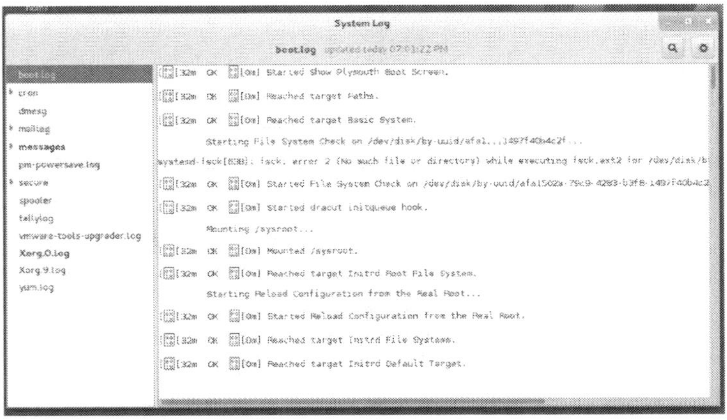

Rotating logs

Logs needs rotation to avoid filling of file systems and make log more manageable.

Once log file is rotated, it will be renamed with new file name. After certain time of rotation older log files will get deleted to save space.

logrotate package manages automatically rotating of log files according to configuration in /etc/logrotate.conf

logwatch

logwatch is program to analyze and reporting short digest via mail. Can be configured vai **/usr/share/logwatch/default.conf/logwatch.conf** configuration file.

Install

```
# yum install -y logwatch
```

Configure

Setting configuration file **/usr/share/logwatch/default.conf/logwatch.conf**.

The email address to which daily digest(report) are sent

mailto =root

Example

```
# Default person to mail reports to.  Can be a local account or
a
# complete email address.  Variable Print should be set to No
to
# enable mail feature.
MailTo = root
```

Chapter 11

Software management

Redhat network

Red Hat Network is a centrally managed service provides facility to deploy software and software updates to Red Hat Enterprise Linux systems. To receive updates for Redhat server you have get subscription of Redhat network.

To register your system with RHN :-

1. Go to Redhat customer portal and create user
2. Add your subscriptions
3. Connect server to internet
4. Give command **subscription-manager register**

```
# subscription-manager register
Username: abc74
Password:
The system has been registered with ID: bb304a30-c30e-4bb7-
9d41-xxxxxx
```

5. Determine the pool ID you want to Add by listing all pools

```
subscription-manager list --available
subscription-manager register
Username: abc74
Password:
The system has been registered with ID: bb304a30-c30e-4bb7-
9d41-xxxxxx
[root@redhat1]# subscription-manager list --available
+-------------------------------------------+
```

```
    Available Subscriptions
+-------------------------------------------+
Subscription Name: 30 Day Self-Supported Red Hat Enterprise
Linux Developer Workstation Evaluation
```

6. Attach your system to desired subscription
   subscription-manager attach --pool=pool_id

7. Now list how many subscriptions are consumed
   subscription-manager list –consumed

Repository

Repository is collection of software for Linux, ether present locally or remotely. The repository can be used to install additional software or to update the current software. When you subscribe to RHN a repository file is created **/etc/yum.repos.d/** directory.

Display all enabled repositories

```
# yum repolist
```

Display all repositories enabled and disabled

```
# yum repolist all
```

yum

Yellow dog updater modifier is command line tool for package management. yum uses repository to fetch the correct version of a particular package compatible for your system. Yum allows automatic update of packages and dependency management. It allows automatically download the packages and install them form repositories either RHN or local repository defined such as CDROM or directory. You can also use third party repositories to install extra packages like open office, VLC etc.

Commands

Package

Install package

Syntax

```
# yum install -y package_name
```

Example

```
# yum install -y firefox
```

Remove package

Syntax

```
# yum remove package_name
```

Example

```
# yum remove firefox
```

Check available updates

```
# yum check-update
```

Update system using yum

```
# yum update
```

Check the file provided by which package

```
# yum provides file-name
```

Get help

```
# yum help
```

list the installed and available software

```
# yum list
```

search the package name with keyword

```
# yum search keyword
```

Display information about the package

Syntax

```
# yum info package_name
```

Example

```
# yum info zip
```

Update all software provided by the repository

```
# yum update
```

Clean the yum cache

```
# yum clean all
```

Interactive shell

```
# yum shell
```

List yum history

```
# yum history list
```

Package group

Package group is group of software, which has same motive to install. It makes administrator's life easy by installing and downloading dependent software automattically. For example, you want to install backup client you give command **yum groupinstall 'Backup Client'**

List all package group available

```
# yum group list
```

Install group package

Syntax

yum group install *package_name*

Example

```
# yum group install 'Backup Client'
```

Remove group package

Syntax

yum group remove *package_name*

Example

```
# yum group remove 'Backup Client'
```

Information about group package

Syntax

yum group info *package_name*

Example

```
# yum group info 'Backup Client'
```

Installing packages with RPM command

RPM

RPM stands for Red Hat Package Manager. RPM packages have .rpm extension. **rpm** command is used to manage software which include list, install, update and remove . RPM is usually used to install packages which has been downloaded locally

Commands

Install

Syntax

```
rpm -ihv  package_name
```

Example

```
[root@redhat1 Packages]# rpm -ihv zip-3.0-10.el7.x86_64.rpm
Preparing...
################################################ [100%]
   1:zip
################################################ [100%]
```

Update

Syntax

```
rpm -Uhv package_name
```

Example

```
# rpm -Uhv zip-3.0-10.el7.x86_64.rpm
```

Remove

Syntax

```
rpm -ev package_name
```

Example

```
# rpm -ev zip
```

Query all installed packages

Syntax

```
rpm -qa
```

Display detailed information about package

Syntax

```
rpm -qi package_name
```

Example

```
rpm -qi zip
Name        : zip                     Relocations: (not
relocatable)
Version     : 3.0                          Vendor:
Red Hat, Inc.
Release     : 1.el6                    Build Date:
Mon 24 May 2010 07:53:44 PM IST
Install Date: Sun 12 Feb 2017 10:05:18 AM IST     Build
Host: x86-005.build.bos.redhat.com
Group       : Applications/Archiving      Source RPM:
zip-3.0-1.el6.src.rpm
Size        : 823612                      License:
BSD
Signature   : RSA/8, Tue 17 Aug 2010 02:05:20 AM IST,
Key ID 199e2f91fd431d51
Packager    : Red Hat, Inc.
<http://bugzilla.redhat.com/bugzilla>
URL         : http://www.info-zip.org/Zip.html
Summary     : A file compression and packaging utility
compatible with PKZIP
Description :
```

```
The zip program is a compression and file packaging
utility.  Zip is
analogous to a combination of the UNIX tar and compress
commands and
is compatible with PKZIP (a compression and file
packaging utility for
MS-DOS systems).

Install the zip package if you need to compress files
using the zip
program.
```

Find the file belongs to which package

Syntax

`rpm -qf  path_to_the_file`

Example

```
[root@redhat1 Packages]# rpm -qf /etc/hosts
setup-2.8.71-4.el7.noarch
```

Find out all dependences

Syntax

rpm -qpR *package_name*

Example

```
[root@redhat1 Packages]# rpm -qpR zip-3.0-10.el7.x86_64.rpm
libc.so.6()(64bit)
libc.so.6(GLIBC_2.2.5)(64bit)
libc.so.6(GLIBC_2.3)(64bit)
libc.so.6(GLIBC_2.3.4)(64bit)
libc.so.6(GLIBC_2.4)(64bit)
```

Repository

To install additional package or update existing package you require repository. It is warehouse all Linux software. Yum repository can hold **RPM** packages located locally like CDROM , directory on local disk or remotely like FTP, HTTP or HTTPS. The configuration files for name, location, status etc. of repository is there in **/etc/yum.repos.d/** directory.

The configuration file present in the **/etc/yum.repos.d/** directory have following fields

Repository ID - Single word unique repository ID

Name - Name of the repository (example: name=CD_media)

Baseurl - URL to the repodata directory. You can use ftp://link, http://link, https://link if repository is located remotely and file://path if repository is located locally (example file:///mnt/ for mnt directory locally)

Enabled - Enable/Disable repository (example: enabled=1 to enable or enable=0 to disable)

Gpgcheck - Enable/disable GPG signature checking (example: gpgcheck=1)

Gpgkey - location of GPG key

Defining repository

1. Create file /etc/yum.repos.d/<*name*>.repo
2. Add following contents

```
[Repository_ID]
name=name_of_repository
baseurl=http://location
enabled=1
```

```
gpgcheck=0
```

Using Red Hat DVD or local directory as repository

1. Mount the RHEL 7 installation ISO to a directory like /mnt, e.g.:

```
# mount -o loop RHEL7.iso /cdrom
```

2. If you use DVD media, you can mount like below.

```
# mount -o ro /dev/cdrom1  /cdrom
```

Where /dev/cdrom1 is DVDROM device you may have different one.

3. Create file name cdrom.repo in **/etc/yum.repos.d/** that should look like the following where /cdrom is directory where cdrom is mounted

```
[installmedia]
name=Red Hat Enterprise Linux 7
baseurl=file:///cdrom/
gpgcheck=0
enabled=1
```

4. Clear the related caches by **yum clean all** and **subscription-manager clean**

```
# yum clean all
# subscription-manager clean
```

5. Now check the repository

```
# yum repolist all
```

Chapter 12

Utilities

Tar

Use to create one archive file of multiple files used for backup on tape or other media. You also create compress file with adding option while creating achieve file.

Create tar

Syntax

```
tar cvf name_of_archive_file files_or_directory_to_archive
```

Where

c create

v verbose

f file name types of achieve file

Example

```
[root@redhat1 share]# tar cvf abc.tar *
applications/
applications/preferred-mail-reader.desktop
applications/preferred-web-browser.desktop
gvfs-metadata/
 [root@redhat1 share]# ls -la
total 96
drwxr-xr-x. 4 root root  4096 Feb 12 10:58 .
drwxr-xr-x. 3 root root  4096 Feb  4 12:46 ..
-rw-r--r--. 1 root root 81920 Feb 12 10:58 abc.tar
```

Create compressed tar file

Create gzip format tar file

```
# tar cvfz nameoftarfile.tar.gz name_of_files
```

Create bzip format

```
# tar cvfj nameoftarfile.tar.bz2 name_of_files
```

untar

```
# tar xvf abc.tar
```

Where

x extract

v verbose

f file name types of achieve file

Uncompressing

Uncompressing gzip format

Syntax

```
tar xvfz filename
```

Example

```
# tar xvfz abc.tar.gz
```

Create bzip format

Syntax

```
tar xvfj filename
```

Example

```
# tar xvfj abc.tar.bz2
```

List the archived tar file

Syntax

```
tar tvf filename
```

Example

```
# tar tvf abc.tar
```

List gzip compressed tar file

Syntax

```
tar tzvf filename
```

Example

```
# tar tzvf abc.tar.gz
```

List bgzip compressed tar file

Syntax

```
tar tjvf filename
```

Example

```
# tar tjvf abc.tar.bz2
```

cp

Command to copy files

Syntax

```
cp <options> source destination
```

Example

```
cp /home/abc.txt /home1/
```

Copy all files in the directory recursively

```
cp -R  /home/* /home1/
```

Prompt before any overwrite

```
# cp -i /home /home1
```

Copy all new files to the destination

```
# cp -u * /tmp
```

Forcefully copy files

```
# cp -f /tmp/abc.txt /backup/.
```

Copy without prompting to overwrite

```
# cp -n * t
```

scp

scp command is used to copy files form one host to other host in secured manner.

Copy files from local machine to remote machine

Syntax

```
scp filename remote_user@remote.host:/some/remote_diectory
```

copy xyz file from remote host to local host

Syntax

```
scp remote_user@remcte.host:/some/remote_diectory/filename .
```

CPIO

Copy files from and to achieve. Used for creating and extracting achieve and for coping files from one place to another.

Creating achieve form directory abc to /directory backup

```
# cd abc
# ls |cpio -ov > /backup/abc.cpio
```

Extracting

```
# mkdir newbackup
# cd newbackup
# cpio idv < /backup/abc.cpio
```

Creating archive of list of specific files.

Example :- archieve all log files

```
# find . -iname *.log -print|cpio -ov > /backup/selog.cpio
```

Using cpio to create tar file

```
# ls|cpio -ovH tar -F abc.tar
```

To extract tar file using cpio

```
# cpio -idv -F abc.tar
```

Dump and Restore

xfsdump

xfsdump utility backup whole file system or files that has changed since last dump ideally dump should be taken on the quiescent file system, so that files are not changing while backup.

Syntax

```
xfsdump <options> target_device  filessystem_tobe backed_up
```

Example :

To take backup of whole root filesystem to device st0

```
# xfsdump -l 0 -f /dev/st0 /
```

Where

0 is dump level. There are ten dump levels from 0 to 9

0 complete

1	increment from last backup
2	increment from last 1 backup
3-9	like that

f for device name

xfsrestore

xfsrestore command is used to restore the backup taken with dump command

syntax

```
xfsrestore <options> backupdevice target
```

Example:

To restore backup stored on /dev/st0 device

```
# xfsrestore -f /dev/st0 /home1
```

where option

f is for device name

ls

Lists the Names of Files

Syntax

```
ls -<options>
```

Example

`# ls -al` To list directories and files

cat

Displays a Text File

Syntax

```
cat filename
```

Example

```
# cat abc.conf
```

rm

Deletes a file, files or directory

Syntax

```
rm filename
```

Example

```
rm abc.conf
```

To delete abc directory recursively

```
rm -r abc
```

More

When you want to view a file that is longer than one screen, you can more utility. More is used for paging through text one screen full at a time.

Syntax

```
more filename
```

Example

```
# more /etc/hosts
```

less

Less is a program similar to more, but it allows backward movement in the file as well as forward movement.

Syntax

```
less filename
```

Example

```
# less /etc/hosts
```

mv

mv command is used to move file form one location to other location. It is also use rename the file without moving it.

Moving file

Syntax

```
mv filename destination_directory
```

Example

```
mv a.txt /tmp/.
```

It will move a.txt file from current directory to /tmp directory

To rename

Syntax

```
mv filename newfilename
```

Example

```
mv a.txt b.txt
```

grep

Searches for a String from one or more files. Display each line which has string.

Syntax

```
grep string file
```

Example

```
# grep '127.0.0.1' /etc/hosts
```

head

Print the first 10 lines of file to standard output. You can also specify how many line it will show.

Syntax

```
head option file
```

Example

`# head -20 /etc/mime.types` it will show first 20 lines of mime.types file

tail

Print the last 10 lines of file to standard output. You can also specify how many line it will show.

Syntax

```
tail option file
```

Example

`# tail -20 /var/log/logfile` it will show last 20 lines

Use tail to monitor file continuously

```
# tail -f /var/log/logfile
```

It will show end of growing file. **Ctrl +c** to interrupt

Diff

Compares Two Files.

Syntax

```
diff First_file  Second_file
```

Example

```
# diff abc.txt bbc.txt
```

File

Determine file type

Syntax

```
file file_name
```

Example

```
# file bbc.txt
```

Echo

Display text

Syntax

echo text

Example

```
# echo hello
```

Date

Print or change the system data and time.

Syntax

```
date
```

Example

`# date`	To check date
`# date -s "24 feb 2017 19:00"`	To set date

Chapter 13

Piping and Redirection

Sending output to file (>)

Normally, we will get our output on the screen, but if we wish to save it into a file the greater than operator (**>**) is used to send the standard out to file.

Example

```
# ls > abc.txt
```

Sending input from file (<)

If we use the less than operator (<) then we can read data from file and feed it into the program via it's STDIN stream.

Example

```
# wc -l < abc.txt
```

Piping (|)

For sending data from one program to another we use pipe (|)

```
# ls | head -10
```

Chapter 14

Compression utilities

There are mainly three utilities to zip the files

Compression	Extension	Uncompress
bzip2	bz2	bunzip2
Gzip	gz	gunzip
Zip	zip	unzip

Compress

Bzip2 format

Syntax

```
bzip2 file_to_backups
```

Example

```
# bzip2 *
```

gzip format

Syntax

```
gzip file_to_backups
```

Example

```
# gzip abc
```

zip format

```
zip zipfile.zip file_to_backups
```

Example

```
# zip abc.zip *
```

Uncompress

Bzip2 format

Syntax

`bunzip2 filename`

Example

```
# bunzip2 abc.bz2
```

gzip format

Syntax

`gunzip filename`

Example

```
# gunzip abc.gz
```

zip format

Syntax

`unzip filename`

Example

```
# unzip abc.zip
```

Chapter 15

Managing services

Daemons

Daemons are processes, which run in the background and not interactively. Daemons perform some predefined actions at predefined time. Generally daemons start at bootup and remain till shutdown. Mostly daemons name ends with **d**.

Services

Earlier versions of Red Hat there used be scripts located in the /etc/rc.d/init.d/ directory and where used to control state of service and daemons.

In Red Hat 7, these init scripts have been replaced with service units, service units resides in **/etc/systemd/system/** directory. Service units end with the .service file extension **systemctl** command is used to view, start, stop, restart, enable, or disable system services.

Service can start at boot time using **systemctl enable name.service** command

Service Status Management

Starts a service	systemctl start name.service Example systemctl start iscsi.service
Stops a service	systemctl stop name.service

	Example systemctl stop iscsi.service
Restarts a service	systemctl restart name.service Example systemctl restart iscsi.service
Restarts a service only if it is running.	systemctl try-restart name.service Example systemctl try-restart iscsi.service
Reloads configuration	systemctl reload *name*.service Example systemctl reload iscsi.service
Checks if a service is running.	systemctl status *name*.service systemctl is-active *name*.service Example systemctl status iscsi.service
Displays the status of all service	systemctl list-units --type service --all or systemctl -at service

Enable and disable service at startup

Enable service	systemctl enable *name*.service Example systemctl enable iscsi.service
Disable service	systemctl disable *name*.service Example systemctl disable iscsi.service

To prevent service from starting dynamically or even manually unless unmasked	systemctl mask *name*.service Example systemctl mask iscsi.service
Check whether a service enabled or not	systemctl is-enabled *name*.service Example systemctl is-enabled iscsi.service
Lists all services and checks if they are enabled or not	systemctl list-unit-files --type service

Service unit information

When we give command **systemctl -status name.service**. it provides following information

Field	**Description**
Loaded	Whether the service unit is loaded, the absolute path to the unit file, whether the unit is enabled.
Active	Running or not
Main PID	PID of the service
Process	Information about process
CGroup	information about Control Groups.

Example

```
# systemctl status abrt-ccpp.service
abrt-ccpp.service - Install ABRT coredump hook
   Loaded: loaded (/usr/lib/systemd/system/abrt-ccpp.service;
enabled)
```

```
   Active: active (exited) since Sat 2017-03-18 06:05:25 IST;
1h 7min ago
  Process: 1013 ExecStart=/usr/sbin/abrt-install-ccpp-hook
install (code=exited, status=0/SUCCESS)
 Main PID: 1013 (code=exited, status=0/SUCCESS)
   CGroup: /system.slice/abrt-ccpp.service
```

systemd Targets

Previous versions of red hat implemented run level .Run level is state or mode of OS in which t will run. Each run level has certain number of services stopped or started providing control over behavior of machine. However, in Red hat 7 it is replaced by **systemd targets** there were seven **Runlevels** replaced by corresponding **target units**

Run level	Description	Target unit
0	halt the machine	poweroff.target
1	single user mode	rescue.target
2	multiuser with command line no GUI	multiuser.target
3	multiuser with command line no GUI	multiuser.target
4	multiuser with command line no GUI	multiuser.target
5	multiuser with GUI	graphical.target
6	reboot	reboot.target

Commands

List currently loaded target

```
# systemctl list-units --type target
```

Change the target

Switch to multiuser

```
# systemctl isolate multi-user.target
```

Switch to GUI mode

```
# systemctl isolate graphical.target
```

Change default target

```
# systemctl set-default <name of target>.target
```

Viewing the Default Target

```
# systemctl get-default
```

Changing the Current Target

```
# systemctl isolate <name of target>.target
```

Managing services startup

To list all services and there status

```
# systemctl -at service
```

To list current setting of specific service

Syntax

`systemctl status name.service`

Example

```
# systemctl status httpdd.service
```

Enabling service

Syntax

`systemctl enable` *`name`*`.service`

Example

```
# systemctl enable iscsi.service
```

To disable service

Syntax

`systemctl disable` *`name`*`.service`

Example

```
# systemctl disable iscsi.service
```

Managing the services status

Determine status of service whether it is running or not

Syntax

`# systemctl status name.service`

Example

```
# systemctl status httpdd.service
```

Starting service

Syntax

```
# systemctl start name.service
```

Example

```
# systemctl start httpd.service
```

Stopping service

Syntax

```
# systemctl stop name.service
```

Example

```
# systemctl stop httpd.service
```

Restarting service

Syntax

```
# systemctl restart name.service
```

Example

```
# systemctl restart httpd.service
```

Install new service

Procedure to install new service

1. Install new service package

   ```
   # yum install service_name
   ```

2. Configure the service to start automatically at startup

```
# systemctl enable name.service
```

3. Start the service

```
# systemctl start name.service
```

Example

```
# yum install vsftpd
# systemctl enable httpd.service
# service start httpd.service
```

Chapter 16

SSH

SSH provides a secure channel over unsecure network in client server architecture. SSH is a replacement of telnet, which is insecure protocol. It allows secure channel to login and execute command securely because all communication between client and server is encrypted.

ssh –x user@hostname

whenever ssh connection is made to system first time the public key of remote system is stored locally so it is identity can be verified next time.

Ctrl + d or exit command will terminate **ssh** session.

If you are connecting form MS windows client to Linux server you require third party software like **putty**.

ssh key

ssh keys helps in identifying yourself to an server using public key cryptography and challenge response authentication. ssh keys are generated in pair one public and private key. The public is for sharing and private key is for you. It must be kept safely.

Server having public key can send challenge, which can only be answered by server holding private key. This allows password less login.

Password less login to server from one server in this example redhat1 to host redhat2.

1. Create keys on **redhat1** host

```
[root@redhat1 ~]# ssh-keygen
```

2. Copy public key from **redhat1** to second server **redhat2** host

```
#scp ~/.ssh/id_rsa.pub root@redhat2:/root/id_rsa.server1.pub
```

3. On second server **redhat2** create directory .ssh in the home directory in our case the user is root its home directory is /root and change permissions.

```
[root@redhat2 ~]# mkdir .ssh
[root@redhat2 ~]# chmod 700 .ssh
```

4. Append the public key file to **authorized_keys** file and change permissions.

```
[root@redhat2 ~]# cat id_rsa.server1.pub >> .ssh/authorized_keys
[root@redhat2 ~]# chmod 644 .ssh/authorized_keys
```

5. Now try login form server one i.e **redhat1** to second server i.e. **redhat2** it will not ask for password.

```
[root@redhat1 ~]# ssh root@redhat2
```

Chapter 17

VNC

VNC Virtual Network Computing is graphical desktop sharing system. Used to get GUI desktop of Linux server remotely. In this VNC client is installed on local machine, which is used to connect to VNC server installed on remote server.

To configure VNC on server whose desktop you want to share

1. install

```
# yum install tigervnc-server
```

2. Copy file from **/lib/systemd/system/vncserver@.service** to **/etc/systemd/system/vncserver@:2.service**

```
cp /lib/systemd/system/vncserver@.service
/etc/systemd/system/vncserver@:2.service
```

3. Edit **/etc/systemd/system/vncserver@:2.service** change <USER> with the local user which will connect to VNC server

```
ExecStartPre=/bin/sh -c '/usr/bin/vncserver -kill %i >
/dev/null 2>&1 || :'
ExecStart=/sbin/runuser -l <USER> -c "/usr/bin/vncserver %i"
PIDFile=/home/<USER>/.vnc/%H%i.pid
ExecStop=/bin/sh -c '/usr/bin/vncserver -kill %i > /dev/null
2>&1 || :'

"/lib/systemd/system/vncserver@.service" 45L, 1744C
```

Change to following in my case it user1

```
ExecStartPre=/bin/sh -c '/usr/bin/vncserver -kill %i >
/dev/null 2>&1 || :'
ExecStart=/sbin/runuser -l user1 -c "/usr/bin/vncserver %i"
PIDFile=/home/user1/.vnc/%H%i.pid
ExecStop=/bin/sh -c '/usr/bin/vncserver -kill %i > /dev/null
2>&1 || :'

"/etc/systemd/system/vncserver@:2.service" 45L, 1742C
```

4. Set VNC password

```
# su user_name
# vncpasswd
```

5. Start and enable the VNC service

```
# systemctl start vncserver@:2.service
# systemctl enable vncserver@:2.service
```

6. Open firewall for vncserver

```
firewall-cmd --permanent --add-service vnc-server
firewall-cmd --reload
```

7. Install vncviewer on the remote machine

```
# yum install tigervnc
```

8. Connect on remote machine

   Go to Desktop of linux box open terminal

```
# vncviewer servername:2
```

It will ask for password we set for vncuser, give password

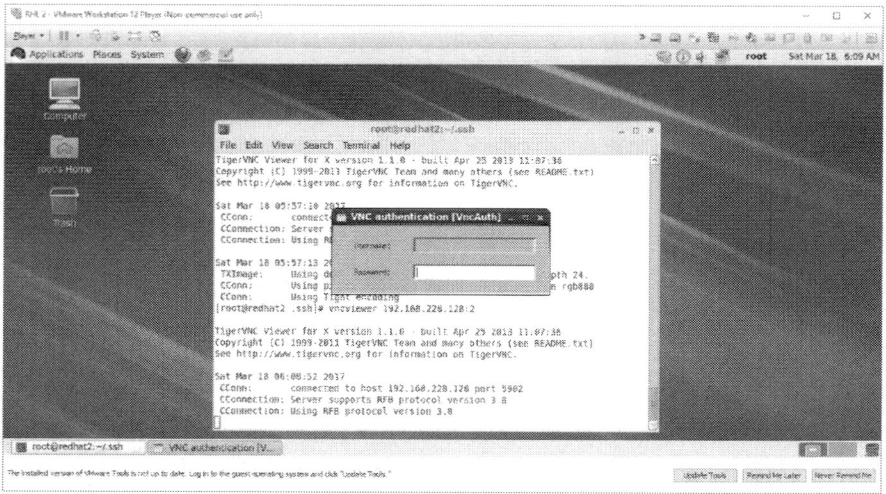

Chapter 18

FTP

FTP is file transfer protocol. It used to transfer files between the computers on the network. It's based on client server model. There can be three type of client

1. GUI
2. Web browser
3. Command line

In Redhat and derivatives distros **vsftp** (very secure FTP) Daemon s used as FTP server.

Deploying vsftp

Install the package

```
# yum install vsftpd
```

Start the server

```
# systemctl start vsftpd
```

Enable the service to start at startup

```
# systemctl enable vsftpd
```

Open the firewall

```
# firewall-cmd --permanent --add-service=ftp
# firewall-cmd --reload
```

Test from remote machine

Syntax

```
# sftp < server IP address or hostname >
```

It will ask for username and password use linux username and password for server

To upload file on ftp prompt

```
sftp> put file_name
```

To download file

```
sftp> get file_name
```

To exit

```
sftp> bye
```

Example

```
[root@redhat2 ~]# sftp redhat1
Connecting to redhat1...
root@redhat1's password:
sftp> pwd
Remote working directory: /root
sftp> cd /etc/
sftp> pwd
Remote working directory: /etc
sftp> get hosts
Fetching /etc/hosts to hosts
/etc/hosts
100%   84     0.1KB/s   00:00
sftp> bye
```

Note You can connect to ftp server anonymously. You can download and upload files to /var/ftp directory.

To configure server to allow anonymous user users ecit **/etc/vsftpd/vsftpd.conf**

Chapter 19

Web server

A webserver is program, which allows web browser clients to access web pages. it uses HTTP (Hypertext Transfer Protocol). In RedHat and its derivatives, Apache HTTP server is used.

Deploying http server

Install http server

```
# yum install httpd
```

Start service

```
# systemctl start httpd
```

Enable the service to start on boot

```
# systemctl enable httpd
```

Open firewall and reload the configuration

```
# firewall-cmd --permanent --add-service=http
# firewall-cmd --reload
```

Default directory where http keeps contents

/var/www/html

Configuration file

/etc/httpd/conf/http.conf

Test

1. Create file in directory /var/www/html/index.html and Write **Hello**
2. Save the file and exit
3. Open the firefox on the address bar write http://localhost
4. You should see hello

Chapter 20

Firewall

According to dictionary, a firewall is a wall or partition designed to inhibit or prevent the spread of fire. In computer world, firewall is network security system used to secure the incoming and outgoing connections. It prevents unauthorized access to the system. It restrict user to access only designated services.

Redhat Linux kernel has built in firewall, which can be used to allow or deny incoming and outgoing network traffic. To configure firewall we can do through GUI or manually:-

In GUI mode

```
# firewall-config
```

Firewalld is the new interface in Redhat 7. It replaces the **iptables** interface and connects to the netfilter kernel code. firewalld stores its rules in various XML files in /usr/lib/firewalld/ and /etc/firewalld/. Firewalld allows security configuration without stopping current configuration. In earlier version with **iptables** every change requires flushing of all old rules and reading new rules from iptable configuration file but in firewalld only new differences are applied without disturbing current connections.

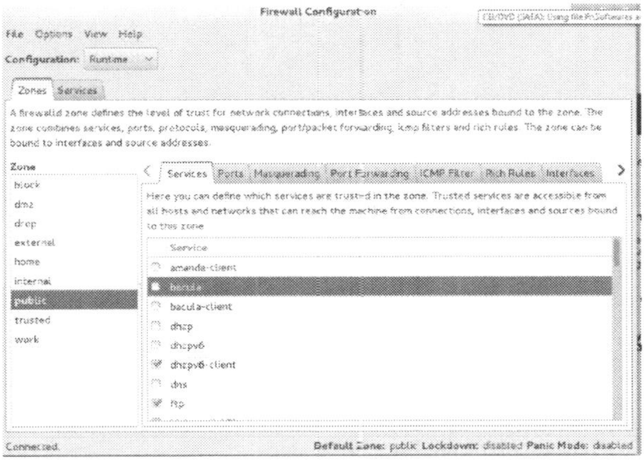

Zones

In firewalld concept of zone is based on network interface all network interfaces can be located in the same default zone or divided into different zones according to the levels of trust defined. By defualt public zone is used for configuration if you have more than one interface than you can create more zones and restrict trafic between zones. Lets take example if we have web server having two interface one connecting to outside world i.e. public zone and second interface in trusted zone that connects to database server.

Note: Without any configuration, everything is done by default in the public zone.

Manual Configuration

A command-line client **firewall-cmd**, is provided. It can be used to make permanent and runtime changes to firewall rules. You require be root or administrative privileges to run **firewalld-cmd** command

Install firewalld

```
yum install firewalld
```

Know if it is running

```
systemctl status firewalld
```

or

```
firewall-cmd --state
```

To display default zone

```
# firewall-cmd --get-default-zone
```

List the available zones

```
# firewall-cmd --get-zones
```

Change the default zone

```
# firewall-cmd --set-default-zone= internal
```

Check the zone interface is associated with

```
# firewall-cmd --get-zone-of-interface=eno16777736
```

Change the interface zone

```
# firewall-cmd --permanent --zone=internal --change-
interface= eno16777736
```

Service management

List of services in the default zone

```
# firewall-cmd --list-services
```

Add a service to permanently to default zone

```
# firewall-cmd --permanent --add-service=http
```

After that, you have to reload the new configuration

```
# firewall-cmd --reload
```

Add service to specific zone

```
# firewall-cmd --permanent --zone=internal --add-service=http
```

Port Management

Firewalld allows configuration to permit traffic through the firewall to a certain port.

List of ports in the default zone

```
# firewall-cmd --list-ports
```

Opening Port in the Firewall

```
firewall-cmd --permanent --zone=public --add-port=5903/tcp
```

then

```
# firewall-cmd --reload
```

Chapter 21

Selinux

Selinux is **S**ecurity **E**nhanced **Linux**. Selinux is kernel module that improves the Linux server security. This is one of the solution for implementation of Access Control in Linux.

Selinux implements **MAC** Mandatory Access Control. Selinux is set of security rules, which determine which process can access which file, directory or port etc. Selinux policy to access process, directory, and files is called as context. One goal of Selinux is to protect data and system. Selinux has three forms of access control:

1. Enforcing
2. Permissive
3. Disabled

Enforcing

Selinux denes access based on selinux policy rules.

Permissive

Selinux does not deny access but deniels are logged for the action that would have been denied if running in enforcing mode.

Disabled

Selinux is completely disabled

Check the installation

```
# rpm -qa | grep selinux
```

Check current mode

```
# getenforce
```

Check the status

```
# sestatus
```

Main configuration file

```
/etc/selinux/config
```

To Change the mode

Edit `/etc/Selinux/config` configuration file and change **selinux=enforcing** to desired mode like **selinux= permissive**. After saving the file and reboot the server.

If you set the mode to **permissive** you can check the log what Selinux is doing.

```
# cat /var/log/messages |grep -i selinux
```

Or

```
tail -f /var/log/audit/audit.log
```

Commands to display context

Description	Command
List process conext	ps auxZ
Display user context	Id –Z
Display files with context	ls -lZ
copy wit context	cp -Z

mkdir with context	mkdir -Z

Install selinux

```
# yum install policycoreutil policycoreutil-python
```

Tool to change context

```
# semanage
```

Show context

```
# semanage fcontext -l
```

Types

The main permission control method used in SELinux targeted policy to provide advanced process isolation is **Type Enforcement**. All files and processes are labeled as a type. Types define a SELinux domain for processes and a SELinux type for files

Example of Types are

httpd_sys_content_t

tmp_t

Add context

```
# semanage fcontext -a -t httpd_sys_content_t  /abc/zzz.txt
# ls -Z
-rw-r--r--. root root unconfined_u:object_r:samba_share_t:s0
zzz.txt
```

Set the context to default

```
# restorecon -v -t /abc/zzz.txt
```

Booleans

Booleans allow a part of Selinux policy to change at runtime without any knowledge of Selinux policy writing

List Booleans

```
# semanage boolean -l
```

Configure Booleans

1. list all

```
semanage boolean -l
```

2. list Booleans weather they are on/off

```
getsebool -a
```

3. Allow ftp read and write files in the users home directory

```
setsebool -P ftp_home_dir on
```

4. Check

```
# getsebool ftp_home_dir
ftp_home_dir --> on
```

Chapter 22

Partition and file system

Partitions

Partition is to divide the storage, mostly hard disk into segments in which you can have more than one type of file systems. Partitioning of storage helps in managing storage properly.

fdisk is used to partition the disk.

List the partition table

```
fdisk -l
```

List the partition table for specific

Syntax

```
fdisk -l <device name >
```

Example

```
fdisk -l /dev/hda1
```

Create new partition on device

In this example /dev/sda2 is added to system

1. First check the new device added

```
# fdisk -l
Disk /dev/sdb: 21.5 GB, 21474836480 bytes
255 heads, 63 sectors/track, 2610 cylinders
Units = cylinders of 16065 * 512 = 8225280 bytes
Sector size (logical/physical): 512 bytes / 512 bytes
```

it will show the all storage device

2. Run fdisk on required device

```
fdisk -cu /dev/sdb
```

3. Check if partition is there on device selected with disk

   Press **p** and **enter** key

```
Command (m for help): p

Disk /dev/sdb: 21.5 GB, 21474836480 bytes
255 heads, 63 sectors/track, 2610 cylinders, total 41943040
sectors
Units = sectors of 1 * 512 = 512 bytes
Sector size (logical/physical): 512 bytes / 512 bytes
I/O size (minimum/optimal): 512 bytes / 512 bytes
Disk identifier: 0xdec2ee90

   Device Boot      Start         End      Blocks   Id  System
```

4. Press **n** for new partition
5. Press **p** for primary
6. Give partition number like **1, 2, 3, 4**
7. Press **Enter** for starting section

   For last sector, give size like +1G to create 1 GB partition

```
Command (m for help): n
Command action
   e   extended
   p   primary partition (1-4)
p
Partition number (1-4): 1
First sector (2048-41943039, default 2048):
Using default value 2048
Last sector, +sectors or +size{K,M,G} (2048-41943039, default
41943039): +1G
```

8. Press **w** to write on disk

File system

File System is method used by operating system to store data and retrieve it. File system helps in managing and arranging data. File systems can be

- shareable
- non shareable

XFS

XFS is a high-performance journaling file system that was initially created by Silicon Graphics, Inc. for the IRIX operating system and later ported to Linux. XFS supports metadata journaling, which facilitates quicker crash recovery. The XFS file system can also be defragmented and enlarged while mounted and active. XFS records file system updates asynchronously to a circular buffer (the journal) before it can commit the actual data updates to disk. XFS is default File system for Red hat 7

EXT File System

Extended file system (ext) is poplar file system used In Redhat 6 and earlier. **Ext3** is journalized file system, it keeps track of changes not yet committed to the file system by recording such changes in data structure to journal which in turn generate circular log. In case of abrupt system down like power failure or crashed file system can be brought back online easily. There are different generation of **ext** File system

- ext2
- ext3

- ext4

.

ext2, ext3 came before RHEL 5 having limitation of file system size as 8TB /16TB and file size as 2 TB

Ext4 came in RHEL 5.6 file system and file size is 16TB. It is efficient reliable and robust.

Creating XFS file system

1. Create partition with fdisk
2. **fdisk -l** check the device name
3. **mkfs -t xfs /dev/sdb1** where **sdb1** is device name and **xfs** is file system type

```
[root@redhat1 ~]# mkfs -t xfs /dev/sdb1
```

4. **create mount point**

```
[root@redhat1 ~]# mkdir /test1
```

5. **Add entry in the /etc/fstab**

```
[root@redhat1 ~]# vi /etc/fstab
/dev/mapper/rhel_rhl--one-root /     xfs     defaults        1 1
UUID=6b761a5f-8c7c-465d-b58c-d29267938403 /boot   xfs defaults
1 2
/dev/mapper/rhel_rhl--one-swap swap swap    defaults        0 0
/dev/sdb1         /test1          xfs     defaults        0 2
```

Where **/dev/sdb1** is device **/test1** mount point, **xfs** for partition type, 0 for dump and 2 order for fsck.

Chapter 23

Swap space

Swap space is used in Linux and UNIX to free physical memory. The inactive pages of data is written to slower storage i.e. hard disk. The area where inactive data is written is called as swap space.

Add swap space

1. Create partition

```
[root@redhat1 ~]# fdisk /dev/sdb

WARNING: DOS-compatible mode is deprecated. It's strongly
recommended to switch off the mode (command 'c') and change
display units to sectors (command 'u').

Command (m for help): n
Command action
   e   extended
   p   primary partition (1-4)
p
Partition number (1-4): 2
First cylinder (307-6132, default 307):
Using default value 307
Last cylinder, +cylinders or +size{K,M,G} (307-6132, default
6132): +1G
```

2. Change the type by pressing **t** of partition selected to **82** which is **linux swap**

```
Command (m for help): t
Partition number (1-4): 2
```

```
Hex code (type L to list codes): 82
Changed system type of partition 2 to 82 (Linux swap / Solaris)
```

3. Check the partition

```
Command (m for help): p

Disk /dev/sdb: 21.5 GB, 21474836480 bytes
171 heads, 40 sectors/track, 6132 cylinders
Units = cylinders of 6840 * 512 = 3502080 bytes
Sector size (logical/physical): 512 bytes / 512 bytes
I/O size (minimum/optimal): 512 bytes / 512 bytes
Disk identifier: 0xdec2ee90

   Device Boot      Start         End      Blocks   Id  System
/dev/sdb1               1         307     1048576   83  Linux
/dev/sdb2             307          614      1050280   82  Linux
swap / Solaris
```

4. Press w to write partition to disk

```
Command (m for help): w
The partition table has been altered!

Calling ioctl() to re-read partition table.
Syncing disks.
```

5. **mkswap /dev/sdb2** where sdb2 is name of the partition which will be used as swap.

```
[root@redhat1 ~]# mkswap /dev/sdb2
Setting up swapspace version 1, size = 1050276 KiB
no label, UUID=c1f98067-9548-4bf1-843d-5f09f5d5ba56
```

6. Add entry in /etc/fstab

```
[root@redhat1 ~]# cat /etc/fstab

/dev/mapper/rhel_rhl--one-root /    xfs     defaults        1 1
UUID=6b761a5f-8c7c-465d-b58c-d29267938403 boot xfs     defaults
1 2
/dev/mapper/rhel_rhl--one-swap swap                        swap
defaults        0 0
/dev/sdb1       /test1          xfs     defaults        0 2
UUID=c392a0fd-528c-46d4-a20f-30881166274c swap swap    defaults
0 0
```

7. swapon -a will activate swap

8. swapon -s will show status of all swap space

```
[root@redhat1 ~]# swapon -s
Filename                Type            Size    Used    Priority
/dev/dm-1               partition       2097144 0       -1
/dev/sdb2               partition       1050272 0       -2
```

To deactivate the swap space

swapoff /dev/sdb2

Chapter 24

Logical Volume Manager

In earlier section we learned about creating Linux partition but we can also create partition type LVM (logical partition manager). When we create LVM type partition, LVM manages space allocated to it. Which is more sophisticated than normal Linux partition. LVM has following benefits

- Grow the File system dynamically
- shrink the File system
- Add disk dynamically
- Mirroring
- Stripping
- Snapshot as backup of File system

Terms used in LVM

Physical Volume

Physical Volume (PV) is physical storage unit of an LVM is a block device such as a partition or whole disk. To use the device for an LVM create partition with **fdisk** as **LVM** type.

Volume Groups

One or more physical volumes combined into Volume Group (VG).

Physical Extent

Storage space from Physical Volume is divided in to small unit of fixed size known as physical extent, which is smallest unit that can be allocated. P.E. will same for all physical volume in the same VG.

Logical extent

Mapping of PE to make up front end of LVM. By default one PE is mapped to one LE But, you can map more than one PE to one LE in case of mirroring.

Logical Volume

Logical volume is group of Logical Extent. It is here we create File system. Logical volume are not restricted to physical disk sizes. In addition, the hardware storage layer is isolated form software.

Steps to create File system with newly disk added to system

1. Create Physical volume (PV)
   Use **fdisk** command and create partition type Linux LVM **8e**

```
[root@redhat1 ~]# fdisk /dev/sdb

WARNING: DOS-compatible mode is deprecated. It's strongly
recommended to
         switch off the mode (command 'c') and change display
units to
         sectors (command 'u').

Command (m for help): n
Command action
   e   extended
```

```
   p   primary partition (1-4)
p
Partition number (1-4): 3
First cylinder (615-6132, default 615):
Using default value 615
Last cylinder, +cylinders or +size{K,M,G} (615-6132, default
6132): +5G

Command (m for help): t
Partition number (1-4): 3
Hex code (type L to list codes): 8e
Changed system type of partition 3 to 8e (Linux LVM)

Command (m for help): p

Disk /dev/sdb: 21.5 GB, 21474836480 bytes
171 heads, 40 sectors/track, 6132 cylinders
Units = cylinders of 6840 * 512 = 3502080 bytes
Sector size (logical/physical): 512 bytes / 512 bytes
I/O size (minimum/optimal): 512 bytes / 512 bytes
Disk identifier: 0xdec2ee90

   Device Boot      Start         End      Blocks   Id  System
/dev/sdb1               1         307     1048576   83  Linux
/dev/sdb2             307         614     1050280   82  Linux
swap / Solaris
/dev/sdb3             615        2148     5246280   8e  Linux
LVM

Command (m for help): w
The partition table has been altered!

Calling ioctl() to re-read partition table.
```

```
WARNING: Re-reading the partition table failed with error 16:
Device or resource busy.
The kernel still uses the old table. The new table will be used
at
the next reboot or after you run partprobe(8) or kpartx(8)
Syncing disks.
```

2. Reboot the server

3. Create PV using command **pvcreate *device_name*** where *device_name* is device created with fdisk

```
[root@redhat1 ~]# pvcreate /dev/sdb3
    Physical volume "/dev/sdb3" successfully created
[root@redhat1 ~]# pvdisplay /dev/sdb3
  "/dev/sdb3" is a new physical volume of "5.00 GiB"
  --- NEW Physical volume ---
  PV Name               /dev/sdb3
  VG Name
  PV Size               5.00 GiB
  Allocatable           NO
  PE Size               0
  Total PE              0
  Free PE               0
  Allocated PE          0
  PV UUID               EQ7ElZ-WiGK-Z0m5-5gSN-gP95-MFSk-
pKyTvS
```

4. Create Volume Group (VG)
   vgcreate *VG_name PV_name*

```
[root@redhat1 ~]# vgcreate vg01 /dev/sdb3
  Volume group "vg01" successfully created
```

5. Create new Logical Volume(LV)
   lvcreate -n *LV_name* -L *size VG_name*

```
[root@redhat1 ~]# lvcreate -n lv01 -L 1G vg01
  Logical volume "lv01" created
```

6. Create File System on LV
   mkfs -t xfs /dev/*VG_name*/*LV_name*

```
[root@redhat1 ~]# mkfs -t xfs /dev/vg01/lv01
```

7. Check the UUID of newly created file system

```
#  blkid /dev/vg01/lv01
```

8. Add entry to **/etc/fstab** mount system automatically at startup

```
UUID=6acaa400-0cd3-4708-ba05-5541139e830e  /newfs
xfs    defaults         1 2
```

9. Mount the file system
   mount -a

PV Commands

Description	**Command**
Display PV properties	pvdisplay
Show all LVM block devices	pvscan
Prevent allocation of PE on PV	pvchange -xn */dev/PV_name*
Remove PV	pvremove */dev/PV_name*

Volume Group Commands

Description	Command
Display VG properties	vgdisplay
Display VG List	vgs
Add PV to VG	vgextend vgname */dev/PV_name* **Example** `# vgextend vg01 /dev/sdb5`
Remove PV form VG	vgreduce vg1 */dev/PV_name* **Example** `# vgreduce vg01 /dev/sdb5`
Activating VG	vgchange -ay *VG_name*
deactivating VG	vgchange -ay *VG_name*
Remove VG	vgremove *VG_name* **Example** `vgremove /dev/vg02`
Recreate a VG Directory	vgmknodes

Moving Volume group from one system to other

1. On first system where VG is currently running unmount all FS which is part of VG

```
umount /newfs
```

2. Deactivate the VG **vgchange -an *VG_name*** command

```
[root@redhat1 /]# vgchange -an sharedvg
```

3. Export the VG with **vgexport *VG_name*** command

```
[root@redhat1 /]# vgexport sharedvg
```

4. After attaching HDD to new system import the VG with **vgimport *VG_name*** command

```
[root@redhat2 ~]# vgimport sharedvg
```

5. Activate the VG with **vgchange -ay VG_name**

```
[root@redhat2 ~]# vgchange -ay sharedvg
```

6. Mount the file systems on the VG

```
[root@redhat2 ~]# mount /dev/sharedvg/sharedlv /mnt
```

7. Check the contents of file system

```
[root@redhat2 ~]# cd /mnt
```

Extending FileSystem

1. Check the current FS size
   df -h /fsname

```
/dev/mapper/vg01-lvC1          1008M   34M  924M   4% /newfs
```

2. Check if you have enough free space i.e free PE on the VG where LV of FS you want extend is there.

```
[root@redhat1 ~]# vgdisplay vg01
  --- Volume group ---
```

```
  VG Name               vg01
  System ID
  Format                lvm2
  Metadata Areas        1
  Metadata Sequence No  5
  VG Access             read/write
  VG Status             resizable
  MAX LV                0
  Cur LV                1
  Open LV               1
  Max PV                0
  Cur PV                1
  Act PV                1
  VG Size               5.00 GiB
  PE Size               4.00 MiB
  Total PE              1280
  Alloc PE / Size       256 / 1.00 GiB
  Free  PE / Size       1024 / 4.00 GiB
  VG UUID               EXKfhW-MfE4-4ZtU-uQuM-v9e4-AJ9k-
Uo6z4B
```

3. Extend the Logical Volume **lvextend -L size /dev/vgname/lvname**

```
[root@redhat1 ~]# lvextend -L +200M /dev/vg01/lv01
  Extending logical volume lv01 to 1.20 GiB
  Logical volume lv01 successfully resized
```

4. Extend the file system using

xfs_growfs /fsname

```
[root@redhat1 ~]# xfs_growfs /newfs
```

5. Check the FS size
   df -h /fsname

```
/dev/mapper/vg01-lv01          1.2G   34M  1.1G   3% /newfs
```

Reduce the File System

1. Check the current FS size
   df -h /fs_name

```
/dev/mapper/vg01-lv01          1.2G   34M  1.1G   3% /newfs
```

2. Backup the File System

```
# xfsdump -f /tmp/newfs.dump /newfs
```

3. unmount the Filesystem
   umount /fs_name

```
# umount /newfs
```

4. Remove the LV

```
# lvremove /dev/mapper/vg01-lv01
```

5. Recreate LV

```
#lvcreate -n lv01 -L 1G vg01
```

6. Recreate the File system

```
# mkfs.xfs /dev/vg01/lv01
```

7. First check the UUID

```
# blkid /dev/vg01/lv01
```

8. Change the UUID of File system in /etc/fstab

9. Mount File System

```
# mount -a
```

10. Restore the backup

```
xfsrestore -f /tmp/newfs.dump /newfs
```

11. Check File System

```
#  df -h /newfs
```

Chapter 25

LVM snapshot

LVM snapshot is a point in time copy of Logical Volume. The snapshot provides static view of original volume. Once snapshot has been taken we can use this snapshot to take backup volume as snapshot is static copy and it will not change while backup is happening unlike the original volume which is dynamic.

The snapshot volume size should be enough to store the data that will change after snapshot has been taken. the volume will store only changes after the snapshot has been taken.

Create snapshot LV

1. Check the LV name and size of File System for which you want to create snapshot

```
[root@redhat1 /]# df -hT /newfs
Filesystem            Type  Size  Used Avail Use% Mounted on
/dev/mapper/vg01-lv01 ext4 1008M   34M  924M   4% /newfs
```

2. Check you have space at least equivalent to 10% of file system you want to take snapshot available on the VG where original LV is located

```
# vgdisplay vg01
```

3. Create LV 8 to 10 % of capicity of original LV
lvcreate -s -n snaplvname -L size /dev/vgname/orginal_lv_name

```
# lvcreate -s -n snaplv1 -L 100M /dev/mapper/vg01-lv01
```

4. if you want to see content of snapshot LV
   mount -o ro /dev/vgname/snaplv /mount_point_snaplv

```
# mount -o ro /dev/vg01/snaplv1 /snapfs/
```

5. Change to directory to check the contents
   cd /mount_point_snaplv

```
cd /snapfs/
ls
```

Remove snapshot LV

1. Unmount snap File system
   umount /mount_point_snaplv

```
[root@redhat1 /]# umount /snapfs
```

2. Remove the snap logical
   lvremove /dev/vgname/snaplv

```
[root@redhat1 /]# lvremove /dev/mapper/vg01-snaplv1
```

Chapter 26

Boot process

Boot process of Linux

1. **BIOS**
2. **Master Boot Record**
3. **GRUB 2**

   Uses /boot/grub2/grub.cfg to select the kernel image. Do not edit this file. GRUB2 menu-configuration settings uses /etc/default/grub when generating grub.cfg
4. **Kernel**
   a. Mounts the root file system as specified in the "root=" in grub.conf
   b. The kernel starts the systemd process with a process ID of 1 (PID 1)
   c. **initrd** stands for Initial RAM Disk. initrd is used by kernel as temporary root file system until kernel is booted and the real root file system is mounted. It also contains drivers, which are required to access hard disk and other necessary hardware.
5. **systemd**

Systemd is a system and service manager for Linux operating systems. It is designed to be backwards compatible with SysV init scripts, and provides a number of features such as parallel startup of system services at boot time .systemd is the parent process of all processes on a system.

systemd reads **/etc/systemd/system/default.target** to determine the default system target earlier it used to called as run level. After determining the target, it performs the initialization of system, which includes

1. Setting the host name
2. Initializing the network
3. Initializing the system hardware
4. Mounting the file systems
5. Starting swapping

Chapter 27

Reset unknown root password

1. At menu press any key any key to enter GRUB menu press arrow keys to stop count down
2. Select first item not the recovery and press **e**

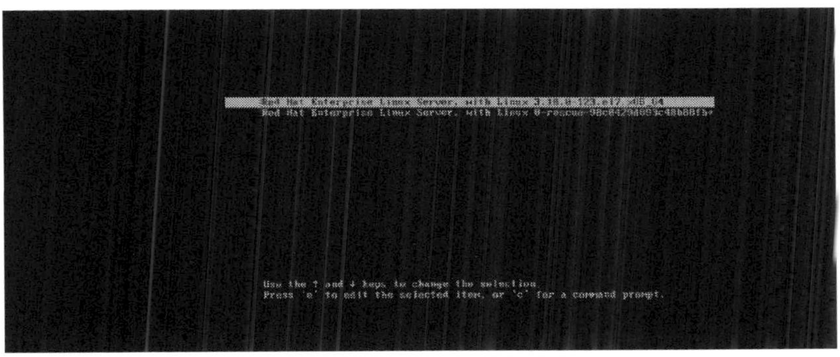

3. Look for line initrd16 above it at the last of line write **rd.break** press Ctrl + x key

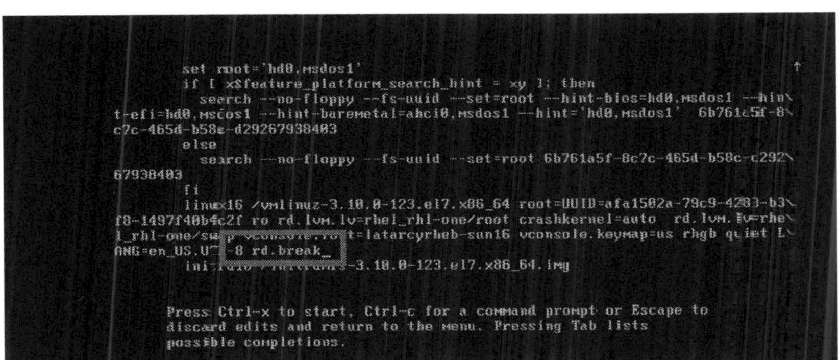

4. It will give prompt but root file system is read only

```
switch_root:/# mount
rootfs on / type rootfs (rw)
proc on /proc type proc (rw,nosuid,nodev,noexec,relatime)
sysfs on /sys type sysfs (rw,nosuid,nodev,noexec,relatime)
devtmpfs on /dev type devtmpfs (rw,nosuid,size=926092k,nr_inodes=231523,mode=755)
securityfs on /sys/kernel/security type securityfs (rw,nosuid,nodev,noexec,relatime)
tmpfs on /dev/shm type tmpfs (rw,nosuid,nodev)
devpts on /dev/pts type devpts (rw,nosuid,noexec,relatime,gid=5,mode=620,ptmxmode=000)
tmpfs on /run type tmpfs (rw,nosuid,nodev,mode=755)
tmpfs on /sys/fs/cgroup type tmpfs (rw,nosuid,nodev,noexec,mode=755)
cgroup on /sys/fs/cgroup/systemd type cgroup (rw,nosuid,nodev,noexec,relatime,xattr,release_ag
pstore on /sys/fs/pstore type pstore (rw,nosuid,nodev,noexec,relatime)
cgroup on /sys/fs/cgroup/cpuset type cgroup (rw,nosuid,nodev,noexec,relatime,cpuset)
cgroup on /sys/fs/cgroup/cpu,cpuacct type cgroup (rw,nosuid,nodev,noexec,relatime,cpuacct,cpu)
cgroup on /sys/fs/cgroup/memory type cgroup (rw,nosuid,nodev,noexec,relatime,memory)
cgroup on /sys/fs/cgroup/devices type cgroup (rw,nosuid,nodev,noexec,relatime,devices)
cgroup on /sys/fs/cgroup/freezer type cgroup (rw,nosuid,nodev,noexec,relatime,freezer)
cgroup on /sys/fs/cgroup/net_cls type cgroup (rw,nosuid,nodev,noexec,relatime,net_cls)
cgroup on /sys/fs/cgroup/blkio type cgroup (rw,nosuid,nodev,noexec,relatime,blkio)
cgroup on /sys/fs/cgroup/perf_event type cgroup (rw,nosuid,nodev,noexec,relatime,perf_event)
cgroup on /sys/fs/cgroup/hugetlb type cgroup (rw,nosuid,nodev,noexec,relatime,hugetlb)
configfs on /sys/kernel/config type configfs (rw,relatime)
/dev/mapper/rhel_rhl--one-root on /sysroot type xfs (ro,relatime,attr2,inode64,noquota)
switch_root:/#
```

5. Mount the / root file system in read write mode

```
switch_root:/# mount -o remount,rw /sysroot
```

6. Chroot /sysroot

```
switch_root:/# chroot /sysroot
```

7. Give **passwd** command to change password
8. If you Selinux is installed create file

```
sh-4.2# touch /.autorelabel
```

9. Write **exit** and press enter
10. Write **exit** and press enter again to start the system in normal mode

Chapter 28

Identify your system

Know version of Redhat

```
# cat /etc/redhat-release
```

Know running kernel version

```
# uname -r
```

or

```
# cat /proc/version
```

List all installed kernel version

```
# yum list installed kernel\*
```

Display CPU information

```
# lscpu
```

or

```
# cat /proc/cpuinfo
```

List all PCI devices

```
# lspci
```

Detailed description of system hardware

```
# dmidecode
```

Display memory information

```
# cat /proc/meminfo
```

or

```
# free -m          shows memory in MB
```

List block device

```
# lsblk
```

List all partitions

```
# fdisk -l
```

List CPU, Memory, Process

```
# top
```

Display Hostname

```
# hostname
```

sosreport

The "**sosreport**" is a tool to collect troubleshooting data on RHEL/CentOS systems. It generates report of configuration of Linux system and most important logs in tarball compressed format which can be sent to Redhat for support related to any problem or performance issues.

Install package

```
# yum install sos
# yum install abrt-cli
```

Generate report

```
# sosreport
```

It prompts for the name of file and logged case number for which you are generating report. If you do not have case number.

28475428R00081

Printed in Poland
by Amazon Fulfillment
Poland Sp. z o.o., Wrocław

FAR ACROSS THE SEA

A family saga that begins in Scotland in 1913, progresses through two world wars and leads to a life in Australia.

Carmel McMurdo Audsley

ABOUT THE AUTHOR

Carmel McMurdo Audsley is an Australian Journalist, Editor and Author who lives in Brisbane with her husband Iain. They both had Scottish fathers, share a mutual love of Scotland and have walked in the footsteps of their ancestors in the country that they love to visit. As a Newspaper Journalist and Magazine Editor, Carmel has written, and had published, thousands of news stories and feature articles and has now turned her research and writing skills to digging up the past and breathing life into the characters she finds. Her first historical fiction novel, *Ours, Yours and Mines*, about the mining families of Ayrshire Scotland, was published in 2012 and captured the hearts of readers as the story unfolded about the harsh living conditions of the mid-1800s and the sad loss of life. *Far Across The Sea* continues the story. Carmel now devotes all her writing and editing time to producing *Scots News Magazine* for ex-pat Scots in Australia, and researching and writing historical fiction.

Published by Theatricks Publishing, Australia. theatricks@iinet.net.au

ISBN 978-1484851715

Cover photo: The SS Brent which carried passengers from Britain to Australia in the 1950s.

Other books by Carmel McMurdo Audsley

Ours, Yours and Mines

FAR ACROSS THE SEA

is dedicated to all the people who took the chance to travel so far across the sea in search of adventure and a new life. Some didn't last the distance and found the Australian way of life too different from their lives in Britain, and so they returned home. Others took up the challenges they faced in their new country, adapted, worked hard and reaped the rewards of their toil. Australia's 'Populate or Perish' campaign after WWII beckoned British people to the 'lucky country' with the prospect of full employment and owning a home – and sunshine, kangaroos and Holden cars. We are a luckier country because of the manpower, ingenuity and culture these new Aussies brought to our shores. I am a first generation Australian, and I wouldn't be here if my Scottish father hadn't decided to take a chance and board a ship to a new land. This book is also dedicated to all the brave men and women who fought in WWI and WWII to keep us safe. Because of our geographic place in the world, Australia remained comparatively untouched after WWII, while the people of Scotland had to live with rationing of food and clothing for years after the conflicts had been settled. I thank them for their tenacity, bravery and resilience.

~Carmel

FOREWORD

I grew up in a time of plenty, in the post-war boom. I knew very little about my father's life in Scotland before I started researching the family history. I knew that I was expected to do well at school and that failure wasn't an option, and I just accepted the expectations of my parents. I had no idea of the responsibility my father carried for the safety of his fellow workers in his dangerous occupation in the mines. I now feel blessed that I was able to build on a good educational foundation and come home to a clean, warm home with plenty of food on the table and clothes in the cupboard. We take it for granted that that is the right of every child. But in Scotland (and other parts of the world) in the earlier part of the 20th century, two world wars devastated towns and villages, physically, socially and economically, and people had to make do with what they had, or go without.

As I have looked back at my grandfather's and father's early lives, the past has become romanticised, as nostalgia is wont to do, but the reality was harsh. I have thought how difficult it must have been for my father to leave his family, friends and country to travel across the world in search of adventure and better prospects. It is only now that I realise how lonely and homesick he was in the first few months of being in Australia, and how easily he could have got on another boat and gone back home, but he stuck it out and eventually things started to look better for him. *Far Across the Sea* is the sequel to my first novel in the McMurdo family trilogy *Ours, Yours and Mines*. You don't need to have read the first novel to be able to enjoy this story, but it would probably give you a greater sense of involvement and continuity to have first read *Ours, Yours and Mines*.

Far Across the Sea picks up after the death of family matriarch Mary Hamilton McMurdo, with her grandson George going down the mines in Ayrshire, despite her wishes. He's a headstrong lad (a McMurdo family trait) and ends up in the trenches in France during WWI. It was a difficult time in Scotland after the war and during the Depression years and WWII. George's son William (known in this book as Willie, and later as Bill) becomes the new hero of the story and you will laugh at some of his mischievous escapades and cheer him on through life's difficulties.

William (my Dad) passed away on April 8, 2012 and I have felt his presence as I have written this book. Information that I had been unable to find would suddenly materialise, and things he had told me over the years came flooding back.

I thank my mother, Myrt, for sharing her recollections of their early life together, as well as stories he had told her about his life in Scotland. My cousin William, in Ayrshire, told me a lot about the Bell family that I would not otherwise have known, and to him and all my cousins in Scotland, I say thank you.

To me, Dad will always be as large as life. He doled out strict discipline just as his grandfather had done, and found it hard to express emotion, but he lived a life full of laughter, music, learning, mateship, generosity and compassion. We all have to travel our own road in life. It takes courage to take the road less travelled.

Carmel McMurdo Audsley

CONTENTS

Oh but I'm longing for my ain folk
Tho they be lowly, puir and plain folk
I am far beyond the sea but my heart will ever be
At hame in dear auld Scotland wi' my ain folk.

Chorus from *My Ain Folk* by Wilfred Mills

Chapter 1 (1913)

STEPPING OUT AS A MAN

Fifteen-year-old George McMurdo entered the colliery gates of the underground mine in his home village of Cumnock in East Ayrshire, Scotland, with the man who had raised him since he was three years old. His uncle, William McMurdo, was the father figure in his life and his grandmother, Mary Hamilton McMurdo, had been his mother figure. George's mother Agnes had died from tuberculosis just three months after giving birth to him, and his father too was taken by tuberculosis when George was just three years old. He had been denied a mother's love and his grandmother, a strong woman whose own heart was hardened by the loss of seven children as well as her husband, gave him all the nurturing she could. Now she too was gone. Her broken heart had finally stopped beating and now the two men were alone.

Mary Hamilton McMurdo had fought hard to keep her children out of the coal mines of Ayrshire, and for a while she succeeded. Her son Douglas (young George's father) had become a Master Baker. Another of Mary's sons, Andrew, followed his brother into the bakery trade, and William had for a time worked as a Bonded Housekeeper's Assistant. After Douglas and Andrew passed away in their twenties, William became the sole wage earner for the family and he knew that he could earn more money working in the mines so, against his mother's wishes, William started work in a coal mine. On her deathbed, Mary had asked William not to let young George ever see the inside of a coal mine, but she also knew that the lad had a mind of his own and would do whatever he felt was best for him.

And so it was, that just one week after his grandmother had been interred in the family plot at Muirkirk Cemetery, young George closed the door on the little two-room house where they lived in Barhill Road, Cumnock and walked proudly along the coal-strewn roads with his Uncle William, to become a colliery man.

He had heard so much about the mines from his uncle, and he knew the family history. His grandfather George, great-grandfather Thomas and great-great-grandfather George had all been coal miners. Despite the dangers involved in working underground, none had perished as a result of a mining accident though all had suffered injury and illness. And now, here he was, at just fifteen years of age, ready to get into the pit cage and descend to the depths below to strike his first blow with a pick and shovel.

Cumnock was a market town for other smaller towns in the district, and almost entirely dependent upon the mining industry to provide employment and economic growth. There were few options for the people of the parish. Many of the men worked for pit operators Bairds and Dalmellington Ltd, and while conditions continued to improve, it was still back-breaking, dangerous work. Despite the large tracts of blackened land that mining had carved across the parish, the hills and glens, open paddocks with black-faced sheep grazing in them, and the clean, flowing rivers were still a thing of beauty and much-enjoyed in hours of leisure.

“Let’s get ye signed on, lad,” said William as he steered George to a thin, grey-haired man called McCottle whose days of working underground were behind him, and who now earned his living ‘up on top’.

“Sign here lad,” said McCottle as he thrust a piece of paper at George. “Ye’ll work yer shifts week about, starting today on the day shift and ye’ll draw yer wages here. The amount ye earn will depend upon how hard ye work, lad. The first week you’ll be partnered with yer Uncle William and then you’ll go where yer needed. Any questions?”

George hastily scribbled his name and handed the paper back to McCottle. “No sir,” he replied confidently.

"Right then, on ye go lad. The men will keep a watch out for ye but yer being paid as a man and you'll do the work of a man."

"Aye, that I will sir, ye've no fear of that. I've a strong arm and I'm willing to work."

"Right then, you'll do well here if ye mean to carry on as ye start. Away with ye now and look out for yoursel' and yer workmates."

George doffed his cap to McCottle and looked at his Uncle William for reassurance. William put his arm around his nephew's shoulders and steered him towards the cage.

"This is what ye wanted lad – are ye ready to see what we do all day?" asked William.

"I'm ready Uncle, and I'm eager to get to it."

The men were lined up ready to go below. The empty cage came up from the black hole and the men piled in, George among them. The door slammed shut, the cage jerked then started its descent into the darkness. The men began to turn on the lamps they wore on their hats and George followed suit. When they reached the bottom, the men got out and went about their business. They all knew what to do. William handed George a pick and shovel and steered him towards a large wall of coal.

"Start picking Geordy, but do it slowly till ye get yer rhythm. I'll no' be far away," William said. For eight hours, with a break to eat the sandwich that he had packed and share a brew of tea with the other men, George eagerly picked away at the coal.

In the afternoon when the whistle blew, the men moved into the cage to take them up top. As they drew nearer the surface, George was glad to see the light of day. Even though the sky was grey and overcast, there was a light as the sun strained to peek beneath the clouds – a light that he had been denied all day and that he was glad to see. When he reached the top, he blinked his eyes in the weak sunlight, as his ancestors had done many times over the years, and breathed in the air. The foreman checked that all men were accounted for, and George and his Uncle William walked the short distance to their house at Barhill Road. It was a typical miner's residence consisting of two rooms, but in better condition than some of the miners' rows in the area. The kitchen measured fifteen feet by ten feet with a fireplace and mantle in front of which stood two home-made chairs and a coal scoop, a table and chairs for six people, a few shelves with a curtain at the front to store potatoes, turnips, flour, sugar and other essential items, and two single bunk beds. The other room, known as a hole in the wall, measured eleven feet by six feet and had a double bed and a single bed and a piece of wood on which to hang clothes. Outside was a makeshift wash-house and coal store. There was no running water and the primitive outside toilet facilities were shared by several families, but it was home. The occupants of Barhill Road were a mix of mainly miners and merchants as well as bakers, coopers and a tailor.

As George entered the house there was no fire and the pots were cold. The house had always seemed so homely when his grandmother was alive. There was always a fire crackling in the hearth and food bubbling in the pot. He pictured his gran sitting in front of the fire, knitting needles in hand, and had always been comforted by knowing that whatever happened in his life his gran would be there to talk it through with him. With the coldness of the house came the realisation that she was really gone. He hung up his cap on the peg by the door and looked at his uncle.

Knowing that the boy was looking for direction, William hung up his cap and placed his piece box on the kitchen table.

"Fill up the pitcher with water and take it through to the wash-house out the back Geordy, and wash yoursel' and I'll get the fire started," William said. "Then hang up yer work clothes for the morrow. I know we have some tatties and neeps so that will be our tea, lad."

George carried the water to the wash-house and poured it into a basin that sat on the roughly-hewn bench, then began to remove the dust and grime of his working day. Once the fire was ablaze, William sat down at the table, pen and paper in hand.

"Now, this is all new to me lad, but we'll be needin' some things so we'd best make a list. I'm no' cook, mind, but we'll make do. We'll no' starve," William said. "We'll be needin' some vegetables and a soup bone and maybe some mutton. And oats for our breakfast.

Aye," he said as he wrote the final few items on the notepad, "that'll keep us goin' for a few days."

As William took his turn in the wash-house there was a knock at the door. George opened the door to find their neighbour Mrs McLatchey standing there with a basket over her arm.

"How are ye, young George?" she asked in her sing-songy voice that slid up at the end of every sentence. "Ye're a workin' man now I see."

"Aye, Mrs McLatchey, would you no' come in?"

Mrs McLatchey walked past George and put her basket on the table. William quickly covered his naked chest and greeted her.

"Now, yer gran was a kind and wonderful woman and I won't see ye starve on yer first day as a working man," she said looking at George. "I've made ye a mince pie for yer tea and some scones to take in yer piece boxes the morrow. At least you'll have a meal tonight."

George's eyes lit up at the thought of something other than just tatties and neeps.

"Oh that's very kind of you Mrs McLatchey," George said.

"Aye, Mrs McLatchey, most kind indeed," William said as he struggled to get his shirt over his head.

"And if you'd like me to fetch ye some things from the shops, just give me yer list and that'll help ye a wee bit till ye get the run of things. It's no' easy with no woman in the house, especially after ye've been workin' hard all day. Now we've all got our own men to do for, but if ye need any help you've only to ask."

"My mother would be grateful to ye Mrs McLatchey, and so are we. As a matter of fact, I've just written a list of things and if ye think we should add anything to it, please say so." Reaching into his trouser pocket William continued: "here's a pound note and if it's no' enough then you'll tell me."

Mrs McLatchey left the house with the list and the pound note, and when the door was closed the two men looked at each other and smiled.

"I can't wait to get into that pie, lad," William said, rubbing his hands together with glee. "It smells so good. Fill the kettle with water and we'll enjoy a pot of tea with our unexpected meal."

At the end of his first day at work, George enjoyed a hot meal and cup of tea then sat back in his chair, smiling.

"Ye know Uncle, I'm very pleased with the day I've had. A hard day's work and a good meal is satisfaction enough for any man, would ye no' say?"

William pushed his plate forward and sat back in his chair. "Aye, there is a satisfaction to be gained from hard labour, but we'll have this conversation again when you've worked for more than one day and then see how ye feel. Now on ye get to yer bed while I clean up here. We've to do it all again the morrow and the next day."

George stood up from the table then looked around the room.

"I think I'll sit in one of the chairs by the fire and think a while, Uncle. I've some reckonin' to do. I want to give you an even share of the rent for the house and any other expenses and I'll still have some money left over, so ye see I need to consider what to buy with it."

William smiled as he cleared the plates. "Aye, you think on it a while lad, for no sooner will ye have the coin in yer hand than it will be gone. Nothing surer."

Chapter 2 (1913)

THINKING ABOUT THE FUTURE

George and his Uncle William had been batching together for almost four months and, although his grandmother Mary may have done things differently, they managed to feed themselves and get to work on time, even though the breakfast dishes were often left on the table till evening and the bed sheets were not washed as often as they should have been. Mrs McLatchey called by the house once a week with one or more of her weans in tow, to drop off some scones or oatcakes, but for the most part they managed by themselves.

On November 16, it was George's sixteenth birthday. His gran would have baked him a cake and cooked a special meal but there was none of that this year. Instead he had invited two of his young workmates to tea with his uncle, and they dined on rabbit stew with tattie scones for afters. The little house was unusually boisterous as the three young men talked and laughed, and William got a word in where he could.

"How are ye finding yer work, lads?" William asked. Jimmy Kline was the first to answer.

"It's hard graft, Will. My faither said the work underground would be hard, but I didnae ken till I went below m'sel," Jimmy said.

"Aye, the days down in the dark are long and when I'm on the night shift I cannae sleep during the day so I'm always tired," agreed Stevie McKay.

"It's a living," George said sagely as he sat back in his chair and pushed his plate to the side. "I'll no' be doon the pits all m' life. I want to travel and see the world."

"And where is it ye've a hankerin' to see, George?" his uncle asked.

George seemed stunned by the question but thought quickly and replied. "They taught us about France in school. Maybe I'll go there." That was all he said for he had no clue about the rest of the world away from Barhill Road in Cumnock, but talk of travel made him sound worldly and he liked to impress. Turning the spotlight away from himself, George asked his uncle "and what of your future plans Uncle Will? Do ye see yoursel' travelling?"

William looked at George and smiled. He didn't need time to think, for he'd never had the luxury of thinking only of himself. "I'll no' be moving far from Ayrshire, lads. I have friends here and a house and a good job. My needs are simple."

George felt a little guilty for he knew that his uncle had had thrust upon him the responsibility for raising his brother's son, when George's father Douglas had died. William, now thirty, had lived his life caring for his ailing mother and his nephew.

"To tell ye the truth, I've never thought much about the future, but now that mither has gone to her reward and young Geordy is almost a man, perhaps I should make some plans," William said.

"Or some woman will make them for ye," George teased his uncle.

A wife, and perhaps some children, William mused. The thought had never crossed his mind. He began to feel a new freedom, a feeling he had never felt before. He looked at George who was dealing out a pack of cards, and his two pals, laughing and joking around the table, and smiled to himself. He would always feel like a father to George but as he thought about one day having his own children, he felt warm inside. From eight children, his mother had been blessed with only one grandchild - George. How she would have loved to have known that her only surviving child, William, was thinking about having children of his own.

Chapter 3 (1914)

HARDIE IN THE NEWS AGAIN

William had been just a lad when family friend and neighbour Keir Hardie had been appointed secretary of the newly-formed Ayrshire Miners' Union, then secretary of the Scottish Miners' Federation. *The Miner* newspaper that Hardie published to give miners a political education, could always be found in the McMurdo household. As well as being a great advocate for miners, William always remembered how grateful his mother Mary had been to Hardie who had sat up through the night in the last hours of his brother Thomas's life, as he succumbed to the dreaded miners' lung at just twenty-five years of age. With all his political aspirations and commitments, Hardie still had time to care for a neighbour in his hour of need. It was in Cumnock that Hardie had formed his political philosophy, writing many of his speeches in the solitude of his summerhouse at the bottom of his garden, overlooking the River Lugar. He was a proud son of Cumnock who had achieved recognition across Britain and beyond.

"Our friend Mr Hardie is in the news again," William said as he read the newspaper in front of the fire one Winter evening after work. George looked up from the shirt he was attempting to patch. "His fellow Labour MPs do not agree with his stance on women's suffrage. He's been a supporter of Mrs Pankhurst and her daughters for years as they fight to get women's rights recognised."

"Aye, and I hear that he's very supportive of Miss Sylvia Pankhurst," George said with a chuckle.

"That's gossip, lad, and I'll no' hear Mr Hardie maligned in that way."

"Oh, Uncle it's all around the pit. The young lads are wondering what she sees in a man nearly twice her age and the old men are wondering what's his secret," George laughed as he continued to sew and pricked his finger with the needle.

"There, that's what ye get for speaking so of such a great man," William said in a way that reminded George of how his grandmother used to chastise him. "I'll no' forget his kindness to Thomas and mither in their time of need. And his wife, Lillie, was a great support to the community during the time of the strikes."

It was common knowledge that Hardie and Sylvia Pankhurst had rented a cottage in Penshurst, Kent five years before and they met there as often as his busy schedule permitted, but in William's mind the meetings were to discuss business and anything else that happened, well it was no one's business.

Hardie, a self-proclaimed Christian socialist, travelled widely throughout Europe to meet other socialist trade union leaders. He was becoming acutely aware of the simmering tensions between Russia and Germany and the potential conflict between Austria-Hungary and Serbia. William read a small article in the newspaper about Germany introducing a new tax to finance the doubling of their armies, but he didn't take much notice of news in other countries. He was never likely to leave Ayrshire, so what happened so far away was of no concern to him.

Chapter 4 (1914)

THE NOT SO GREAT WAR

As the last of the Summer sun shone high in an August sky, William and George headed off to the mine for the afternoon shift. Barhill Road Cumnock was abuzz with people chattering in groups as the piercing voice of the local paper seller broke through the hum.

"Great Britain Declares War On Germany", "Special Edition Paper", "Great Britain Declares War On Germany".

George looked at William in disbelief. "What's that all about, Uncle?" he asked.

"Get a paper off the lad and we'll find out," William said, then he crossed the street to talk with his neighbours, while George ran to the corner to fetch the paper. There, in huge capital letters, were the six words that struck fear into the hearts of people all over Britain. George joined the group where his uncle was talking and they gathered around to read the news.

"Declaration last night after unsatisfactory reply to British ultimatum that Belgium must be kept neutral," William read as he scanned the paper for the salient points. "The King's message to his Navy – Government to take control of all railways. Admiral Jellicoe to be in supreme command of the Home Fleets. Great Britain is in a state of war with Germany. It was officially stated at the Foreign Office last night that Great Britain declared war against Germany at 7pm. The British Ambassador in Berlin has been handed his passport."

"What does that mean for us?" George enquired. William continued to read.

"It was reported yesterday evening that Germany had taken the first hostile step by destroying a British mine-layer. At the present time Germany is in a state of war with Great Britain, Russia, France and Belgium." He hesitated.

"Well go on, Uncle," George urged.

"Men are required to enlist for one year, or as long as the war continues." William closed the newspaper and a neighbour grabbed it out of his hand and continued to scan the pages to try to make sense of the news.

William signalled to George to be on their way to the pit. They were already late to start their shift but he thought that most of the men would have been caught up with the shocking news. They walked in silence and as they reached the pithead, two of George's pals called out to him.

"We're joining up, we're going to fight," they said excitedly. George was not yet seventeen but his pals were a few years older. His eyes lit up with the news, then his shoulders slumped as he realised that he was too young. "Will ye join us, George?" his pal Stevie asked.

George looked at the ground and kicked a piece of coal. "Aye, I'd love to go but I'm no' old enough."

"Cheer up pal," said Stevie, "with a bit of luck this war will last fer years. You'll get yer chance," and they walked off making plans for their enlistment. William walked towards George who was now standing alone.

"I'm too young to join up, Uncle. They'll no' take me," he said dejectedly.

"And a good thing it is," William said sternly. "I didnae raise ye up to be cut down in yer boyhood. Now put such things out of yer mind. We've a night's work ahead of us and ye need to be thinking about the job. There'll be some changes ahead for us, that's for certain, but fer now we can only take it one day at a time – and pray for yer pals."

Chapter 5 (1914)

POLITICS IN THE HOUSE

As the news of the outbreak of war was digested, members of Parliament and people in the street debated Britain's need to enter the war. Keir Hardie disagreed with many members of the Labour Party over the outbreak of war. He was a pacifist and was determined not to let his two sons join up. As always, he appealed to the working man and tried to organise a national strike against Britain's participation in the war.

William followed Hardie's views with interest, and he wanted George to have a balanced view of the war.

"Mr Hardie is no' fer this war, George," William said as he assumed his regular nightly post in front of the fire and behind the newspaper. "He's issued a statement saying 'the long-threatened European war is now upon us. You have never been consulted about this war. The workers of all countries must strain every nerve to prevent their Governments from committing them to war. Hold vast demonstrations against war, in London and in every industrial centre. There is no time to lose. Down with the rule of brute force! Down with war! Up with the peaceful rule of the people'".

"Uncle, I don't truly understand what the fighting is fer and on that I agree with Mr Hardie. But if the Government thinks it's worth the fight, do you no' think that Mr Hardie could be wrong?" George asked.

"I'm as bewildered as you, Geordy," William said shaking his head. "I know that we have to stick with our allies in times of need and

I've been trying to make some sense of it. Near as I can tell, Austria-Hungary declared war on Serbia and Russia got involved to defend Serbia. Because Germany was an ally of Austria-Hungary, they declared war on Russia. France was an ally of Russia so they were drawn in against Germany. The Germans attacked France through Belgium and, as allies of both France and Belgium, Britain got pulled into the war."

"So it's nothing to do with us really then," George said as he sat down in the chair beside William.

"Aye, well then there's the issue of fighting for King and Country, lad, and when yer country is at war you are duty-bound to do yer part, whatever that may be."

"So Mr Hardie is wrong then," George said.

"Mr Hardie is doing what he feels is right. He doesnae want the workers of this country to be pulled into this fight. There's no right or wrong answer here, George. I believe that each man must follow his conscience."

Seeing his nephew's despair at being too young to serve his country, he continued. "There'll be plenty to do here on the home front. If everyone was fighting there'd be no one left to support industry here at home."

George wasn't happy with that answer and sat in silence with a scowl on his face. He was prepared to listen but what he really wanted was to join up and fight.

Hardie's health had begun to fail, and despite taking part in several anti-war demonstrations, his pacifist views did not sit well with some of his former supporters. While still a loved and respected figure among the people, his dominance as a great Labour leader was fading. The competent and experienced speaker debated no more. Where once people listened to his every word, his stance against the war had seen him branded, by some colleagues, as a traitor. It all became too much and in December, Hardie suffered a stroke. The war was dividing people across Britain and affecting the health of the nation.

Chapter 6 (1915)

THE PASSING OF A GREAT MAN

Six months had passed since Britain declared war on Germany. When so many coal miners volunteered for the Army at the beginning of the war, they swapped their lives working in the heat, damp and stale air underground for a life of dodging bullets, but at least they felt the sun on their skin and the air in their lungs. If any good had happened so far, it was that the Government had taken coal mines across Britain under their control. The miners who continued to work the coal seams, at first cautious, grew to realise the benefits of this action as safety standards increased and higher wages were introduced in all areas.

With a strange irony, the war that Keir Hardie detested was helping to achieve some of the aims that he had fought for all of his adult life.

Before he had made a full recovery from a stroke, within two months Hardie returned to the House of Commons in February, 1915 but his health was so frail that he kept falling asleep in meetings. He knew that the time had come to leave political life and the hustle and bustle of London. In his quiet and careful way, he arranged for the disposal of his furniture and books and gave up his rooms, and returned to Scotland.

When William opened the newspaper on September 26, 1915 he was visibly shaken by the news. He dropped the paper into his lap. George picked up the newspaper, sat down beside his uncle and began to read out aloud.

"James Keir Hardie, born of poor Scottish parents on August 15, 1856, died in hospital in Glasgow yesterday from pneumonia." He looked up from the newspaper at his uncle who was sitting in the chair beside him, gazing into the fire.

"Oh, I'm sorry Uncle," George said.

"Keep reading, Geordy," William said sadly.

"He lived to be such a force in British politics, particularly as far as concerned the Labour Party. From the time he was seven years of age until he reached twenty-four he worked in coal mines, and then he was elected secretary of the Lanarkshire Miners' Union. He was the pit lad of politics and refused to be anything else. He went down the pit and shaft, a little lad of seven, to win his bread. He never had a day's schooling. His mother taught him to read, but he was seventeen before he could write his name. He taught himself shorthand, practising the characters on the face of the coal seam where he worked. He came out of the pit at twenty-four with an idea, a purpose and a vision. Eventually his dream was accomplished. Keir Hardie was Chairman of the Independent Labour Party and he has represented Merthyr-Tydvil in the House of Commons since 1900. For some time he was Chairman of the Parliamentary Labour Party and he was looked upon as the chief figure and inspirer of that group. In 1892 James Keir Hardie rode up to Westminster from West Ham, clothed in cloth cap, tweed suit and flannel shirt, accompanied by a brass band. It was said of Hardie that he was the most typical Scotsman in the House, both in appearance and outlook. One day, when entering the House, a policeman asked him: 'Are you at work here, mate?'. 'Yes,' was the laconic reply. 'On the roof?', the policeman asked. 'No, on the floor', came the reply and he passed in, happy in the pride that he had not revealed himself."

George started to laugh and looked over at William who was also chuckling. He turned back to the newspaper.

"His home is still in the little cottage at Cumnock where he was once a pit lad. He clung to his poverty with the pride of a Highland Chieftan."

George put down the newspaper. "He was some man."

"Aye, that he was and he was one of ours – a friend, strong and true. Never forget that, lad," William said.

George rose from the chair and took a pair of scissors out of a drawer. He cut out the photo of Hardie that accompanied the obituary and stuck it to a piece of cardboard. He took a piece of string and attached it to the back of the cardboard then hung the picture on the wall near the door.

"That's a nice gesture, Geordy," William said. "You know he carried an old silver watch he had worn in the mine, with teeth marks from a favourite pit pony that had tried to eat it. He was very caring and sentimental and that's why this business with the war hit him so hard. People can say what they will, but in this house James Keir Hardie will always be a hero."

Chapter 7 (1916)

A YOUNG LAD OFF TO WAR

The willingness of the Scots to fight was legendary. When the call to arms was raised in 1914, thousands of Scots joined the armed forces. The bulk of soldiers from the mining areas were in their physical prime, and ideally suited to the rigours of army life. Colliers in their thirties who had worked underground were seen as physically unacceptable to the army, and many a man was disappointed when he turned up to enlist. By February 1916, over a fifth of all miners had left coal-mining and enlisted in the army, but Britain needed more coal. The government realised that too many coal miners were joining up as infantry and not enough coal was being produced for the navy's ships. The Defence of the Realm Act was introduced and coal mining was classified as a 'reserved occupation' and miners as a whole were no longer allowed to join the army. There would be exceptions as the miners' digging skills were proving invaluable in trench warfare in France, but it became clear that miners were needed to keep the coal mines operating and to keep the home fires burning.

William, now aged thirty-three, was considered too old to join the armed forces and he was happy to play his part in producing coal for the Empire. He was concerned about George, though. George had turned eighteen the previous November and he was still champing at the bit to sign up to serve his country. William knew that he wouldn't be able to hold on to him for much longer as conscription had been introduced in January of that year. He feared for his safety.

The Military Service Act specified that single men, eighteen to forty-one years old, were liable to be called up for military service unless they were widowed with children, or ministers of a religion or providing a service in a reserved occupation such as coal mining.

The British Government had posters drawn up to entice young men from all over the United Kingdom into the army. Each poster was specific to the country and the culture of Scotland, Ireland, England and Wales.

As George walked home from the flesher's shop, he stopped at the tobacconist's to look at the brightly coloured poster of a soldier in full Scottish military dress, knapsack on his back, proudly holding his rifle and bayonet. 'Your King and Country Need You' shouted the poster, 'To Maintain The Honour and Glory of the British Empire'. And to add the colloquial touch, the poster declared that 'a wee scrap o' paper is Britain's bond'. Mr Miller, the tobacconist, started to bring in his signage from outside the shop and saw George studying the poster.

"I suppose you'll be off on the big adventure soon lad," Mr Miller said. "Away to far climes to see the world," he said as he clenched his pipe between his tobacco-stained teeth.

George didn't answer as he stood there, hearing Mr Miller's words but lost in his own thoughts. Mr Miller shook his head and smiled and continued on with his work. George started walking down the street to his house, still daydreaming. When he reached the house and stepped inside, his uncle was sitting at the table peeling potatoes for their tea. William looked at George and then at a brown envelope sitting on the table next to the white enamel bowl, as he kept peeling potatoes. George picked up the envelope which was addressed to him and saw the words 'The War Office' in the top left corner. He eagerly tore open the envelope and read the letter. A smile crossed his face.

"I've been called up to serve, Uncle," George beamed. "I'm to report to the recruitment section of The War Office in Ayr for further instructions."

"But you're in a reserved occupation, Geordy," William said. "You've only to tell them that and you will be excluded from war service." William knew that his words would fall on deaf ears, but he had to try to dissuade George from joining up. He could see by the look on the lad's face that it was no good.

William put down the knife and wiped his hands on a cloth. He stood up and extended his hand to George. "Looks like you'll get to see France after all, lad. May God go with ye."

Chapter 8 (September 1916)

YOU'RE IN THE ARMY NOW

The recruitment office was bustling as George timidly stepped through the door. He watched in silence for a few minutes, trying to get his bearings and listening to the chaos that surrounded him. A thin, young lad with red hair and freckles walked a few steps past him, up to one of the many recruitment officers who stood straight-backed, resplendent in their uniforms.

"I'm here to join the army and serve at The Front," the lad shouted over the din.

"How old are you, son?" asked the recruitment officer.

"I'm eighteen," said the boy. The recruitment officer looked him up and down.

"You'd better take a walk down the street, pick up a birthday while you are out and come back and try again." The bewildered lad did as he was told and after a few minutes he was back standing in front of the recruitment officer.

"I'm here to join the army and serve at The Front," the lad said again.

"How old are you, son?" asked the recruitment officer.

"I'm nineteen," said the boy.

"Right, take this paper and see the sergeant." The boy beamed and grabbed the piece of paper and walked over to the sergeant.

George still had a couple of months to go until his nineteenth birthday, but he was desperate to serve overseas. He had been watching the pageantry unfold between the thin young boy and the recruitment officer.

'Aye, well he'll do me,' George said to himself and strode confidently over to the recruitment officer and presented his call-up letter. He knew that you had to be eighteen to join the army, but nineteen to be sent to The Front. By the time he finished his basic training he reckoned he'd be old enough to be sent into the thick of the action.

The recruitment officer looked him over and then he was directed towards a cubicle where a doctor weighed and measured him and gave him a general health check. Then he was handed some papers and moved on to the next station. The sergeant looked him up and down, read the papers and thrust them back in front of George.

"Sign on the dotted line. Welcome to the army, son." He was handed one of the papers and a travel warrant. "Now hold out your hand," said the sergeant as he placed two six-penny pieces on George's palm. "Here is the King's shilling," he said as George's eyes lit up, "and I'll be taking a sixpence for myself." George looked at him. "It's called commission, son. Every man for himself in this man's army."

Chapter 9 (1916)

ACROSS THE WATER

At the beginning of the war, when volunteers had been asked to come forward, men put down their tools of trade to answer the call. Full of patriotism and enthusiasm, and eager for adventure and regular pay, they left the fields, offices, mines, factories and universities from all over Scotland to fight for King and Country. But few had any military experience. Basic training was given over several months but as the war dragged on year after year and new recruits were needed at The Front, the training became very basic. Young lads who had barely left their mothers' knees were handed a rifle and shown how to use it, then shipped across the sea to face the enemy.

When George arrived at the Training Reserve at Bordon Military Camp in Hampshire, England in the early Autumn of 1916, he was assigned to a unit within the 9th (Scottish) Division Infantry of the three brigades of the Scottish Command. He lined up with the other civilians and soon they were listening to instructions from the sergeant. They were a ragtag bunch of men, some who looked as though they hadn't had a decent meal in days. The men were shown how to stand at ease, stand to attention, right turn, left turn and quick march. Next they were issued with uniforms and kit and taken to their barracks to get settled in. The men of the 9th (Scottish) Division wore a glengarry rather than a service cap. George proudly pulled the traditional thick-milled woollen Scots cap on to his head, and caught a glimpse of himself in the mirror. The cap, decorated with a pom-pom known as a toorie on top, and a rosette cockade on the left side, and with ribbons hanging down behind, was the most interesting piece of clothing he had ever owned.

It was now about 2pm and most of the men hadn't had their midday meal, but they were told they would have to wait until tea time at 5pm. While standing to attention in the barracks, one of the lads fainted. When he came to, it was discovered that he hadn't had anything to eat for nearly two days, such was the poverty from which some of these new soldiers came. Three square meals, a roof over their head and clothes were the very reasons that some of them had decided to join up, while others had had no choice as they were required to answer the call, due to the new conscription laws.

The next day they were on parade in front of a loud-mouthed sergeant who passed out comments to almost every man to 'smarten up',' get a haircut', 'sew on a button' or 'wipe that smile off your face'.

"You'll no' have yer mithers here to dress ye and pick up after ye, so smarten up lads. You'll soon be facing Jerry," said the sergeant. The German Army had been given the nickname 'jerry' because the shape of their helmets resembled chamber pots or jerries.

The weeks passed in a blur as George learned how to use a rifle and, perhaps more importantly, how to take orders. When the request came for men to go to The Front, George was glad of the opportunity. He stood before the sergeant to be assessed.

"McMurdo, you were a coal miner before joining up," said the sergeant. "You'll be needed in France."

George's heart skipped a beat. He was going to France. How exciting. Ever since he learned about France at school he had wanted to see the countryside and maybe ride a bicycle through the streets with a pretty girl. He was going to fight but there would be some rest time, surely, when he could explore this exotic new land. He was off on the great adventure.

"Wipe the dreamy look off your face, McMurdo," growled the sergeant. "Move along."

At mail call on the morning of his nineteenth birthday on November 16, George received a letter from his Uncle William. He sat on his neatly made-up bunk and took the notepaper from the envelope.

'I couldnae let yer birthday go without sending ye a greeting', the letter read. 'Things are much the same here though some things are now in short supply. I'm not much of a writer, but I wish you a happy birthday and say to ye don't be a hero, and keep yer heid doon.'

George tucked the letter into his pocket and took out a writing pad and pen.

'Dear Uncle,' he wrote. 'I miss the birthday cakes that Gran used to make fer me, and I miss you, but they're a good bunch of lads here and I'm learning so much, out in the fresh air – and rain. I cannae say too much but I'll be heading off soon. Let me just say that I may get to see some of the sights I've mentioned before. You keep the home fires burning and I'll do my bit to keep Jerry on the run. Yours, George.'

With the most basic of basic training completed, George was issued with a rifle and ammunition and taken with his unit to Southampton Docks where he boarded a troop ship bound for somewhere in France. Even being in England was exciting as he had never ventured outside of Ayrshire. The lads in his unit chattered excitedly but were told to keep the noise down. They travelled through the night across the channel and were only allowed up on deck when the shipped docked. Most of them had never been abroad before and as the sun rose over a new landscape, they took in the sights and sounds.

Like cattle they were herded off the ship and marched to the British military camp at Rouen. Along the way the local people lined the streets and cheered. George spotted many a pretty girl in the crowd and lots of bicycles. Now if he could just get a pretty girl and two bicycles together he could complete his fantasy. He felt glad to be alive. Here he was in a new and exciting country, the sun beaming down on his face, being lauded just for being there. As they marched along he stole a glance at his pal Angus Blair, the boy who'd picked up the birthday so quickly at the recruiting office, and they both smiled and marched proudly with an added spring in their step.

Looking straight ahead, Angus whispered out the side of his mouth "do they call this place Roo-in. It could be the ruin of us, George," and they both smiled.

Upon reaching camp they were given a meal and showed where to stow their kit. Then came news that left them all stunned.

"You have a few hours leave this afternoon to visit the local town," shouted the sergeant. "Remember that you are British soldiers and your conduct will be on display. Don't break any hearts and be back here by 1100 hours. Dismissed."

"Well Angus, let's go!," said George and they started to walk faster and faster out of the camp until they were on the road to Rouen's town centre with its cobbled streets and interesting shops. They spent a pleasant afternoon and evening feasting on bread and cakes from the boulangerie and cheese from the fromagerie, and George and Angus had their first taste of wine.

"I've no' had wine before – in fact, I've never had any of the drink before. It was never allowed in oor hoose," confided Angus. "I don't mind a drap."

"Aye, it's no' bad, Angus, but I think I'd prefer a nip o' whisky," George said.

"I've just been told the wine is free Georgie boy, so drink up."

George took another sip of the wine. "Ye know, it's beginning to taste better and better."

Chapter 10 (late November 1916)

EYES FRONT

The next morning, George woke with a bit of a headache but there was no time to recover. They were just miles from the Western Front and soon they would be marching to the Front Line.

George and Angus gathered their kit ready for inspection then lined up with the other men to await their instructions.

A well-groomed captain appeared from an officer's tent, his middle-aged face lined and his brow furrowed. He stood in front of the latest recruits and silently marvelled at how young they were.

"Men," he began in his southern English accent. "You are about to take on a task that will require great mental and physical strength. The men in the trenches, your countrymen and your allies, are tired and bloodied and they need reinforcements. You are young and strong and fresh from home. Be in no doubt that your contribution to the war effort is greatly appreciated and greatly needed. The conditions will be difficult and comforts few. We are making it as hard as we can for Jerry to make progress. But it has come at a great cost. We have lost many brave men, and we will lose many more." Each man in the unit felt as though the captain was speaking directly to him.

"You have a long march ahead of you. When you reach The Front each of you will be assigned a task. The officers under whom you will serve are experienced men so take your orders like the soldiers that you have become, and watch out for your mates. May God go with you."

The captain raised his right arm to his forehead in a salute, which the men returned, then turned on his heel and marched back to his tent.

"Attention," called the sergeant, "right turn, quick march!" and George and Angus marched side by side into the unknown.

"I've no idea what we're heading into Angus, but we need to keep an eye on each other," George said as he marched. He could see that the boy was trembling.

"It's all getting a bit real now, isn't it?" Angus stuttered.

"You'll be fine – keep yer heid doon," George said and smiled at Angus. He was only a few months older than the boy but he felt a protectiveness towards him. As an only child, George had always been a loner and knew how to take care of himself, but he had learned from his conversations with Angus that the boy had always been protected by his older brothers. George decided to step into the older brother role for Angus. They were going to need each other.

***

They had marched for five miles when the noise began. The guns became louder as they neared the battle. The further they walked the more ear-splitting the noise became. When they reached battalion headquarters they descended into a deep dug-out with roughly-hewn, uneven steps to find a cleanly-shaven officer sitting at a table, drinking tea from a china cup and reading a newspaper.

'Awfully civilised,' George thought. 'Maybe it will no' be so bad.'

The officer drained his tea cup, folded the newspaper which he placed neatly on the table and stood up. He moved his upper lip from side to side and his thin little moustache twitched.

"Fresh blood," he said in his upper-crust English accent, as he looked the men up and down. "Dirty and sweaty, but fresh blood."

As the officer walked around the table to stand in front of the men, George noticed a tunnel leading off to the left and a bed and dressing table. The officers' quarters were well decked out but he was about to find out that his lot would be very different. The officer continued.

"Life in the trenches is rough on soldiers – and you lot are barely soldiers. Food can be in short supply and you'll be wet and cold. You'll see men dying in agony around you. You'll see limbs amputated to save a life because it can take too long to get to a medical station. You'll experience body lice, and your ears will ring from the deafening shell fire."

George was exhausted from the long walk and momentarily let his gaze drop to the floor. The officer walked down the line and stopped in front of George. "And if you do get time to fall asleep there'll be rats crawling over you. You, soldier," he snapped at George. "What's your name?"

"McMurdo, sir," George replied.

"Have you ever had rats crawling over you, McMurdo?" asked the officer, leaning his face into George's.

"Aye, sir. There are many rats down the pit. We share our piece with them and keep them as pets."

Angus sniggered and the officer turned his attention to him. "And you, son – are you a coal miner too?"

"N-no sir," Angus stuttered. "I'm off a farm."

"Well then. I have just the job for you McMurdo, and you can take your sniggering friend with you. You see this tunnel?" he said as he moved his head to the right.

"Aye sir," said Angus with a smile.

"This is nothing like the tunnels you'll be working in." The officer stopped smirking and became serious again as he turned his attention back to addressing all the men.

"Anyone who disobeys an order runs the risk of being executed. Make a mistake and it could cost your life or that of the other men. Keep that in mind and keep your wits about you."

He sat back down at his desk. "Each man will receive a small daily ration of rum. You'll need it as this Winter sets in. That's all, sergeant." And with that, the men were lead along another tunnel ready to begin work.

"Just my luck," George said to Angus. "I left the coal mines looking for adventure and end up in a tunnel under France, digging again."

"I've never been underground before, George," Angus said nervously.

"I'll make a deal with ye. You take care of the 'yes, sir, no sir' part of the arrangement, and I'll teach ye to take care of yoursel' underground. I'm no' real fussed on taking orders from tea-sippers."

Angus laughed and George was glad to see the boy relax.

They arrived at a dugout where they stored their kit and had their first meal in many hours. The old beef, peas and pickles was tasteless but filling. Prunes were on offer for dessert but as Angus reached to take one from the glass jar, he was cautioned by a soldier who had been there for some months.

"You won't be needing them here," he said. "There's dysentery throughout the trenches."

Angus returned the prune to the jar and sat back quietly. Dysentery, rats and lice aside, George thought it was rather thrilling to be so close to the German Army – the enemy that was threatening peace in Great Britain.

***

Specialist miners were required to dig tunnels under an area known as No Man's Land, and to place mines beneath enemy defensive positions. When detonated, the explosion would destroy that section of the trench, allowing the infantry to advance towards the enemy Front Line, hoping to take advantage of the confusion that followed the explosion of an underground mine. It was dangerous work.

As they sat huddled in the muddy trench, the ground started to shake as guns belched out shells.

George was glad of the distraction when one of the men in the line spoke to the group. He was a fellow Scot and obviously someone in charge though you'd never know it from his mud-caked, sweaty appearance.

"You've to maintain the trenches – it's a job that never ends," the man in charge said softly. "You're always digging, whether the trenches need widening, deepening, repairing or strengthening, or new trenches need to be dug. We have been digging trenches since we came here seven months ago - it's bloody hard work."

George picked up a handful of the wet earth.

"It's clay, and heavy clay at that," he said.

The man-in-charge's eyes widened. "So you've some experience of tunnelling?" he asked expectantly. George nodded. "Well, however hard you've worked before you can double it. Yesterday I had to dig a trench seven feet long and four feet wide and the deeper you get the harder the clay is to shovel over your head." The man leaned back against the side of the trench and put his head in his hands in exhaustion and desperation.

"Show us what to do and take a break yoursel', man," George said quietly. "We'll do our part."

Chapter 11 (February 1917)

IN THE TRENCHES

The miners worked in cold, cramped conditions, in six or twelve hour rotating shifts. The tunnels were dark, small and often flooded with water. The entrances to the tunnels were a closely guarded secret. The men operated in near silence to avoid detection, and with electricity in short supply at the Front Line, tunnellers were forced to work by candlelight in small spaces up to a foot deep in freezing water.

The Winters in Scotland were cold, but the past few months had been the most uncomfortable and cold that George had ever felt. The trenches, where most of the men lived and worked, were deep with snow and the men were always wet. Only the young and strong could withstand the conditions for a long period. Even so, his body ached from the constant digging, and his mind was numb from the daily routine and constantly taking orders. After a meagre breakfast each day, and weapon cleaning and inspection, an officer would appear with details of the duties to be performed, then it was another day spent on pick and shovel. Only the direction of the tunnel changed to break the monotony.

As more men were wounded from fighting, the youngest and strongest were sent to replace them.

In June, word came through for reinforcements. George and Angus were being sent into the thick of the fighting.

"Finally, we'll see some action," George said as he dropped his shovel and wiped the sweat from his brow. "I didnae come to France to dig tunnels. I could have stayed at home and done that. Now we'll see some real action."

George looked over his shoulder to find Angus cowering in the mud. 'The boy should never have been sent to The Front'. George thought. He knelt down beside Angus.

"Angus, do ye no' think we are all afeared?" George said as he placed his hand on Angus's shoulder. "Pull yoursel' together lad, and make your family proud. We are here now and we've to take our orders and fight, the same as every other man here. Stay with me, and remember..."

Angus looked up at George. "I know, 'keep yer heid doon'."

"Aye, that's right. Now on we go."

The British Army worked on a sixteen-day timetable. To give the men time away from the intensity of the fighting, each soldier usually spent eight days on the Front Line and four days in the reserve trench. Another four days could be spent in a rest camp that was built a few miles away from the fighting, but as the years of war dragged on and the army was short of men, soldiers had to spend far longer periods at The Front. By the time George and Angus reached their trench, the men had been in the Front Line trenches for over thirty days.

"The danger period for attack is usually dawn or dusk when they can see well enough to move forward and cover a good distance before being spotted," a sergeant told them. "About half an hour or so before dawn and dusk you'll hear the order, 'Stand to', which will be passed throughout the length of the Battalion Front. Then the whole Allied Front Line system will be on alert."

The sergeant could see the fear in their eyes and remembered how he had felt when he took his first shot.

"You are here to kill the enemy, make no mistake. It's kill or be killed. Remember that," he cautioned.

It was nearly midday and all about was curiously quiet. George took in the scene around him. Bedraggled men sat or squatted in the trenches, drawing on cigarettes, cleaning weapons, reading letters or writing letters home. Angus seemed to have recovered from his anxiety attack and George sat back against the trench clutching his rifle.

"Cigarette?" asked the soldier next to him, in a Yorkshire accent.

"Aye, thank you," said George as he took a slim cigarette from the muddy packet.

He saw the strain on the older man's face.

"Do you have a sweetheart at home?" asked the man.

"Oh, no," George said shyly.

"Oh, you're lucky. It's bad enough for any man here but when you have a wife and children to worry about - if I'm killed, like - what will happen to my family? My wife has always depended on me."

George didn't know what to say and dragged on his cigarette as he let the man compose himself.

"I'm George, by the way," he said extending his hand.

"Fred," replied the man. "You'd be advised to write a letter to someone back home, George. The mail does get in and out of this place. That's what we do in the quiet times, write letters home."

"Thanks for the advice, Fred. Can you no' get some sleep while Angus and I keep watch?"

"No, I must keep alert," Fred said as he slowly finished his cigarette and dropped it in the wet clay. Then his head dropped onto his chest as his tired body took a few minutes to replenish.

Chapter 12 (July 1917)

THE ADVENTURE LOSES ITS GLOSS

The fighting continued across the trenches and George and Angus had fired many shots, not knowing if any had reached their targets. That was about to change.

On June 7, the Battle of Messines resulted in the capture of the ridge which spurred the allies on to capture Passchendaele Ridge. The first and second battles at Ypres had been launched by the Germans, but it was now felt that the morale of the German troops was broken and their numbers weakened, virtually guaranteeing the allied capture of the ridge.

Word filtered through that a major offensive was to take place in late July. As if the task at hand, to capture the ridge, was not difficult enough, the heavens opened and heavy rains turned the lowland soil into a thick muddy swamp, severely limiting the mobility of the infantry. Heavy preliminary artillery bombardment was effected for ten days prior to the launch of the attack which was scheduled for July 31.

The fighting intensified, and the German Army introduced a new weapon in the form of mustard gas. As the artillery shells rained over and into the trenches, the gas began to take its effect. Men started vomiting and were temporarily blinded by the gas.

"My throat's closing up," cried Fred as he struggled to take a breath, "and I can't see."

All around, men were writhing in pain as the shots continued to rain in. George kept his head, and fired across the barren wasteland.

Angus lost his mettle and began to climb up out of the trench in an effort to get away from the smell of blood, vomit and death. Clutching his rifle in his right hand, George stretched out his left hand to grab at Angus's belt but as soon as his head was visible above the parapet, Angus was struck by an enemy bullet and he was dead before he fell back into the trench. George looked at his young friend, now only recognisable by his red hair, covered in blood. He didn't suffer and George was thankful for that. He choked back a tear and took a sharp intake of air, then collapsed on the ground beside his dead friend. He had been hit by mustard gas and his throat was on fire. His eyes started to stick together and the skin on his hands was raw. He could hear the cries of his fellow soldiers, some burned to the bone.

The next voice George heard was that of an orderly who carried him to the Battalion Medical Officer who examined him and sent him on to the Regimental Aid Post a few metres behind the Front Line in a dugout. Once again, George found himself underground in a room with six beds for short-term holding and men lying all over the floor, some suffering gunshot wounds and others in various states of affectedness from mustard gas. The most serious cases were treated first and by the time George had received first aid, large blisters had started to develop on his hands and face. He was taken by field ambulance to the Casualty Clearing Station, then on to a hospital in Rouen.

His eyes were bandaged and he could scarcely speak from the burns he had suffered to his trachea.

On the fourth day after receiving his injuries, George awoke in the hospital. His throat felt like it was closed and the pain from his hands was searing. Both eyes were still bandaged but the gas burns on his hands, arms and face could not be touched and he was covered with a tent of propped-up sheets to avoid the cloth making contact with his skin. All around him men cried out in pain. As he stretched out his right hand to feel his way in the darkness, he felt a gentle hand touch his cheek.

"Hello there, George," the soft English voice said. "Nice of you to join us."

George thought for a moment that he may have died and gone to heaven. He had not heard a woman's voice in many months.

"You are in a general hospital in Rouen, George. You've been injured from mustard gas. We put you to sleep for a few days to give your throat a chance to heal. My name is Nurse Anderson and I've been looking after you – well, you and twenty other young men." She propped up the pillows behind George's head and sat him up. "Here," she said raising a glass of water to his lips, "take small sips."

As George gratefully took the water he was aware of her closeness. She smelled of lavender and antiseptic.

"Tomorrow, the doctor will take the bandages off your eyes and we'll see how we go from there. Now you rest," she said as she gently laid his head back on the pillow.

A faint smile crossed his face as he sank back into the pillow. For a moment he allowed himself to feel safe. He was away from the mud and the blood of the trenches – how far away he did not know – but for now he could relax.

Nurse Anderson fed George some mashed vegetables for his dinner and, with a whiff of lavender lingering in his nostrils, he fell asleep. At about one o'clock in the morning he jumped up in his bed and started screaming. Nurse Anderson ran to his side.

"George, your throat - don't scream, quiet now," she said as she cradled him in her arms. "Calm down now. You are safe here. No harm can come to you."

"Angus," George whispered. "Angus, he's covered in blood. Ooh, they're comin' fer us, stay low Angus," he continued to call out. Nurse Anderson soothed his brow and soon he was sleeping peacefully. The physical wounds would heal but the mental and psychological effects of trench warfare would take longer to repair.

The following morning Nurse Anderson was at his side again.

"Good morning George," she said cheerfully.

"Do ye never sleep, woman?" was all that George could whisper.

Nurse Anderson ignored the question and smiled as she introduced Dr Thomas.

"You've sustained some lung damage George, but you are lucky that that is the only internal damage and it will repair itself over time, if you don't smoke or breathe in stale air," the doctor said. "Just relax George, and we'll remove these bandages and see what we are dealing with." First the bandages from the left eye were removed. "What do you see, George?"

George blinked. "Not a thing," he replied. The doctor removed the bandages from the right eye.

"How about this eye?" he asked.

George blinked hard and in the darkness he saw a flash of light and the starched whiteness of Nurse Anderson's uniform. She leaned her face next to his. "Can you see me, George?" she asked.

George smiled as he smelt the familiar lavender. She had short, wavy blond hair and pale blue eyes and, he thought, the smile of an angel.

"Aye, I can see you," George smiled. Dr Thomas and Nurse Anderson also smiled.

"Now your hands, George," Dr Thomas said as he pulled back the propped-up sheet and examined the burns which had been replaced by white marks on his skin.

"You've healed well George. You're lucky that you are young and strong. There may be some scarring on your hands but they'll heal up well. Your eyesight will fully recover, though you are to stay out of bright light for a few days. Now open your mouth and let's have a look at this throat."

Dr Thomas removed the tongue depressor from George's mouth and turned out the torchlight. He mumbled something to Nurse Anderson that George did not hear.

"Nurse Anderson will take care of you George, and will advise you of my assessment," Dr Thomas said.

'I'll be happy to be in Nurse Anderson's care any time,' George thought.

As the Doctor turned on his heel to leave he called over his shoulder, "Is your shift finished now, darling."

“Yes, dear,” replied Nurse Anderson. “I’ll see you after your rounds and we’ll have some breakfast.”

George’s heart sank. His angel had a man – and a doctor to boot.

‘Och well,’ he thought. ‘A man can dream.’

***

Three days after the Doctor’s visit, Nurse Anderson gave George his assessment.

“It’s good news, George,” she said. “You’re to be shipped back across the channel. You’re going home.”

George took a while to process the information. He thought for sure he would be back on the Front Line within weeks.

“We can’t keep you here much longer as we need the beds, so tomorrow you’ll be taken to a hospital ship and transported to a hospital in England until you are fit to return home. Where is home, George?”

“Cumnock, Ayrshire,” George whispered. “It seems so long since I was there. I’ll need to let my uncle know what’s happened to me.”

“We’ll get a message to him. I’m sure he’ll be pleased to know that you’ll soon be back in Scotland.”

“Aye, that he will.”

Chapter 13 (November 1917)

GOING HOME

William had just returned from the day shift at the mine and was still covered in coal dust. As he made his way from the kitchen, through the hole in the wall to the wash-house, he heard the door open. He placed the white enamel bowl of water on the table and stood open-mouthed.

"Hello, Uncle," George said in a quiet, raspy voice.

William eyed the young man up and down, noting the smartness of his uniform and the slump of his shoulders.

"Geordy, lad, you've been returned to us," William said and walked towards George, right hand outstretched. Instinctively George put both hands behind his back as he still suffered shooting pains. William swallowed hard as the impact of George's injuries suddenly hit him and instinctively hugged his nephew in a rare display of affection. Grabbing George by the shoulders he said, "Here, let me look at you. Oh Geordy, it's so good to have ye back." Motioning George to a chair at the kitchen table, he continued, "Tell me all about yoursel'." William sat at the table, black-faced, listening as George told his uncle, in whispered tones, as much as he wanted him to know. There were some things he would never tell him and some things he would never forget. He was a raw boy when he left Scotland in September 1916, and just over a year later he had returned a scarred and burdened man.

George was tired but as William made him a cup of tea and a sandwich, he looked around the little house and took in its familiarity. He got up and stood at the window looking up and down the street which seemed eerily quiet.

"We've lost a lot of friends, Geordy," William said sadly. "There's barely a family in Cumnock that hasn't lost someone."

He placed the pot of tea on the table. "I've been saving the sugar and tea for yer return," William said eagerly. "We were asked to limit the amount of bread, tea, sugar and meat we used, and most people have been careful, but of course some have not, so the government introduced rationing just this year. It seems fair to me that we should all be doing what we can."

George sat back down at the table and took a sip of tea, but didn't touch the sandwich. He was very quiet and looked drawn.

"Aye, and things have changed at the mine," William continued, eager for the conversation he'd been denied as he lived alone for the past year. But he could see that George wasn't well enough to talk and steered him towards his bed.

"There's yer bed lad, just the way ye left it. Now you get a good night's rest and we'll talk more in the morning."

George lay in his bed as William cleared the dishes. He took in the smell of the fire and the quietness of the house. He was home.

Chapter 14 (February 1918)

A SLOW RETURN

George had been back in Cumnock for three months and taken time over the Winter to recover from his physical wounds. His hands and eyes had healed and his voice had improved. For all outward appearances he was back to normal, but inside his head the memories lingered of dead bodies, buried in the mud where they fell, rats gnawing at the flesh of the fallen and Angus's face – always Angus's face. George had always been a self-assured lad with big ambitions, but the war had changed him. He kept to himself mostly, taking long walks in the deep snow to no particular destination. He had no employment and no inclination to take any. He helped William around the house, bringing in the coal for the fire and hand-washing clothes and making the occasional meal, but while he had physically returned to his old life, mentally he was far away.

William had brought friends to the house for card games and taken George to the Craighead Inn to try to get him to socialise, but he would speak only when spoken to and barely made an effort. What could he speak of with these people? The men who had gone to war either did not return or, like him, had no interest in discussing their experiences. He had fallen into a lonely abyss that only he could get himself out of.

William was frustrated that his efforts to cheer George up had failed. He thought back to what his mother, Mary Hamilton McMurdo, would have done. She had a no-nonsense way of cutting to the heart of the issue. He thought George's biggest problem was that he was idle and didn't have an occupation to fill his waking hours. One night after tea, as George sat staring into the flames in the fireplace, William decided to speak to him.

"They're needin' men up at the pit, George," he began. "Good men, with experience, like you. And things have changed Geordy. There are more safety precautions now and the wages are better, although the taxes are higher to help pay for the war. What I'm sayin' is, there's a job for ye and I think it would do ye good to get back to work."

George continued to stare at the flames. He knew his uncle was right but he didn't know how to make the next move in his life.

"Ye've served yer time for the country George, and paid the price. Now you can continue to serve, as the country needs coal and men to dig it. This war can't go on much longer and ye've got to live yer life."

"Harsh words, Uncle," George said. "Ye've no idea what I've seen." He rose from the chair and stood over his uncle. "Do ye know I was working underground in France? Aye, that's right, I went from one underground hell to another. Did ye know that there were people dying all around me? Did ye know that I saw a lad's face blown clear away by an enemy bullet?" He slumped back down into his chair.

William swallowed hard, and thought before he spoke. "I sometimes forget how young you were - you are still - and the horrors that ye've seen at such a young age." He paused choosing his next words carefully. "But the fact is you are now a man, with yer whole life ahead of you and ye can choose to sit around here all day or get back into the land of the living which, George, if ye don't think it's too harsh of me to say, you are lucky to be a part of. I wasnae there to help ye in the trenches but I'm here to help you now, if ye'll let me. There are some wounds that won't heal, lad, but ye'll never know what ye can make of yer life if ye don't try." William stood up and headed for his bed. "That's all I'm saying," he said over his shoulder.

George sat by the fire for half an hour, just staring into the flames and thinking. Slowly he stood up and went to his uncle's bedside. "I'll make up two piece boxes the night for tomorrow's shift," was all he said. His uncle knew that meant that George would be heading off to the pit with him in the morning. He knew that the past would never completely leave George, but a step towards the pit was a step in the right direction.

Chapter 15 (November 1918)

FIGHTING STOPS, BUT MEMORIES LINGER

At the eleventh hour, on the eleventh day of the eleventh month in 1918, all hostilities ceased and The Great War - 'The War to End All Wars' - was finally over. George and William and the other men of the day shift were on their way home as they saw the village buzzing with people shouting and dancing. The newspaper boy held the broadsheet aloft. 'Germany Surrenders' read the headline in bold capitals. 'The war is over', shouted the newspaper seller.

George bought a newspaper and the men all headed for the Craighead which was already bursting at the seams with people laughing and rejoicing. The ale and whisky were flowing and George was glad it was over. He took his whisky and retreated to a table in the corner of the inn to read the newspaper.

Around 557,000 Scots had joined up to help keep Britain safe. One in four had died. Scotland had paid a very high price for its warrior tradition. The Scottish casualty rate was 26 per cent, while the British Army casualty rate was 11 per cent. 'The war may be over,' George thought, 'but the battle has just begun'. There was a long road to recovery ahead but no more young men would be forced to leave the bosom of their families and be sent far away to fight a merciless enemy. No more men would be separated from their wives and children in the pursuit of a bloody victory. Perhaps the world could be at peace now, and the raging war inside the heads of the men who took part in the conflict could also end. As the noise of the celebrations invaded his thoughts once again, George looked up from the newspaper and saw his uncle beckon him over to a group of men. Life would go on.

Chapter 16 (1920)

A CHANGE OF PACE

The coalfields of Scotland had been important to the overall war effort, especially providing fuel for the Clyde shipyards, and while the country still relied heavily on coal production, the world economy slump was magnified in Scotland due to its reliance on the export of heavy industry such as coal, shipbuilding, iron and steel. George and William were lucky to have jobs in the mines, as unemployment levels rose when soldiers returned from the war. While the coal industry received a short boom period after the war, the price of coal per ton on the Scottish coalfields dropped from £4 to £1 and mine owners cut wages to keep the mines profitable.

After a boom there's always a bust, and despair and hopelessness gripped the country as the economy began to crash. Around 100,000 men in Scotland were unemployed. Many sought to emigrate to America, as former soldiers found nothing but unemployment and poverty in their futures.

The war had also had an impact on the role of women in society as, with many of the men away fighting the war, women took jobs in factories and coal mines. When the men returned to their traditional jobs after the war, many women, often widowed, were left without an income. People with homes and income were encouraged to take in strangers to alleviate unemployment and homelessness.

"Things are bad," William said one evening as he and George sat playing cards. "I see the state of some of the weans about here.

They're dirty, no proper clothes and starving. Some families are barely keeping body and soul together."

"Aye, it's bad alright, but there's no' much we can do," George said matter-of-factly.

"I've been thinkin' on that," William said as he put his hand of cards on the table face down. "We haven't had a female touch in this house since yer Gran died – seven years we've been batching for oursels' and I don't feel my cookin' has improved at all."

"Aye, I'd agree with that," George said with a smile. He put his cards down on the table, face up to show a full house, and sat back in his chair. "Spit it out Uncle, I know you've a plan."

William smiled. He'd raised George from a boy and they knew each other well. "What would ye say to us gettin' a housekeeper?" he asked.

George began to laugh. "A housekeeper – for a two-room house? Why would we go to such extravagance?"

"Let me put it to ye this way. How would ye feel about comin' home to a clean house, no' one strewn wi' dirty clothes and dirty dishes, with a hot meal on the table and hot water ready for a wash? Then gettin' into clean clothes and stepping out with yer pals, to come home and find yer piece box made up ready for the next day's work, and a good breakfast on the table before ye head off to the pit?"

"I can see ye've thought about this," George said as he remembered the pies and stews his Gran used to make, and the feel of clean sheets on the bed. "And where do we find this housekeeper – and what do we pay her?"

"There are so many people out of work and without a house, we won't have any trouble finding someone. And I doubt it will cost us much as we'll probably get a widow woman whose children are grown and she'll just be thankful for a roof over her head and food in her belly, and someone to care for," William said confidently.

"Sort of like having Gran here again," George said. "That's fine by me."

Two weeks later, on a bright Sunday morning, William answered a knock at the door. She was wearing a brown bonnet with wavy nut-brown hair peeping out of it, and a brown, long-sleeved, ankle-length dress with cloth-covered buttons down the front, and well-worn brown shoes. Her skin was pale and her hazel eyes bore the gaze of a woman who had seen much.

"Mr McMurdo," she said sharply, "I've come about the position."

"Aye, come in," William said gently. She looked about the two-room house and then back to William.

"Not that I'm no' in need of the position, but are you sure you need a housekeeper, Mr McMurdo?" she enquired.

"It's William, and yes we, that is my nephew and me, we need a housekeeper," he said confidently. He could tell by her down-at-heel shoes that she had probably tramped many a mile in search of work in this desperate climate of unemployment, but she had her pride and he would deal with her delicately.

"I'm Jean," she said. "So there are just the two of you, then?"

"Aye," said William. "I'm afraid there'll be some very dirty washing as we are both coal miners."

"That's nae bother," she replied firmly. "My faither is a coal miner and I'm from a family of nine children. I know a hard day's work when I see one."

William studied her appearance. She was younger than he thought the housekeeper would be. About 30, he guessed. In fact, Jean was 35 and a spinster.

"Where is yer family, Jean?" William enquired.

"They stay at Waterside Place here in Cumnock. I see them often but I've been making my own way in the world for quite some time," she said.

The door opened and George walked in, a coal bucket in each hand.

"George," William said, "this is Jean and she's here about the housekeeper's job." George put down the buckets, and wiped his right hand on his trousers before extending it to Jean.

"Please sit down with us Jean, and we'll talk this over. Ye know the terms and I'm hopin' yer happy with them," William said.

Jean had softened her tone considerably since she'd walked in the door. She hadn't been too sure of what she would be walking into, but she needed a place to stay and was willing to give it a go.

"I'll no' lie to you. I need a place to stay and I'd be pleased to care for both of you. But I do have one condition. I cannae live here alone wi' two men. Even with the unemployment and housing situation as it is, people still like to gossip and I'll have none of that. I have a friend, Helen, who would be pleased to move in as well."

William shifted uncomfortably in his chair. "Now before you say anything," Jean began, "you should know that Helen takes in dressmaking for a big store in Glasgow. Mind you, there's no' the demand for her work that there was. She travels up there by train once a week to collect and deliver dresses but she wants to stay in Cumnock to be near her family. We won't take a penny in payment, just our room and board in return for keeping house. That's how it must be," she said firmly.

"To speak plainly, Jean," George began, "the only woman we've ever lived with is my Gran and that was some time ago. We're no' used to having women in the house."

"Well," Jean said, "it won't be all bad. In fact, I think we could all get on quite well," she said looking at William. They were all silent for a few minutes, and then George spoke.

"It will no' cost much more in food, and the female company might do us good," he said.

"I like a man who speaks plainly, George," Jean said, "but I'm drawn to the strong, silent type," she said as she fixed her gaze on William. William didn't know where to look. His experience with women was minimal and now he would have two women living in his house. Times were changing.

Chapter 17 (1920)

A WOMAN'S TOUCH

Three days after their meeting in early December, Jean and her friend Helen arrived on the doorstep of 48 Barhill Rd, Cumnock ready to share the house with two bachelors. They re-arranged the rooms so that Jean and Helen had the privacy of the hole in the wall bedroom, and William and George took the bunk beds in the kitchen. The women cleaned and dusted and sent William and George to the inn, to get them out from under their feet. When they returned there was a hot meal ready to be served and they tucked in as the conversation flowed. George laughed more than he had in two years. He had never had a sister, but now he felt that he had two.

William had never had a wife, but his feelings for Jean grew every day. He started bringing her home little gifts of flowers or ribbons and gradually she changed his awkward bachelor ways. The household fell into a happy domestic routine with the women looking after all the household chores and William and George bringing home money to pay for the rent and food. Helen had her own money from her dressmaking and was happy to run up a dress for Jean or a shirt for William or George, when extra material was available.

After so many years on his own, William thought he would find it difficult to share the household with a woman, and he was surprised at how easy he felt in Jean's company. They could talk to each other and William found himself accompanying Jean to the shops and carrying back any parcels, or helping her to lift heavy buckets of coal and water. He just enjoyed being in her company. He thought that Jean felt the same, so one night he plucked up the courage to ask her to a dance.

"Oh, I'd be pleased to step out with you William," Jean said.

"That'll get the tongues waggin'," said Helen.

"Aye, and I'm no' takin' you Miss Helen, if that's what you're thinkin'," George said.

"Nobody asked you to take me, George – besides I'm meeting someone there. I do have a life outside of this house, you know," Helen said.

They all laughed the way that a family laughs together.

Over the passing months, William and Jean grew fonder of each other and would often steal away by themselves for some privacy. They were falling in love and both were ready for marriage.

In August 1922, as William celebrated his fortieth birthday at home, Jean called him outside after their tea. It was a cool, clear night at the end of Summer, and a night that William would never forget.

As Jean held her knitted shawl loosely around her arms, she stood facing William who was leaning against the outside wall of the house.

"Now, William," she began. "I've something to tell you. I think you'll be pleased. I've a special birthday gift for you," she said crossing her arms against her chest. "Now, I didnae think that I'd be able to give you this gift – because of my age – but...," she seemed lost for words, then she spoke quickly. "Your fortieth birthday present is the news that you are going to be a father."

William stood up straight and looked at Jean briefly, before lifting her in the air and twirling her around.

"Put me down," Jean insisted, "the neighbours will think you've gone mad."

"Ye've made me so happy, Jean," William said. "I never thought this day would come. Let's tell the others."

William took Jean by the hand and led her inside the house to where George and Helen were still eating cake and drinking tea.

"Jean has just given me the most wonderful birthday present," William announced as he stood with his arms around Jean. "I'm to become a father."

George and Helen looked at each other.

"I'd had an inkling," Helen said.

"I just thought you were puttin' on the puddin'," George said and the room went quiet, then they all started laughing. Trust George to say what was on his mind.

William and Jean joined George and Helen at the table. "My parents will no' believe it. At thirty-seven, they'd given up hope of me ever getting married and having a child," Jean said.

"Oh, my mither would be so pleased," William said. "Of her eight children, the only grandchild she ever had was George and now to think she'll have another grandchild to carry on the family name. Oh, she'd be so pleased. Well, I'll go and see the minister tomorrow. Oh, Jean I'm walkin' on air," he said as he kissed her cheek.

The next day William went to see Mark Robson, the Congregational Minister in Cumnock, about publishing Banns at the church. Jean went home to tell her parents, Robert and Annie Hyslop, the happy news. They decided to hold the wedding at the Hyslop family home at Waterside Place, Old Cumnock on November 3. William met the whole family, including her six brothers who were all coal miners. George and Helen were witnesses to the marriage.

After the wedding, the sleeping arrangements at the house at 48 Barrhill Rd had to be changed to accommodate the married couple. They all arrived back home after the wedding and Helen had an announcement to make.

"Well, I've some news of my own," she said. "I've been offered a full-time job as a dressmaker in Glasgow and I'm to start tomorrow."

"Tomorrow," Jean said. "Oh, Helen, I was hoping you'd be here when the baby arrived."

"Oh, you've got yer mither and yer sisters who'll see you right. No, it's time I moved on and got on with things. Now for tonight, I'll sleep on one of the beds here in the kitchen while you two have the other room to yourselves. Mind yer business tonight, George," Helen cautioned.

"Ah, ye've nothin' to fear from me," George said indignantly.

After Helen moved out, the house was re-arranged again. William bought a cradle to place beside their double bed in the hole in the wall, and George made himself comfortable on a bed in a nook of the kitchen. Just a few weeks after their wedding, their first child, a son, was born in the house where Mary Hamilton McMurdo had died nine years before.

"We'll call him Douglas Percy Hamilton McMurdo," William declared. "George, that's in honour of your faither (and my brother) Douglas, my grandmither's maiden name, Percy, and my mither's maiden name Hamilton. The family names will go on."

"Aye," George said, "just as I am George Percy Hamilton McMurdo. They are good strong names, Uncle, and the little lad is sure to do ye proud."

With the new life in the house, it seemed to take on a glow. William and Jean were besotted with the baby and George loved his wee cousin. He was now twenty-five years old and thinking it may be time that he too was married, but he wasn't sure if he was ready for the responsibilities that a wife and family would bring. He still had nightmares about the war, and the air in the house at Barrhill Road was often punctuated either by his screams or that of the baby.

Chapter 18 (1923)

BONNIE MARY

She had the sweetest face he had ever seen, and a trim pretty figure. Her light brown hair was swept up in a loose bun at the back while soft tendrils bounced as she walked briskly along the cobbled pavement, a woven basket swinging over her arm. George could see her from his seat across the road at the inn where he was tenderly nursing a glass of whisky. It was a Saturday, just after noon when the inn had opened. He often went to the Craighead to wash away the coal dust from a long week's work, and to give William and Jean some time alone with the baby. He liked to sit at the same window seat each week, just to watch the passing parade. It was August, and the last days of a cheerless Summer were drawing to a close. The beautiful girl crossed the street as she headed for the flesher's, and George shifted in his chair as she approached. She was even more beautiful up close, her skin creamy and flawless and her eyes as blue as cornflowers. He smiled in the hope that their eyes would meet, but she walked on purposefully, not even glancing into the inn. He hoped that she would walk back the same way to go home, so he downed the last of his whisky, straightened his coat and cap, and walked outside the inn to stand against the wall, his hands in his pockets. He waited and waited but still she did not come. He thought about retreating back into the inn for another whisky, and then he saw her. The hem of her grey dress skimmed the top of her well-polished black ankle boots as she hurried down the street, her basket full of meat, fruit and vegetables. As she got closer, George rehearsed in his mind how he would approach her. When she neared the inn, she crossed the street to the other side and George hastily followed.

He caught up with her. "Excuse me," he said politely, dipping his cap. "Could I carry yer basket for you?"

She eyed him cautiously. "I can manage quite well," she said and continued on her way.

"Then may I walk with you?" George ventured, his cap still in his hands. She looked at him again, studying his face. It was a pleasant face with a hint of sadness behind his eyes. He looked trustworthy, she thought, but her father wouldn't take kindly to any man walking her home.

George broke the awkward silence. "I'm George McMurdo, how do you do?" he asked extending his right hand. As she reached out to take his hand, apples poured from the basket she had balanced on her right arm. "Oh no," she cried. "Faither will be cross."

George bent down to pick up the apples. "Oh, it's all right lass, they're no worse for wear," he said as he examined the pieces of fruit and put them back into the basket. "There, nae harm done."

She looked into his hazel eyes and saw a kindness in him. "I'm Mary," she said smiling. "Mary Bell."

'Well, Mary Bell, since I've caused you all this fuss, let me take yer basket and walk you the rest of the way home."

Mary handed her basket to George and they strolled through the streets towards Mary's house at Townhead Street. They talked easily together, then she suddenly stopped a few houses from hers and took the basket from George.

"Thank you George, but I must be going now," she said hastily looking further down the road.

"Oh, aye. It's been a pleasure to meet you, Mary," George said. "Could I call on ye sometime?"

Mary became agitated. "Oh no George," Mary said quickly. "Faither would never approve."

"Of me?" George said, somewhat surprised.

"No, of any man," she said. "It's difficult, George."

George wasn't going to give up so easily. "Could we meet somewhere, then. Could I take ye for tea next week. Do ye visit the shops every Saturday?"

Mary smiled and blushed. "If I'm there and you're there, then we shall see," she said, then turned and hurried down the street towards her house.

George was charmed by her beauty and she fascinated him. He headed back to the inn for another whisky, but stopped and turned for home. He'd better save his coin for the following Saturday to take Mary to tea.

All week at work, deep below the surface of the earth digging coal, he could think of nothing but Mary. He'd never seen anyone so sweet and delicate. Even the girls he'd thought were beautiful in France, paled into insignificance to the lovely Mary.

The next Saturday morning, he was at the inn, but not at his usual table. He didn't want whisky on his breath, so he bought a newspaper and stood propped up against the wall outside, pretending to read, meanwhile peering over the top of the paper, ready to catch a glimpse of her. Then she appeared around the corner, her empty basket swinging on her arm. He folded up the newspaper, tucked it under his arm and hurried across the road to greet her. They smiled at each other and without saying a word, George ushered Mary a few doors down to the tea room. He ordered a pot of tea and cream cakes and Mary seemed to enjoy their time together.

"Oh George, look at the time," Mary said as she glanced at the clock in the tea room. "I've got to get back and I've no' done my shopping," she said as she took the napkin from her lap and placed it back on the table. As she picked up her basket, George put his hand on hers and she looked up at him.

"We'll get it done, lass. Don't fret. I'll come wi' ye. Just tell me what ye need and we'll do it together." Her arm relaxed under his touch and she nodded in agreement. George did the rounds of the shops with Mary and walked her home as far as the top of Townhead Street.

"That's far enough," Mary said, taking the basket from George. "I've had a lovely morning."

"Aye, let's do it again next week," he said. Mary agreed, then hurried off down Townhead Street.

Every Saturday morning for a month George was waiting for Mary and after tea and cakes he'd help her with the shopping and walk her home as far as she dared allow him. He wanted to find out more about her. He needed more time with her, so he hatched a plan for the following Saturday. When Mary arrived, he took her basket and her shopping list and beckoned down the street. A small girl of about ten appeared. She was a neighbour's child from Barrhill Road. George bent down to speak to her and handed her the basket and shopping list.

"Now lass, just as I've told ye, take this list and get all the things on it and bring it back to the tea room. If ye have any trouble, just tell the shopkeepers it's for Miss Bell and they'll know. Here's a penny for now, and another penny when you bring back the basket with everything on the list."

The child's eyes gleamed as she took the penny in her grubby hand then thrust it into the pocket of her worn dress. She skipped off barefoot with the basket and the list. Mary looked at George, waiting for an explanation.

"Right, now we have more time to be together. We can drink tea, eat cake and talk for longer while yer shopping is getting done," George declared as he steered Mary in the direction of the tea room.

Mary liked a man who could take charge, and she was liking George more every time she met with him. She didn't say a word until she was seated comfortably at the table and George had placed the order.

"Ye've no idea how I've come to look forward to these Saturday meetings, George," Mary said. "I'm on my feet from daylight to dusk with never a moment to rest."

George listened intently. He wondered what her home life was like and why he could not walk her to her house. "If ye don't mind me asking Mary, are ye ashamed to take me home to yer family?"

"Oh no George," Mary said as she put her hand on his. "It's just that…well…faither is very strict. He doesnae approve of me or my sisters having any idle time and he'd think it was frivolous if he could see me sitting here getting waited upon."

George could see the fear in her eyes and he listened as she told him about her home life. Her father, William McMaster Bell, had emigrated from Ireland and, as well as working at the local Ironworks, he owned some land nearby to his house and ran a variety of businesses.

Her mother, Mary McNeish Bell, was a local lass whose health was poorly, and she often took to her bed. Mary and her sister Sarah ran the household and worked hard in the businesses.

George listened intently, gazing into Mary's eyes and hanging on her every word. His concentration was broken as he felt a tugging on his shirt sleeve. The neighbour's lass had returned with the basket which he handed to Mary with the list. Mary checked that everything was there, as the little girl stood wide-eyed. Mary nodded to George who reached into his pocket and pulled out a penny. The little girl held out her hand.

"There ye go lass, for a job well done," George said. The little girl looked at the penny, then back at George. Mary took a cream cake from the plate and held it out to the little girl, who grabbed it and stared at it. "Now on ye go home," George said, and the little girl skipped out of the tea room as the two pennies jingled in her pocket.

"Maybe we could employ her next week," Mary said timidly.

"No," said George. "Next week I'm calling at yer house for you."

"Oh George, you cannae," Mary began.

"Let's get ye on home now and I'll call for ye next week," George said emphatically as he rose from the table. Mary relaxed and smiled and nodded her head. She liked him more and more.

***

The following Saturday morning, George was up early and took a bath in front of the fire before William and Jean and the baby were out of bed. He was sitting at the table with a cup of tea when

William joined him. As he reached for the teapot, William eyed George up and down.

"A starched collar," William said as he poured the tea. "You cannae be off to the inn this morning, Geordy."

George set down his tea cup. "No, I'm off to impress someone," George said solemnly. William sat back in the chair, his hands wrapped around the hot teacup.

"If you're in yer Sunday best, it must be a girl," William smiled.

"Oh, I think she's suitably impressed," George said with a smile. "It's her faither I've dressed up for. I hear he's very strict and I want Mary to feel comfortable about stepping out with me."

"Oh, Mary is it?" William said as he leaned into the table. "Tell me more."

George looked out the window. "She has the face of a wee angel, the tiniest waist and long brown hair. She's a bonnie wee thing." With that, he rose from the table and took his cap down from the peg beside the door. "I'm away," he said and walked out the door.

Jean joined William in the kitchen, with the baby on her hip. He poured her a cup of tea and she drank it standing up as the baby fussed.

"Our Geordy's got himself a lass," William said.

"I wondered why he seemed a bit happier lately," Jean said.

William placed his arm around his wife's waist. "It took me a while but I found my happiness and I hope he finds his. God knows he deserves it."

Chapter 19 (1923)

STANDING UP

George walked the few streets from Barhill Road to Townhead Street and knocked on the door of Mary's house. It was in a brown brick building with shops and other houses side by side. Her sister opened the door slightly and introduced herself as Sarah.

"I've come to see Mary and your faither," George said as he stood erect at the doorstep. Then the door opened wider. George was imagining a tall, stout, foreboding man but instead there stood before him the thin frame of William McMaster Bell clad in trousers, braces and a flannel undershirt.

George extended his hand. "How do you do, Mr Bell," he said confidently. "I've come to ask yer permission to take Mary out fer tea."

Mr Bell looked George up and down, then slowly raised his right hand to shake George's hand. It was a strong grip and George could tell the handshake of another working man.

"In you come, lad," Mr Bell said gruffly. Mary smiled timidly in the background as she clutched at her sister Sarah's hand. They all followed Mr Bell, and the first thing George noticed was that they had a living room. In fact, there were five rooms in the house – a kitchen, living room, a small bathroom and two bedrooms - unlike the two-roomed miners' houses he was used to. "Sit," Mr Bell said to George, motioning him towards a large arm chair. Sitting opposite George was Mrs Bell, who was clearly not well. "This is my Mary – Mrs Bell." George listened to the lilt of Mr Bell's Irish accent. He knew so little about Mary and her family, but he was keen to learn. They all sat in silence for about a minute then George, growing impatient, turned to Mr Bell.

"I've been meeting Mary at the tea room for the past few Saturdays for tea, and I wanted to make sure that ye knew about it," George said. He looked across at Mary who was horrified that George had shared their secret. She knew her father's temper and struggled with his over-protectiveness.

Mr Bell sat forward in his chair. "Have you now," he said. "Ye need to know something, lad. I have seven daughters and one son. Two have left home and Mary is now the eldest. Mary, Jeannie, Sarah, Janet, Maggie and my lad Robert all work with me in the businesses while I also work at the Ironworks. We all work in this family and no one can afford time to go gallivanting off when they please. We've not a lot of time for 'tea' in this household."

Mrs Bell began to cough and Sarah rushed to her side. She looked worn-out and sad, George thought.

"And as you can see, her mam is not well at all, so Mary's needed here just as everyone else is."

George had been used to his Gran's strict discipline when he was a lad, but now he was a man and he had no problem speaking up for himself.

"Aye, Mr Bell, I can see you're a hard working family, but Mary's chores will no' suffer if she steps out wi' me. Last week I arranged for a wee lass to do the shopping while Mary sat wi' me in the tearoom, so one way or another her work will still get done."

Mr Bell's eyes narrowed. If Mr Bell was stubborn, George was even more so. He'd held his own in physical fights and he wasn't afraid to speak his mind. Mr Bell could see that George was a determined sort.

"It takes Mary one hour to walk to the village to do her shopping and back again. You can have one hour of a Saturday and the shopping must get done. And you will be held personally responsible for her safety, young McMurdo," he said and got up and walked out of the room.

George looked across at Mary and smiled. He stood up and bid goodbye to Mrs Bell then held out his arm for Mary to take. She picked up her shawl and basket at the door and off they strode into the town.

"You were marvellous, George," Mary said. "I was expectin' a fight from faither."

"I've met many a tough old bird. He'll no' get the better of me."

Chapter 20 (1924)

A WELCOME SURPRISE

Not content with merely taking tea on a Saturday, George began to call for Mary more regularly, despite her father's protestations. He was smitten with her and the more he heard about her family life, the more he wanted to take her out of the house and enjoy their time together. They would take long walks along the River Afton, and George would occasionally bring Mary home to Barhill Rd for Sunday dinner with William and Jean.

Jean was well pregnant again, with toddler Dougie fussing at her legs as she was bent over the fireplace stirring the pot. As the door opened, she stood up and brushed back the errant strands of hair that fell about her face.

"Oh Mary you're here. Sit down lass," Jean said as she picked up young Dougie. Jean enjoyed the female company after caring for her husband William and nephew George.

"You've not long to go now, Jean," Mary said as Jean instinctively touched her growing belly.

"Aye, here I was just two years ago a spinster of thirty-seven and I'm soon to be the mother of two," Jean said as she looked lovingly at William. She looked back at Mary who was smiling at them. "How's yer mither Mary? Is she doin' any better?"

"Oh, Jean she's no' well at all," Mary said as the smile faded from her pretty face. "The doctor wants her in the hospital but m' faither will no' hear of it. She's awfully tired."

"Aye, a rest in the hospital would do her good," Jean said as she looked at George who knew what she meant.

A week later, when George called for Mary, he had some happy news.

"Jean's had the wean," he said. "They've called him William after his faither. Another strong lad."

George and Mary enjoyed the long days of Summer, picnicking by the Afton in a secret spot among the long grass, sheltered by an outcrop of rocks. After one of their trysts Mary settled back in George's arms and looked at the sky.

"What do you think of the new wean?" Mary enquired.

"Oh he's like all babies – cries and sleeps," George said.

"But do you like babies, George?" Mary asked.

"Oh, I've never thought much about it. They're all right, I suppose."

Mary leaned up on one arm and looked into George's face. "I'm going to need your help George," then leaning back she continued. "I'm terrified. Absolutely terrified."

George sat up and looked at her sweet face as her tears fell.

"Why Mary, what are you afeard of?"

"I'm to have a wean George, and worrying about your reaction is frightening enough, but what will faither say. He'll no' take this news well."

George looked at Mary while the news sank in. He wasn't sure how to feel, for he'd never thought about becoming a father. But as he thought, he began to smile.

"A wean," he said to Mary. "A wee one to look up to me, and for us to care for." He thought a while more.

"And when will this take place?"

"Around Christmas," Mary said through her tears. "I've helped enough women in the village through pregnancy and childbirth to know about these things."

"We'll marry as soon as possible," George said. "I'll speak to your faither today."

"Oh no, George," Mary said as she stopped crying and stood up, "please don't say anything to faither. I'll find a time to tell him, but not now. Not with mither so ill and …," she stopped talking, took a breath and continued. "Oh, there'll never be a good time to tell faither. I can hear his shouts already. We'll run away, far away."

George took Mary by the hands. "Settle down, lass," he said gently. "We'll no' tell him for now, if that's what you want. But there is one thing that needs settlin'. Will you marry me, Mary?"

"Aye George. When the time is right, I'll marry you." They held each other in a lasting embrace then George walked her home.

Late in July, Mary's mother was admitted to the hospital in nearby Mansfield Village. She had a bad heart and had taken to fainting. Each day she grew weaker. On July 29, 1924 Mary McNeish Bell died of heart failure. Mary had been close to her mother and the news hit her hard. Her father, for all his hard ways, had loved her too but he wasn't one to show emotion. After the funeral, it was business as usual for Mr Bell, but his daughters were expected to increase their workload to make up for the loss of their mother.

"I'll never get away now," Mary told George as he once again broached the subject of telling her father about her advancing pregnancy. "Faither expects us to run the household now that mither is gone and we've scarcely a minute to ourselves. I'm worn out at the end of the day."

"Aye, I can see that. You need to take care of yourself, Mary."

"Wait just a while longer, George. We're all still so upset with mither passing."

George agreed to wait to tell her father, but he did confide in William and Jean one evening as they sat down to their meal.

"Mary's in the family way and we are to be married," George blurted out matter-of-factly. William looked at his nephew. He was not a child that needed his guidance. He was a grown man of twenty-seven and he knew his own mind. Jean broke the silence.

"I'm very pleased for you both, George," she said as she fed Dougie his dinner. "When's the wedding to be?"

"Well right away if I had my way, but Mary is so afeard of her faither that she willnae let me speak to him," George said.

"Aye, I've heard tell of old Bell," William said. "He's got a reputation as a hard old man. Just confront him George. It's not as though you and Mary are children. Mary has a right to a life of her own."

"I'm glad to hear you say that Uncle, for it's what I feel mysel'," George said pushing his plate aside. "I'll be telling him this Saturday. It cannae wait any longer."

By now Mary was five months pregnant and could scarcely hide her condition. She carried a heavy load of washing to the clothesline and dropped the basket, with clothes spilling into the dirt. Her father stopped chopping wood and looked at his daughter as she stood, hands on hips, staring at the ground. Mary caught his glance and saw the anger in his eyes. He drove the axe into the wooden stump and walked towards her. Mary cowered with fear and looked for a place to run.

"Have you something to tell me, girl?" Mr Bell asked. "Is there something you're hiding from me, girl. Well, you can't hide it any longer for it's plain for all to see." He advanced on his frightened daughter, his right hand raised to slap her. But before his hand could make contact with her cheek, Bell felt a strong hand around his wrist.

"Touch her and you'll fall where you stand," George said as he looked old Bell in the eye, still holding him by the wrist. Bell raised his left hand in a fist and took a strike at George but he ducked out of the way and grabbed Bell's other hand.

"I've no wish to fight with ye Mr Bell, but I won't see Mary hit. Do you hear me? Don't lay a finger on her. The poor lass is frightened out of her mind to tell ye something that I've wanted you to know for months. Mary and I are to be married and we're having a wean."

Bell released himself from George's grip and took a step back. His gaze never left Mary.

"The girl knows her place is here with me helping to run things. She's needed here."

"No, her place is making a life for herself and our wean. She's twenty-six years old, man. You cannae hold her here."

Bell knew he was fighting a losing battle, and he calmed down.

"Take yourself inside girl, and show your sisters your predicament." He turned to George pointing a finger at him. "You're responsible for this, but she's my daughter and I'll say when she is free to marry. And that time is not now." He stared at George then walked past him into the shed. Mary was standing on the back steps of the house with her sister Sarah.

"Will you look after her, Sarah?" George said. "See that he doesnae touch her." Then he turned to Mary. "It will all be all right, lass. Don't fret. Just look forward to being a wife and mother and I'll arrange the wedding as soon as I can." He nodded towards the shed. "And if he gives you any trouble, I'll sort it."

Mary's life in her father's house grew more and more uncomfortable as he scarcely spoke to her. She longed for the day when she could marry George. Her sister Sarah was a great comfort to her and helped her let out the seams of her dresses to accommodate her growing girth. The months rolled by but still Bell would not release his daughter to marry.

By Christmas, Mary was heavily pregnant. She had helped her mother raise the children and had become one of the unofficial midwives in the village, so she knew what to expect.

At 11.05pm on December 29, 1924, George and Mary's daughter Mary McNeish Hamilton McMurdo made her way into the world at the Bell family home. George and Mary, both in love, were still living apart. On seeing the beautiful child, old Bell smiled and left the room. He didn't offer congratulations, but he was moved when he saw the baby.

"We'll have no more trouble with him," George whispered to Mary as they both gazed lovingly at the child cradled in Mary's arms.

Without telling Mary or her father, George had arranged with the minister for the wedding to take place on January 20. Mary, and baby Mary, remained at the Bell home until the day of the wedding and then they moved into the house at Barhill Road with William, Jean and their two wee boys. The house was full again with crying babies.

"Oh if only yer Gran could see this," William said to George as he looked at the children.

"Aye, she'd be proud of them all," George said.

Chapter 21 (1926)

IT'S A BOY

By the Winter of 1926, Mary knew that she was pregnant with their second child. They were visiting friends in New Cumnock when their son William Bell McMurdo was born at the end of Spring on May 12, 1926. He was a good strong lad and old Bell, the only grandfather the child would ever know, was especially pleased to have a grandson. He was named both for his grandfather William Bell and his great-uncle William McMurdo, the man who had raised his father. He was christened in the Church of Scotland in the new, white christening robe that Mary bought for him. The lad would be known as Willie. The baby grew into a curious toddler and was the apple of his mother's eye and doted on by his older sister Mary. He had a smile that could soften the hardest heart.

In 1928, two years after Willie's birth, William and Jean welcomed another son – Andrew Hamilton McMurdo, this child named after William's older brother Andrew who had been a baker but died from tuberculosis.

***

The economy and way of life in Scotland had not recovered fully after the war and people were often destitute, without work and in some cases starving. William and George worked hard in the mines and earned enough to keep their families housed and fed, but there was never anything left for more than some pipe tobacco and a dram for the men, and the occasional new bonnet, dress or shirt for the women and children. Despite the poverty of many families, the babies kept coming and Mary's skills as a midwife were becoming more in demand. She was often called upon at all hours of the night to tend to a labouring woman or help layout a deceased person in the village. The small amount of money she was paid went into a glass jar in a cupboard in the kitchen. In the coming years she would need every penny.

Chapter 22 (1930)

SWAPPING OLD FOR NEW

A stock market crash on the other side of the world meant little to most of the people of Scotland, however the financial crisis that gripped New York in October 1929 would have consequences that would be far reaching. All of Britain was still trying to recover from the economic and personal losses caused by the Great War, but this Great Depression had a devastating effect on the industrial areas in Britain, particularly the coalfields and shipyards of Scotland, as demands for British products collapsed. Still struggling to cope with the cost of the war, British heavy industry was out of date and labour intensive. When orders dried up, the only course of action was for employers to lay off workers. Meagre government benefits were available for the unemployed, and a state pension of ten shillings a week had been introduced for people over sixty-five, but in truth many families went without food, and coal for heating.

The mining industry was one of the hardest hit and many men lost their jobs. George and William had a wealth of experience in the mines and were always willing to take on extra responsibilities. Their jobs were secure, and it was just as well for as the snow began to clear at the end of Winter in 1931, George and Mary welcomed their third child on February 15, a daughter whom they called Margaret after her great-great-grandmother Margaret Stevenson McMurdo.

The little house at Barhill Rd, with its two small rooms, now housed William and Jean and their three wee boys, and George and

Mary and their three small children. The mine owners had installed electricity and a tap in the kitchen which made life a little easier, but it was crowded.

"It's like old times," William said one evening as the adults sat down to their tea, each holding a child. "I remember mither telling us of how our grandmother Margaret Stevenson McMurdo raised eleven children in a wee miner's house and here we are two generations later, ten people squeezed in together."

"It's no' by choice," George snapped. When he felt the eyes of William, Jean and Mary upon him he felt compelled to explain.

"It's no' that I mind sharing the house, but I would like to have a home of our own some day – and I'm sure you'd like the same, Uncle Will," George said.

"Aye, of course Geordy, but wi' the way things are going for this country at the moment, and jobs being so hard to come by, I think it best that we stick together for the time being," William said. "We've two incomes to house and feed our families and we're managing. Not like some poor devils who are on the streets because they've lost their jobs. All in good time lad, all in good time."

While he'd heard stories of how his father and mother, and his mother's five children from her previous marriage, had moved in with Mary Hamilton McMurdo and her children and they all lived happily together, George had only ever lived with two people – his grandmother and his uncle. He needed his own space and some privacy.

Mary reached across the table and squeezed George's hand. He sometimes became moody and Mary never quite knew the cause, but she suspected it had something to do with the war, and she was right. Although on the outside he functioned perfectly well, he still had nightmares that woke the household and he often wandered off on his own for hours. 'It's just his way', she thought.

The Great Depression took its toll on Scotland, and unemployment reached twenty-five per cent. Particularly hardest hit by economic problems were the industrial and mining areas and nationally more than three million people were out of work. Many families depended entirely on dole payments from the local government and many a man's pride was irreversibly damaged. George and William clung to their jobs at the pit, and Mary and Jean saved every penny they could. They cut down the men's old clothes to make shirts for the boys, and made the two wee girls dresses of the cheapest material they could buy.

In 1932, there was another wee girl to make dresses for, with the birth to William and Jean of their daughter Agnes Margaret Mary.

With the arrival of the new baby, George felt the time had come to move and he was confident that, with his wage from the mine, and the pin money Mary earned from her midwifery duties, that they could afford to rent a home of their own. It was a brave decision to make in the current economic climate, but he was tired of waiting for things to get better, and he wondered if they ever would.

He had heard about new council housing at Lochview in Pathhead, New Cumnock, just a few miles from Barhill Road, Old Cumnock, and went to have a look. There were four flats in the block – two up, two down – separated by a close. The roof was made of tiles and the outside was built from bricks that had been clad in grey stucco, a material made from lime and sand. George was shown a flat upstairs. He opened the door and entered the flat through a hallway into a large lounge room measuring fourteen feet by thirteen feet, with a kitchen ten feet by ten feet, off to the side. The kitchen contained a solid, coal-burning cooking range and cupboard space. There were two windows at the front of the flat and two windows at the back. Down the hallway were two separate bedrooms, each measuring about thirteen feet by ten feet, and there was room for a garden at the back. If a cooking range in the kitchen and separate bedrooms wasn't enough, the flat also had running water in the kitchen and in the indoor bathroom, an inside toilet and electric lighting. The water was heated by a coal fire with a back boiler. Compared with the family's long history of living in two-roomed miners' rows, with only one or two windows, no running water or electricity and toilet facilities shared between many large families, this new council flat was a palace. The rent would take more than half his wage, but George was still convinced that the money was worth spending to ensure the family's privacy and to give his children room to grow. And, he thought, for all of old Bell's faults, he had provided his family with a good house with several rooms, and he wanted Mary to have the best house that he could afford. He paid the agent the first week's rent and went home to tell Mary.

As they were all seated at tea that night, George gave them his news. "Mary, lass," he began. "I've a surprise for ye – one that I'm sure you'll be pleased about." Mary continued to feed baby Margaret her mashed vegetables, while eight-year-old Mary helped her brother Willie load peas on to his fork. Willie started to throw peas at his sister and his mother Mary scolded him and reached across the table and took the fork out of his hand. "I'm sorry, George, what was it you wanted to say?" Mary said as she looked at her husband who was growing impatient at having to wait to get her attention. George took a deep breath and continued.

"I've rented a council flat and we are moving tomorrow," he said. The adults were quiet while the children continued laughing and playing.

"Tomorrow, George, but I've not even seen it," Mary said.

"Ah, you'll be well pleased Mary. I can't begin to tell ye about it," George said smiling. After he'd recounted every detail of the flat to Mary, he sat back in his chair.

"And how much will this cost?" Mary asked.

"Och, is that all you can think about – the cost. I want ye to have the comforts it can offer," George said, suddenly aware that William and Jean were staring and him. "And I want Uncle Will and Jean and their weans to have their own space." He paused and began eating his tea.

"Well, it's a fine set of walls you've arranged for us, but what are we to sleep on and eat off?" Mary asked. George continued eating and realised that that was something he hadn't thought about.

"We'll manage," he said, not knowing how. Then a thought dawned on him. "I don't like other people's miseries to be our good fortune, but there's a lot of people had to sell perfectly good furniture to the second-hand shop and we'll do well to pay them a visit tomorrow."

He had already spent half his pay on the rent and now he would need to buy furniture for the flat, but he was convinced that it was the right move for his family.

The following morning, Mary and George with their children Mary, Willie and Margaret in tow, prepared to leave the little house at Barhill Road Cumnock, bound for a new life at 20 Lochview, Pathhead, New Cumnock. George was leaving behind the two-room houses of the miners' rows – the only home he'd ever known – and striking out on his own with a family to support.

As Mary gathered up their few belongings, William stood at the door with his hand on George's shoulder.

"It's no' the first time I've said goodbye to ye, lad, but I feel as though my first son is leaving us," William said as he fought to hold back a tear.

"Oh, Uncle Will, I'll no' be far away and we'll visit often. Better still, you can visit us and see the new place."

"Oh, I'd like that, George," Jean said. "It sounds wonderful."

William walked over to the wall and took down the photo of Keir Hardie that George had cut out of the paper fifteen years before. He handed it to George.

"It's old and yellowed but it will remind you of the past, and I think that's a good thing," William said.

George looked at the photograph and the years came flooding back. He took it without saying a word. He picked up young Willie, while his older daughter Mary carried baby Margaret, and Mary held four large paper bags containing their clothing and a few household bits and pieces that Jean had given her.

"We'll get to the flat then I'll go out and get some furniture," George said.

"You've chosen the flat – do ye think I might be able to choose the furniture, George?" Mary asked.

"Oh, aye. We'll do it together," he said as he winked at William.

Chapter 23 (1932)

A NEW LIFE IN NEW CUMNOCK

The village of New Cumnock lay six miles south of Old Cumnock, where the Nith River, Afton Water and Moorfoot Burn met. Though essentially a mining village, New Cumnock was flanked by green fields rising to rocky and vegetated hills. On the left wing of the town, north of the plain, the village of Pathhead had shops, a hotel and a railway station. About a mile to the east sat Mansfield Village and at the south side of the plain lay Afton-Bridgend. The striking and beautiful Corsencone Hill rose on the north side of the River Nith, and locals used it as a barometer – 'When Corsencone puts on his hat, you may be sure it will be wat'. Robert Burns had been a familiar visitor to New Cumnock and even wrote *Flow Gently Sweet Afton* about the river that runs through the village. But for all its beauty, and even with the new council flats that had been built, the mining village of nearby Connel Park was testament to the poverty in which some families were still living.

When Mary saw the flat she could not believe her eyes. She ran from room to room like a child at Christmas. When she finally settled in the kitchen, she lovingly ran her hand along the range and kept turning the tap on and off with delight. For a brief moment she didn't care how much it would cost, and threw her arms around George.

"Don't tell me yet how much this is costing, just let me enjoy it for a while," Mary said.

'That's just as well', George thought, but it gave him pleasure to see her happy.

While Mary settled the children, George took the photograph of Keir Hardie and hung it on a nail by the front door.

They set about making a comfortable home for their family and Mary soon learned that the range which was supposed to make her life easier, was a coal burning monster that had to first be fired up with paper and wood and the ashes cleared away each day. The iron parts of the range had to be black-leaded and the steel parts rubbed with emery paper. Some days her hands were as black as her husband's from a day spent down the mine. She had to admit that heating water for baths was easier and for that she was thankful. Still there was no respite from household chores. Clothes and sheets were scrubbed and rinsed, and the heavy garments carried downstairs to be hung out to dry on a sunny day or hung overhead by the range to dry most days. The clothes were ironed with a flat iron that was heated on the range and, with an adventurous young son, and a husband working down the pits, there were always clothes to be mended and socks to be darned.

George had moved from the mine in Cumnock to take up work at the mine in Connel Park. The after-effects of his injuries during the war were more mental than physical, and he still had periods where he was withdrawn and Mary couldn't draw him into conversation. He liked to take long walks by himself and had started smoking a pipe. After his injuries from mustard gas, he was told by the doctor not to smoke or breath in stale air, yet here he was ingesting tobacco smoke and working underground all day. But drinking and smoking were among the working man's few pleasures.

While the living standard in Scotland was generally still poor, there were new innovations after the war that added comfort to living, for those who could afford it. Electricity in homes was available but some people could still not afford it. Mary learned to cook on the range and it became the focal point as it radiated heat in the most used room in the house. It was just as well as, even though George received a supply of coal as part of his wages at the mine, it was costly to run the fireplaces and so the range was kept well stoked from morning to night to provide warmth and food.

Eight-year-old Mary and six-year-old Willie were now enrolled at the local school in New Cumnock. Mary was a studious girl and always strived to do her best, but for Willie it all came too easily and he was often bored. Boredom often led to mischief, but he had such a bubbly personality and sweet smile that he often got away with his cheekiness.

Since the war, family sizes had decreased but Mary was still very much in demand as a midwife. While she attended to the poorer women in the village, the local doctor called on her at all hours of the day and night to assist with the laying out of corpses, a job that usually fell to midwives. It was not unusual for her to trudge through snow in the middle of the night to birth a baby, and return home just in time to cook breakfast for her family and get George's piece box ready for his day's work. She received a few shillings at most, which she added to the jar in the kitchen, but she was glad to help where she could. After all, she was starting to feel better off than many.

Chapter 24 (1935)

SOME BOY

The dour, long face of the school teacher, Mr Murdoch, was red with anger. He peered over the top of his rimless glasses, as the veins in his neck bulged out of the starched collar of his shirt.

"McMurdo!" he shouted as he walked quickly from the front of the classroom, a text book under his left arm and a switch of cane in his right hand. "What do you think you're doing?" he enquired as he stood beside Willie's desk.

"I'm no' doin' anything, Mr Murdoch," said Willie angelically with a flip of the long, blond fringe that fell across his forehead.

"Show me your hands," demanded Murdoch. As Willie slowly uncurled his hands Mr Murdoch could see that they were covered in ink. Then he looked at the girl called Jenny, seated at the desk in front of Willie. He opened his mouth to speak but words would not come. He gasped as he saw that the ends of Jenny's pigtails had been dipped in ink and that the ink had stained her dress.

"Stand to, McMurdo," Mr Murdoch shouted. Willie rose from his seat with his hands in his pockets. "Hold out your hands," commanded Murdoch. Willie slowly took one hand from his pocket. "Both of them." Willie took the other hand from his pocket. As Mr Murdoch raised the cane above his head, Willie quickly spat on both of his hands as all the boys did in a vain attempt to avoid the sting of the cane. Whack! Whack! Whack! Whack! The noise echoed across the classroom as the little girls gasped and the boys looked on in horror. After four good whacks with the cane, Mr Murdoch regained his composure. "Now sit down, and in future you will listen to what I am saying when I am teaching you about Britain's greatest ever poet and playwright, and not get up to any of your foolishness."

Willie sat down, holding back tears but smiling to his friends in the class. He was angry and wanted to strike back at Murdoch, but there wasn't much physically that a nine-year-old could do against an adult. So Willie thought that he would torment Mr Murdoch with the only weapon at his disposal – his sharp tongue.

"Mr Murdoch," Willie called to the teacher who was now standing at the head of the class. "Why are ye teaching us in English, when ye should be teaching us in Scots?" he asked cheekily. Murdoch began to turn red again. Willie continued. "Are we no' in Scotland, and not England, so why do we no' speak in oor ain language? Why are we learning aboot Willie Shakespeare when we have oor ain Rabbie Burns, the greatest poet of all, who hails from right here in Ayrshire?"

"McMurdo!" shouted Mr Murdoch. "To the principal's office – now!" Willie started for the door, swallowing a smile. Hands in his pockets, he walked calmly past Mr Murdoch – then winked. Mr Murdoch threw up his hands in exasperation. "That boy will either be a saint or a sinner", he said. "A saint or a sinner."

Willie loved life and shook it by the throat. He turned every challenge into an opportunity and wasn't afraid to share his opinion, even if it was not wanted. He was old for his tender years. His father provided for the family but he had become, at times, cold and distant, while his mother showered young Willie with love and affection. He would do anything for her. He had also become close to his Grandfather Bell, and while he was a hard taskmaster, Willie idolised the old man. He could be found most weekends, and after school, working the old man's land with his Bell cousins, for no more than the satisfaction of pleasing the old man. He had never known his McMurdo grandparents for they had died when his own father was just a toddler, and his attachment to his Grandfather Bell was strong. There was something about the old man that Willie loved. He was not averse to taking off the wide belt that he wore, to strap it around the legs of any of his grandchildren, but he made a good living through sheer hard work, and it was a lesson in life that Willie was learning.

He was a free spirit who wandered the streets of New Cumnock and the hills and glens around, looking for fun and adventure. He made friends easily and had his own little gang of lads that he got about with. They went fishing and they played soccer at the Glenafton Athletic Club and he enjoyed being part of a team. They didn't have much in the way of material comforts, but they didn't know that that was supposed to make them sad, so they just made do with what they had and enjoyed life with the carefree attitude of children. It was the way it was supposed to be.

Chapter 25 (1939)

NOT AGAIN

The number of workers at the mines had diminished and some mines across Ayrshire closed. While he sometimes had his shifts cut, and therefore his take-home pay, George remained employed at the Bank No. 6 Mine at Craigbank, New Cumnock where he had moved when he was enticed to leave Connel Park with the prospect of more responsibility and job security. He had escaped serious injury a few months earlier when a number of hutches in which the men were being brought back to the surface broke away from the haulage rope near the summit of the incline, and crashed after careering down the mine for about a quarter of a mile. Five men had been killed and twenty-one injured – one was a lad of fourteen, not much older than Willie, who had been employed at the pit for just a few days. George had been on an earlier hutch and made it to the surface unscathed, but the whole pit was saddened by the deaths and did all they could for the widows of the three married men who perished.

The family now owned a radio and every night they gathered to listen to the news, after which they would enjoy the music of the day. But the economy was still in decline with many people out of work and the housing conditions had not improved much for some. George sometimes became impatient and spent more time at the inn than Mary would have liked. These days he was often involved in fights, but the boxing lessons his Uncle William had given him as a boy stood him in good stead and he was usually the one standing over his opponent. He earned some respect in the village as a man who could handle himself and he became known as 'Hooker' for the ferocity of his right fist. It was a skill he passed on to his son Willie whom he taught to box, and the boy could take care of himself in the schoolyard or in the street. There were some tough lads in New Cumnock, raised in poverty and toughened by necessity, but Willie felt confident in dealing with them all.

"The lad's a natural," George used to say to Mary.

"I want him to be able to defend himself George, but I'll no' have you creatin' a bully," Mary cautioned.

"Och, away wi' ye woman," came the standard reply from George when he didn't agree with Mary. "A man's got to defend himsel', especially in this village."

And Willie learned well the lessons his father taught him. He felt that to make his way in the world he should be equipped with three weapons – his sharp tongue, quick wit and his strong fists.

While George honed his son's physical skills, Mary wanted to reach Willie's tender side, so for his thirteenth birthday she gave him a puppy. The labrador was part of a large litter and the owner was glad to give the pup away. She was pitch black and Willie immediately called her Raven.

"Oh, mither, she's braw," Willie said as he cuddled the little pup. "I'll teach her to do tricks and she'll go for long walks with me to Corsencone."

"Can I play with her too, Willie?" asked eight-year-old Margaret.

"Oh, aye, you can feed her and give her a bath and brush her coat," he said.

"Part of having a dog is looking after it Willie, so you'll be doing some of those tasks yoursel'," Mary said. Willie just smiled at her and she smiled too, as Margaret made a face at her older brother.

On September 3, as the family gathered to listen to the radio, the news was announced that war had been declared by Great Britain against Germany as they had invaded Poland. Most people had never heard the voice of the Prime Minister Neville Chamberlain, and they sat spellbound as the news was broadcast. The original radio announcement had been broadcast just after 11am that morning when many people had been at work, and so it was repeated in the evening.

"I am speaking to you from the Cabinet Room at 10 Downing Street," the Prime Minister began.

"This morning the British Ambassador in Berlin handed the German Government a final note stating that, unless we heard from them by eleven o'clock that they were prepared at once to withdraw their troops from Poland, a state of war would exist between us. I have to tell you now that no such undertaking has been received, and that consequently this country is at war with Germany."

George listened to the news, pipe between his teeth, then stood up and took his cap down from the peg and walked out the door without saying a word. The children all looked at Mary.

"Yer faither was in the first world war and he was injured," Mary began. This was news to the children for they had never heard of their father's war service.

"This news of war will bring back terrible memories for him and we'd best be mindful of it."

"Will faither have to go to fight?" Willie asked.

"No son, he's done his bit. It's time for young men to step up now."

"Will they take me?" Willie asked in all sincerity.

"No, son, not at your age – and besides I wouldnae want you to go. I need you here, and I couldnae bear not to see that cheeky face every day," Mary said as she smiled at Willie.

The talk at the inn from the young men was all about joining up, and there were tales about the horrors of war from the old men. George ordered a large whisky then drained the glass. He ordered another and drained it too.

"Fill it up again," he said to the barman. He raised the full glass above his head and shouted: "Here's to any man fool enough to think there's any glory in war, for I'm here to tell you there's no'," and he downed his third whisky. Some of his pals sidled up beside him at the bar, nodding in agreement, but a young voice responded.

"Take it easy old man. There's some of us still got it in us." George turned quickly and before the young man could wipe the smile off his face, George landed a right hook on his jaw and flattened him. With his fists still raised he called "anyone else have something to say. Huh, any one of you?"

No one responded and George turned back to the bar. "Another one," was all he said.

The alcohol dulled his pain as the memories of his young friend Angus, and the horrors of his time in the trenches, came flooding back – and just when things seemed to be going so well.

Even if he'd wanted to join up again, George was too old, as only men aged between eighteen and forty-one were liable for conscription into the armed forces, and he was already forty-two. Mining was once again considered to be a reserved occupation, which exempted him from conscription anyway. The government was determined not to repeat the mistakes of World War One, when the indiscriminate recruitment of too many men into the military had left major war production schemes short of the necessary workforce.

'It's a young man's war, and they are welcome to it,' he thought.

Chapter 26 (1939)

STILL FUN TO BE HAD

The Christmas of 1939 brought little cheer to most homes in Scotland. Food and clothing were rationed and some things were not available at all as Germany blocked supplies to Britain. In the three months since war had been declared, the people of Scotland had learned to live with the blackouts, drawing black curtains at night to keep out the light so as not to provide targets for the enemy in the air. Everyone had been issued with a gas mask as the British Government feared that gas would be used to injure or kill people as had happened in World War One, and children sat in their classrooms with the windows taped in a criss-cross fashion to save them from being sprayed with glass should a bomb fall. Willie hated the suffocating feeling of the gas mask drills at school. The children were encouraged to drink the free milk provided to the school by the government, in an attempt to improve the diet and health of Scottish school children. They lined up each morning for their little bottle of milk, the only sustenance many of them had had since waking up that day.

"Oh, I dinnae like milk," said Jenny to no one in particular.

"Hand it over here Jenny, and I'll drink it," said Willie.

"Oh, thank you, Willie," said Jenny as she blushed. "Now, I'll no' be in trouble from Mr Murdoch."

Willie smiled at her and wondered why she was looking at him with such a silly look on her face. It never occurred to him that she may like him.

Despite the gloom that had overtaken the village, Willie's life went on much as normal. He took Raven on long walks up to Corsencone, along the banks of the Afton and through the streets of New Cumnock.

The local picture theatre was a welcome distraction for everyone and one of the few affordable pleasures for ordinary folk. Still, Willie and his pals rarely had the price of a ticket so they would sneak in a back door and sit quietly in their seats so as not to be noticed. As the News of the World played before the start of the feature film, Willie would get out of his seat and walk slowly to the foyer, his hands thrust into his pockets. The cigarette machine was positioned facing away from the ticket and refreshment counter. He had no money so he took a piece of wire from his pocket and jiggled it in the slot from which the single cigarettes would fall. Jiggle, jiggle and the first cigarette fell. A few more jiggles of the wire and he had four cigarettes which he placed gently in his trouser pocket, together with the piece of wire, and walked slowly back into the theatre. Once inside, one of the boys produced a box of matches and the four sat happily puffing on their cigarettes as the film began. It was dark in the theatre and most people smoked so they could puff away and watch the film without attracting any attention.

On the way home from the picture house, they would climb fences to take apples from backyard trees then happily kick stones along the streets, as they made their way home. The local police officer, Sergeant Robert Leslie, would often give them a kick up the backside if he saw them scampering over fences with vests full of apples, then send them on home. They were restless lads in need of an occupation, but they did no real harm.

Chapter 27 (1941)

TIME FOR MOVING ON

On the night of March 13 1941, two hundred and fifty German bombers gathered over Clydeside in Glasgow, as Scotland became a target. Warning sirens wailed as the first incendiary bombs were dropped. The people of New Cumnock could see the glow in the night sky as the bombs hit their targets and exploded. The Luftwaffe returned the following night to inflict even more serious damage. Over 1,200 bodies were retrieved from the rubble and half of Clydebank's population had become homeless, with few of its twelve thousand houses escaping damage. With fierce determination, and some carrying injuries, men climbed through the wreckage to work in the shipyard the next morning. Within a fortnight, the Clydeside industries were back in operation and the shipyards were again supplying the British Navy. The German campaign to inflict major damage on Scotland's factories, coal mines, engineering works and shipyards, so important to the war effort, had failed, but in the process had resulted in massive loss of life.

So many children in Glasgow were left homeless and motherless, and with their fathers away fighting in the war they were virtually orphans. The Headmaster's wife, Mrs Dow, tried to match sad children with New Cumnock families who were willing to open their homes to them, but as many local families could barely keep body and soul together themselves, some of the children ended up being sent to the poorhouse.

Although they had a roof over their heads, things in the McMurdo household were tough. George was still working in the mines, but the rent on the flat had risen and money was tight. Their daughter Mary had left school at fifteen and was working on a farm at Stewarton, some twenty-one miles away, and only came home once a month, but she received little more than room and board at the farm and there was little money to bring home. The bombing affected George even more, and his times spent at the inn were becoming more frequent, even though the money he spent could have been put to better use.

Willie's relationship with his school teacher, Mr Murdoch, had not improved and he grew bored with school life. The only thing he really enjoyed about school was reading Rabbie Burns' poems and he would proudly stand up in class and recite *Flow Gently Sweet Afton* and *My Love is Like a Red, Red Rose* and *Tam O'Shanter,* for he loved the image of the witches dancing around and the old grey mare, Meg, losing her tail as she galloped across the Brig o' Doon at Alloway. But he could see the toll that the war was taking on his parents and he wanted to help. In two months' time he would be fifteen. He was growing into a strong lad and he knew that an extra pay packet would help his mother immensely.

One Friday morning in March, Willie dressed for school as usual and walked off with his sister Margaret to the school house. He sat through the day's lessons and as the bell rang in the afternoon to go home, instead of meeting his friends for a game of soccer, he marched straight to the Headmaster's door.

"Enter," said the Headmaster, on hearing the knock at the door. "Ah, young McMurdo, what is it today? Dipping girls' pigtails in ink? Reciting Burns in the middle of an English history class?"

"No sir. Mr Murdoch didnae send me. I'm here to speak to you."

The Headmaster sat back in his chair and took off his glasses. "Well then, you'd better sit down," he said, gesturing to a chair.

"I'll stand if you don't mind for I'll no' be here long," Willie said confidently. "This will be my last day at the school and I've come to tell you."

"Are your parents moving away from the district?" the Headmaster enquired.

"Oh, no, it's just that I've learned all I can here and I feel I can do more on my own," Willie said.

"Is that right," the Headmaster said. "And do your parents feel the same way?"

"Aye, they will when they find out," Willie said.

"You get a letter from your parents and I'll release you from school." The Headmaster picked up his glasses and looked at the boy. "You are making a grave mistake, Master McMurdo. You will be sorry for this decision."

"I don't believe I am making a mistake, sir. There's a whole world out there and my mither could do with the help of another man's wages. No, it's a good decision. Good day to you Headmaster," Willie said pulling his cap down on his mop of blond hair, then he turned and walked out the door leaving it open behind him.

The Headmaster sat back in his chair again and sighed. Then he laughed out loud. He didn't know what would become of the boy, but he wished him well.

As the family sat down to a tea of watery soup and bread, Willie dropped his own bomb.

"Are they needin' men at the pit, faither?" Willie asked.

"Aye, they're always needin' men now that most of the young 'uns have joined up," George said as he took another swallow of soup.

"Then I'll have no trouble getting a start there on Monday," Willie said as he ate his bread.

Mary looked at her son, then at George. He was almost old enough to leave school and she knew that he was a bright lad. It seemed inevitable that he would work down the pits one day, and she didn't have the strength to argue.

"You'll get a start," George said. "The hard work will do ye good. It's the pits for you then is it, like the rest of us?"

"Aye, it's the pits for me. I cannae wait to get started."

And that was the end of the conversation. Willie would go down the pits, like the generations of men before him. There were few options in Scotland for the working classes and while mining was all he knew about, it was just a start for him – he had big plans.

Chapter 28 (1941)

LIVING ON RATIONS

Coal mining had suffered a severe shortage of manpower because of the war, and inexperienced men were brought in to do the less skilled tasks such as unloading coal from the tubs. It was here that Willie got his start in coal mining, working as hard as any man.

From almost anywhere in New Cumnock, you could see the shaft with its great wheels and cable carrying the cage that took the miners below, but as Willie entered the colliery gates it was as though he was seeing it for the first time. Once signed on, he was given his safety lamp and a token to string around his neck as identification in case of an accident. He watched the men having a last smoke and many of them crouching as he had seen his father do many times. It was known as the miners' crouch, and it eased stomach muscles which became tight and sore from working in confined spaces. Once down below, the men walked to the seams until the roof became too low and they covered the rest of the journey at a crouched walk. There were passages going off at all angles, following the seams of coal. They were met by the deputy who had been down the mine for some time to ensure a proper air supply for the miners. He assigned the men their tasks for the shift and continued to write his report. Willie was taking it all in. His father had told him that the coal was mined using bell pits – digging down the coal seam then digging out the coal creating a bell shaped underground excavation, which had to be done before the roof gave way and the air ran out.

He got to his job of filling tubs and when it came time for a break, Willie sat with the men, 500 feet below the surface, to eat his bread and jam sandwiches and listen to the older miners as they talked a language he didn't always understand, but he intended to learn all that he could. They talked about how mining methods had improved over the years with the use of machinery, but because not enough money was being spent by the mine owners on equipment, a lot of coal was still cut by hand.

He was black and tired at the end of the day, but his mother always had a hot meal, however meagre, and a welcoming smile for him. As he walked, or sometimes cycled, through Connel Park on his way to the mine, he was glad that his father had moved the family to the council flat at New Cumnock. He had heard stories of the bleakness of the miners' rows and from what he could see, nothing had improved much in Connel Park. At the end of his first week of work, he proudly handed over his pay to his mother. She took it gratefully and hugged him hard. She had two working men to feed now, and she would try her best to get them some meat.

Like every family at the outbreak of the war, Mary had been issued with a rationing book so that the government could control the provision and distribution of food and ensure that everyone received an equal share. She was required to register with each shop supplying the rationed food - bacon, ham, butter, margarine, sugar and cheese - so that local food committees could calculate the amount of food a shop required each week. Coupons in the ration books could be exchanged for a certain amount of food each week. Sugar and butter were measured by weight, however the amount of meat allowed was measured in money, and was restricted to one shilling and tuppence worth of meat per week. Mary chose the cheaper cuts of meat so it was mostly mutton and she created mutton stew, mutton pie, fried mutton and tatties, boiled mutton and neeps, and mutton meatballs. When meat was not available, she fried oatmeal and onions in the pan to make poor man's haggis, and stale bread would be toasted to make a coating for the fish that Willie would often catch in the Afton River.

Despite her creativity, the family grew tired of eating mutton, but it was the cheapest meat available and all that they could afford.

Clothing was also rationed and people were given coupons they could exchange for clothes. Mary became adept at unpicking the seams of her dresses and cutting them down for a 'new' dress for Margaret to wear. She kept flour sacks, washed them and transformed them into pillow-cases decorated with insertion lace which was available cheaply at the haberdashery. She worried about how Jean was coping as William needed to take a lot of time off work. He had developed asthma and the stale air and coal dust in the mine made it impossible for him to work some days as he struggled for breath.

Willie fitted in well with the other men at the mine and knew many of the other boys. While he worked hard, he was never far from mischief and would often play pranks on the other men, but he was learning more about mining each day and took a great interest in not just his own tasks, but all of the work that was going on around him.

Mary took on extra work as a midwife but her duties were first and foremost to her family, and she kept a clean home and as much food on the table as she could.

As the radio continued to bring news of the war into the homes and hearts of the people of New Cumnock, George grew more irritated. He listened to the graphic descriptions of the bloody battles, and his face grew stern. On most evenings he would leave the family to sit by the radio, while he pulled his hat from the peg near the door and walked alone for hours, observing the men in their Home Guard uniforms who practised their drill in case the Germans ever made it to New Cumnock. He could see the young men of the village being conscripted, and it brought back painful memories.

Chapter 29 (1941)

A HARD BLOW

Willie still spent a lot of time with his Grandfather Bell, helping him with his businesses. The old man had worked as a coal miner and ironworks labourer but was now retired. Though he could barely read or write, he was an astute businessman and used his grandchildren as free labour. For some years he had owned a house on a four-acre plot on which he planted potatoes and other crops. He had managed to open a shop where he sold hot potato chips and also a grocery shop, down the burn in Mansfield Village. All week long he made his grandchildren gather sticks of wood from the surrounding area and cut them into six-inch lengths to make kindling which he would sell to people in New Cumnock to light their home fires. If the wood was cut too short or too long, he would take off the belt that he wore around his waist and hit the fingers of his free labourer. Every Friday night, he would have them pile it all into five horse-drawn carts and go around New Cumnock and surrounding areas selling logs and kindlers for people's fires. He also ran a fish and chip cart that was pulled by a horse.

All of his grandchildren, male and female, took a turn at ploughing the fields and if they stopped he would whip them around the legs with the horse whip that he carried with him. There was a hardness about the old man. His family had lived through the potato famine in Ireland in the mid-1800s and the effects had filtered down the generations. He knew what it felt like to go without and he was determined that his family would always have food on the table and a roof over their heads, but he was equally determined that they should all know the value of a hard day's work and appreciate what they had.

Willie was growing to become a 'man's man' and he idolised his Grandfather Bell. The old man ruled with an iron fist, but he got results. He was feared and respected by his children and grandchildren, and became an important part of the commercial fabric of New Cumnock as his businesses were reliable suppliers that people had come to depend upon.

Even after a long day down the coal mine, Willie could be seen by the old man's side, helping him plough the field or taking in the harvest or cutting sticks to size.

"I'm away to grandfaither's house," Willie said one Saturday morning as he grabbed his coat from the peg by the door.

"There is work here to be done," George said.

"Aye, and I'll do that too, but I promised grandfaither. I'll see ye at tea time, mither," Willie said and closed the door behind him. George looked at Mary and shook his head. Mary smiled and continued washing the breakfast dishes. "I wonder where he gets that wilful streak from," Mary said looking at George.

"Huh," was all George could say, for he had been as independent as Willie when he was that age.

Willie walked to his cousin Davey's house, said hello to his Aunt Sarah and then the two were on their way to Grandfather Bell's house, kicking stones along the road and telling jokes as they went.

"There's a field to plough and bundles of sticks to tie up," the old man said without any sort of greeting. "Mind you get to it and no playing about." The boys looked at each other for they were used to their grandfather's ways. As a young man, he had emigrated from County Down in Northern Ireland and settled in Kilbirnie, Ayrshire. The Irish were blamed by many Scots for taking precious jobs and many were not welcomed, but old Bell was made of tough stuff and he wasn't going to let the snide remarks of neighbours stop him from making good. He worked hard and he expected his family to have a strong work ethic.

Willie and Davey worked for eight hours bent over a plough, and were exhausted at the end of the day. Grandfather Bell appeared beside them.

"I'm away for a whisky with my pal, Andy. You can finish up now, lads. You know where the tap is around the back of the house for you to take a drink." The lads, tired and sweaty, drank thirstily from the back yard tap while the old grandfather sat on his veranda with Andy and watched them, whisky in hand.

"Why do we do it, Willie?" Davey asked as they set off on the road home.

"We're building character," Willie said.

"Where did you hear that one?" Davey asked.

"It was in a book I read. It makes perfect sense. If ye work hard ye build up yer muscles for the lassies to admire, and ye build up yer constitution so that if ye are ever in a bad situation ye can think of how hard ye worked at Grandfaither's and overcome the problem," Willie said confidently.

Davey looked at his cousin who was strutting along with his usual air of importance.

"Yer full of it, Willie McMurdo," Davey said as he pushed Willie, and they continued laughing as they walked towards home.

Old Bell sat with Andy on the veranda of his house and as the light of day began to fade, he finished up his whisky and headed down the couple of steps to round up his chickens and put them in the coop for the night. As he reached the ground, his right foot stood on the prongs of an upturned garden rake and the heavy wooden handle swung up and hit him on the head. The old man fell to the ground and Andy ran to his side. He saw the blood pouring from the head wound.

"Call the doctor," Andy shouted. Bell's youngest daughter Maggie appeared at the door and let out a scream. "No time for screaming, lass, call the doctor," he shouted.

An ambulance was despatched and Bell was taken to the Kilmarnock Infirmary. Maggie sent word to her brother Robert who went immediately to the hospital.

"Your father has a fractured skull," the doctor said, "and he's lost a lot of blood. He's an old man and not in the best of health."

"Aye, but he'll be all right," Robert said.

"You should call the family," the doctor said. Robert got word to Maggie to let the rest of the family know. One by one they crept to the old man's bedside.

When word reached Mary, she gathered up her shawl and started out the door. "You'll no' go alone, mither. I'll go with ye to the infirmary," Willie said.

"You're a good lad, Willie," his mother said as they set off in the evening twilight.

Family members were allowed in, one at a time. When his turn came, Willie stood beside his grandfather. The old man's head was swathed in a white bandage and his eyes were closed. His face was pale and lined, and Willie had never seen him look so vulnerable. He gently touched the old man's hand and choked back a tear. Willie sat with him for an hour and was then asked by the nurse to leave.

The old man lasted throughout the night. Willie hurried home from the pit and just as he and his mother were about to set off for the infirmary once again, there was a knock at the door. It was Maggie.

George opened the door and there she stood, tears streaming down her face.

"Come in lass," he said.

"He's gone," Maggie said between sobs. "At 1.15pm this afternoon. Robert was with him."

Mary went to her sister's side and put an arm around her shoulders. Willie, who had been standing nearby, ran from the room and took off down the street. He walked for miles on his own, up to Corsencone, but not around the streets of New Cumnock, lest anyone see his tears. It was dark when he returned home and he went straight to his bed.

"The lad's taking it hard," George said to Mary.

"Aye, my faither was a hard man but Willie saw something in him that the rest of us missed," Mary said.

"I don't know what he did to earn the lad's respect but he seemed to think more of the old man, than he does of me," George said bluntly.

"Our Willie's tough on the outside but he has a soft heart," Mary said. "He loves you George but he idolised my faither, for all his faults. The lad is just like my faither in a lot of ways. Let him get over it in his own time."

A lot of the townsfolk turned out for the funeral. Old Bell's body was taken by his own horse and cart and buried in the New Cumnock Cemetery beside his wife Mary. While the adults held a wake at the inn, Willie took Raven up to Corsencone. He wandered through the hills and fields, and over old fences to the lime kiln ovens and pulled his jacket around him to keep out the cold as the wind dried his tears. He sat on a rock, just to think.

'If I can be half the man grandfaither was, I'll be happy,' he thought.

Chapter 30 (1942)

FIGHTING SPIRIT

The wealth that Old Bell had accumulated throughout his life was not divided between his children. True to form, he had his own way to the end and left his estate – assets and debts – to his daughter Sarah. No one, including Sarah, knew why he took this course of action and there was rancour within the family. Willie, however, took a series of life lessons from the old man that would stand him in good stead.

As Winter set in, William's health did not improve and in early January, it was time for George to say goodbye to the strongest man in his life. William had moved his family to a house at 7 Emrys Avenue, Cumnock, named in honour of Keir Hardie's son-in-law Emrys Hughes who, together with Hardie's daughter Nan, had been very active politically in the area. William was working as a Head Surfaceman in the mines, but years of breathing stale air and smoking cigarettes, had taken their toll. His asthma had worsened and then he developed emphysema. George hadn't spent much time with his uncle since they both had families of their own, but his love and respect had never wavered for the man who had raised him. William was just fifty-nine years of age when he drew his last breath on January 5, 1942. His wife Jean had her sons and daughter to comfort her, and George had Mary and his children, but once again he felt alone in life. The man who he had relied upon for the first twenty-eight years of his life was gone, and he felt his passing as though he had lost his own father.

Young Willie had missed his Grandfather Bell every day since his passing and while father and son could have comforted each other in their sorrow, it was not to be. He had matured from a strong-willed fifteen-year-old to a stronger-willed sixteen-year-old and now, with his grandfather gone, he was ready to strike out on his own.

His countrymen were fighting overseas and he wanted to join the fray. One Saturday morning he walked into the War Office in Ayr with the intention of enlisting in the army.

"How old are you, son?" asked the recruitment officer.

"I'm eighteen years old," said Willie raising himself up to his full height of five feet seven inches.

"And where is your birth certificate?"

"That sir, was lost in a fire. Tragic it was – I just got my dog out in time but the papers were burned," Willie lied.

"That was very heroic of you," said the recruitment officer. He scribbled on a piece of paper then handed it to Willie. "Here are your enlistment papers. Report back here on Monday morning."

Willie took the papers and smiled broadly. He was in the army! He got off the bus and ran the rest of the way home. When he reached his house, he opened the door and hung his coat and cap on the peg.

"Why are you so red-faced, Willie?" asked his mother.

"Mither, I've joined up. I'm in the army," he said proudly and showed her the enlistment papers. George emerged from the other room, his pipe clenched firmly between his teeth. He took the papers from Mary's hand and looked at them. Mary's face went white with shock at the thought of her beloved son heading into battle. George could see her distress.

"Dinnae fash yoursel', woman," he said. "Your laddie's no goin' anywhere near the war." Turning to Willie he continued.

"You're a boy of sixteen. Did they no' ask to see yer birth certificate?"

Willie hesitated for a few seconds. "No, I didnae need one."

"Is that right?" George said. "They didnae ask for proof of yer age when I joined up, but these days they do. We are on the night shift next week, so first thing Monday morning we'll go together to the recruitment officer and show him your birth certificate. Then we'll see how clever you are, lad."

The following Monday morning as Willie and George stood before the recruitment officer, he perused the birth certificate, took back the enlistment papers and ripped them to shreds.

"Nice try, son," said the officer. "Now away hame wi' yer Daddy and come back when yer older."

"He'll no' be back," George said over his shoulder as he and Willie walked out the door.

"Oh, yes I will," shouted Willie as George's hand came down across his ear. He didn't like things not going his way and he vowed to return to the recruitment office the day he turned eighteen.

Chapter 31 (1943)

A LIFE IN DANGER

Willie had proven himself as a hard, reliable worker at the pit and was popular among his peers. A year after his attempt to join the army, the war still raged on.

"Do ye think this war will last?" Willie said to George as they started a shift together on a warm Summer's morning in July.

"It cannae go on much longer," George said shaking his head.

"Well I hope it lasts another year so that I can join up," Willie said as he placed his carbide lamp on to his hat in readiness to descend into the darkness of the mine. His father put down his piece box and grabbed Willie, with both hands, by his shirt.

"You're no' going to war so put that out of yer mind. All ye need to do is concentrate on yer work here today and never heed this notion of guts and glory. There's no glory in dying," George said as he gazed into Willie's eyes, then he let go of his shirt and picked up his piece box and walked towards the cage. Willie pulled his shirt back into place and adjusted the lamp on his hat. His father had a temper for sure, but something about the war really got his blood boiling. Willie walked to the cage with the other men and descended into the mine to start his shift. His father would be working in a different section from him today, and he was glad of it. They weren't seeing eye to eye at all lately. Willie was becoming a man and he had inherited his father's stubbornness. The trouble when they argued was that each thought he was right and neither would back down.

It was mid-morning and Willie and two other men were cutting coal in a high section of the mine, which made a pleasant change from crouching in a space three feet high. John MacDonald and Neil Carey were experienced miners in their early forties. Willie enjoyed a joke and a laugh with them as they worked. MacDonald suddenly stopped working and cautioned Willie and Neil.

"Wait up a minute – stop picking," he said. He looked up and they heard a crack. Before they could run, a huge slab of coal fell from the roof of the mine and Willie and his two workmates were trapped. The slab shattered as it fell, but a large piece had pinned Willie up against the wall of the mine. Neil Carey was buried under the rubble and John MacDonald had been knocked unconscious, but was slowly coming back to life. He looked around and saw Willie pinned in a standing position and in pain.

"Can you speak to me, lad?" asked MacDonald as he tried to move some of the large pieces of coal from around Willie's chest. "Where's Neil?"

Willie tried to speak but the pain was unbearable. He motioned with his eyes towards the rubble. MacDonald began digging in the rubble and uncovered an arm. He began to dig faster but it was too late for Neil Carey. MacDonald sat for a moment on his haunches, then turned his attention to Willie who was by now losing consciousness.

"Hold on lad," MacDonald said, "we'll get ye through this." MacDonald knew that a rescue team would be looking for them and began to shout. "Here, we're here." His head hurt from his own injuries but he knew that time was of the essence to save Willie. When his voice gave out, he grabbed a shovel and began tapping on a wooden support beam, slowly so as not to dislodge any more coal from the roof. He heard another crack and waited – but there was no coal fall this time.

Meanwhile all the men had been called back up on top. The deputy had done a head count and knew that three men had been trapped. George, who had been working in a different part of the mine, searched the crowd for his son's face but he could not be found. He approached the deputy.

"Have you seen my lad?" he asked.

"He's trapped, Hooker. We're goin' in now to try to find him," said the deputy.

George sat down on a bare patch of earth as people rushed about him. 'I shouldnae have lost my temper with the lad this morning,' he thought. 'His mither will be frantic when she hears the news.'

George stood up and approached the deputy again. "I want to help with the rescue," he said.

"No, stay back and let the other men do their work, Hooker," said the deputy as he put a protective arm in front of George to stop him going back into the mine. "Look, man, I think you should go and get yer wife. She'll need ye and we'll do the best fer yer son."

Tears came to George's eyes as he started to walk quickly out of the colliery gates. When he reached the house at Pathhead, Mary was baking scones as the radio blared and she sang along to a familiar tune. She didn't hear the door open and as she turned from the range, George was standing in the kitchen beside her.

"Oh, George, you frightened me...," she said then realised that he should be at work – unless something had happened. She put down the hot tray of scones on the table. "Where's Willie?" she asked as she went to the front door.

"Did you no' hear the siren, lass?" George asked as he walked after her and took her gently by the arm. She looked at him with wide eyes. "There's been a cave in – and Willie's trapped down below."

Mary grabbed her shawl and walked quickly with George to the pit. Mrs MacDonald and Mrs Carey were already there, unaware that at least one of the men would not be coming out alive.

Below the surface, Willie managed to remain conscious as MacDonald talked to him. MacDonald tapped on the beam when he dared and hoped that help would arrive soon. He knew the mine well – he knew that air was in short supply and they could not last more than a couple of hours longer. After four hours caught in the rock fall, MacDonald heard voices.

"Can ye hear us?" the voice called. "Anybody hear us?" The rescuers had followed the tunnel as guided by the men who had managed to get out before the fall, and were met with a wall of splintered coal, blocking the way to where the three men were trapped.

"Aye, we're here," MacDonald said as loudly as he could. "In here, we're in here."

"Hold tight and we'll get you out," came the rescuer's voice and his team took their picks and shovels and carefully began shifting the coal, as one man listened out for further cracking in the roof. After an hour they had broken through the barrier and saw the lights from two helmets and then the face of MacDonald peering at them.

"We're comin' man, hold on," said the rescuer.

"It's the lad – he's awfully bad. And Carey's gone to meet his maker." There was silence from the rescuers as they took in the news. "Send to the surface for three stretchers," said the rescuer. Another fifteen minutes and they had made their way through to MacDonald who reached out to grasp the hand of relief. By now, Willie's breathing was shallow. MacDonald held the lad's one free hand and with renewed energy began to pick away the pieces of coal with his other hand. Then he felt a tap on his shoulder.

"We'll take over now," said the rescuer as he guided MacDonald to the team and out through the hole the rescuers had made. The air supply was all but exhausted so the rescuers were ordered not to speak. Three of them worked to help Willie, while two more extracted Carey's body, lay him on a stretcher and covered him with a sheet. When Willie's chest had been freed the three men lifted his broken body up out of the coal. He screamed in pain.

"Ye'll have broken ribs, lad, and maybe internal injuries," said the rescuer. They lay him down on a stretcher and wiped his parched lips with water then told him to sip slowly. MacDonald was already on his way to the top and two men stayed with Carey's body as Willie was stretchered along the dark tunnel and into the waiting cage to take them to the surface.

Mary and George saw a man get out of the cage and fall to the ground. It was MacDonald who gave in to his injuries and fatigue. Then, a few minutes later, the men carrying Willie on the stretcher emerged. Mary saw a rescuer walk over to Mrs Carey and she assumed that the man on the stretcher was her husband. Mrs Carey fell on the ground and Mary could take it no longer. She ran to the stretcher and looked down at the blackened face of her beloved son, as he winced in pain. She gently took his hand and squeezed it.

"Oh, Willie ye've been returned to us, son," she said as tears streamed down her face.

"Could you stand back please, Mrs McMurdo," said the rescuer. "Your lad is in a bad way and we are on our way to the Kilmarnock Infirmary." The ambulance backed up and Willie was loaded into it for the twenty-four mile ride to the hospital in Portland Street, Kilmarnock. The mines' manager offered his car for George and Mary to be taken to the hospital and when they arrived they were ushered to a waiting room. For an hour they sat there, with no one telling them anything. Then a doctor emerged, his white coat smudged with coal dust. He looked serious as he strode towards them, a pile of papers under his arm.

"If there are any other family members I suggest that you call them," the doctor said sadly. "I'm not confident that Willie will make it through the night."

George caught Mary before she fell to the floor. A nurse brought her a glass of water. "If there are any phone calls you'd like me to make I'd be happy to," said the sweet young nurse gently.

George sat down to regain his composure. "Aye, our daughter Mary is at Stewarton, she'll need to be phoned. And my Uncle William's family in Cumnock – they will want to know." George said. He didn't know the phone number for the farm where Mary worked but the nurse tracked her down, and other miners had been to William's house to tell Jean of the accident.

"Can we see him?" Mary asked.

"He's been heavily sedated to help him cope with the pain," the doctor said. "He has sustained several crushed ribs and he has internal bleeding. Both of his lungs were punctured in the fall. He also has a lot of damage to his back, though at this stage we can't say how much."

George put his arm around Mary's shoulders as they walked to the hospital bed. There lay Willie, his face still black from coal dust, lying on the white sheets, the oxygen tank at his bedside hooked up to a mask covering his mouth and nose. Mary took in a breath in fright as she saw her son lying unconscious. She sat and looked at him while George stood beside her.

"I'm staying here the night," Mary said. "He'll need my strength."

"Aye, I'll be right here beside you, lass," George said as he pulled a chair from the next bed and sat down beside here. Later that night Willie's sister Mary arrived and gasped when she saw him. Even though she was the eldest, Willie had always tried to take control when they were children, but she never let him get away with it. They teased each other but she loved her brother and it pained her to see him lying there, hovering between life and death. Their younger sister Margaret was just twelve years old and as children were not allowed to visit patients in the hospital she could not be there, but was comforted by a neighbour.

A new day dawned. Mary awoke from a moment's sleep to find her son still hooked up to the oxygen tank, but breathing nevertheless. The doctor appeared at Willie's bedside, in a newly-laundered and starched white coat. He checked Willie's heart with his stethoscope and opened his eyes to shine a light on them, then studied his breathing.

"To tell you the truth Mr and Mrs McMurdo, I didn't expect that this lad would make it through the night. His injuries are very serious. It's still one day at a time to see if he can pull through this. We will be watching him very closely, so I suggest that you go home and get some rest. We will call for you if there is any change, but right now he needs his rest."

Mary and George and their daughter Mary caught a bus back to the flat at Lochview. Young Mary put on a pot of tea as her mother gathered together some of Willie's clothes to take to the hospital.

She didn't know why, but it seemed a positive thing to do and she needed to busy herself.

Just as the tea was poured there was a knock at the door. It was Jean and her eldest son Dougie, who wanted to be there to comfort George and Mary.

"He made it through the night," Mary said excitedly. "He'll pull through."

Jean hugged Mary and joined her in a cup of tea, while George took Dougie aside.

"It's still touch and go," George confided. "I don't think Mary could cope if anything were to happen to Willie. He's the apple of her eye."

"Oh Geordy, think of the stock he comes from," Dougie said to his cousin. "If there's anyone who can survive this, it's our Willie." George nodded and they joined the women in the kitchen.

In the afternoon George and Mary and their daughter Mary arrived at the hospital during visiting hours. As they approached the bed where Willie had been the night before, it was empty. Mary began to fret, and then the sweet, young nurse was at her side.

"He's been moved to another part of the infirmary," she said as she led them to another room.

Willie's face and body had been washed of coal dust and he looked much better, though his wounds were now more visible. He was still heavily sedated and on oxygen. The doctor arrived, listened to Willie's heart, then wrote on his chart.

"This lad has a heart as strong as an ox," he said shaking his head. "He has youth on his side and he was in good physical condition before the accident, so I can say that with each passing hour the prognosis is looking brighter."

Mary breathed an audible sigh of relief. The doctor continued.

"That's not to say that he'll ever make a full recovery. We don't know if he'll walk again and the damage to his ribs and lungs is extensive."

George choked back a tear. “Never you heed about that,” he said. “He gets his strong heart from his great-gran. If there’s anyone who has a will to live it’s our lad. He’s got the whole world waiting for him – he’ll tell you that hissel’ given half a chance.”

“Well, if I was a religious man I’d say that there’s someone looking down on him,” the doctor said. “He’s a very lucky lad – very lucky indeed.”

Chapter 32 (1943)

A FIERCE DETERMINATION

Within a week of the accident, Willie was conscious and taking soft food. He still had trouble breathing but he was unhooked from the oxygen tank. It stood by his bed, a silent sentinel, ready to spring into action should the need arise.

His ribs were tightly wrapped in bandages and the scratches on his face had already begun to heal. After another week he wanted to get out of bed.

"They're feeding me baby mush," Willie said to his mother one afternoon as she visited. "And I want to get out of this bed."

"You'll do as yer told for once in yer life, son," his mother said sternly. "The doctors know what they're doing. They say you're getting stronger every day." She patted down the sheets on the bed. "I maybe can sneak you in some tattie scones on my next visit," she said. Willie smiled.

"Mind you don't forget, now," he chided her. His sense of humour was coming back but Mary could see that he was being brave for her and that he was still in great pain.

After a further two weeks, x-rays revealed that his ribs were mending well and there were no broken bones in his back. His lungs were healing well too, although if they would ever function at capacity, only time would tell.

"I've a surprise for you, Willie," the doctor said on his morning rounds. "We're going to try to get you up on your feet today."

"Right," said Willie throwing back the bed clothes with only a slight wince. "Let's get to it."

"Nurse is bringing in the wheelchair."

"I'll no' be sittin' in that thing," Willie said indignantly when he saw the wheelchair approach. "Give me a hand," he said as he slowly sat up. As the nurse and the doctor steadied him, he tentatively placed his right leg on the floor, then swung his left leg over until he was sitting on the bed. Taking in a breath of air, he pushed off on his legs and with the help of the nurse and the doctor, he was raised to a standing position. He faltered, but the doctor held him under the arm. He attempted his first step, then another and a smile crept over his face. After five steps the doctor intervened. "That's enough for today, lad," he said. "Nurse, bring the chair."

"Never heed wi' that. I'll walk back to the bed," Willie said and he turned around, summoned up all the strength he had and slowly walked back to the bed, still assisted by the doctor and nurse. He was exhausted and in pain by the time he lay down, but he wouldn't let them know that.

"Very good. We'll try again tomorrow," the doctor said.

"Twice as far tomorrow," Willie said. "I'll walk twice as far tomorrow, and twice as far again the next day." The doctor looked at the nurse and smiled.

"I wish all of our patients had your determination, but don't overdo it."

Willie slept for most of the afternoon. It was a satisfying sleep. He was glad to be productive again. He was working on a new project – himself - and as always, he would do the best job possible.

Chapter 33 (1943)

A LONG ROAD TO RECOVERY

Willie had been released from hospital in time to celebrate Christmas 1943 at home. His mother would have killed the fatted calf if there'd been one available, but rationing grew more severe with each passing year that the war dragged on. Eggs were in short supply and they were rationed to one egg per person per week. Some families were reduced to eating dried eggs which had been crushed to a powder and rejuvenated with water. They were imported from America and tasted nothing like eggs, but with a bit of toasted bread they were passable. Mary was lucky that her daughter Mary worked on a farm and was able to bring a few eggs home with her once a month. She made sure she got her rationing of three pints of milk a week to help Willie build himself back up. Small amounts of tea and sugar were available and any kind of sweets were rationed to just half a pound every four weeks. Even soap and washing powder were rationed and this was felt sorely by the miners' wives who had more than their fair share of dirty clothes to wash. Regardless of the meagre pantry supplies available, Mary did her best to provide nutritious meals for her family. Willie grew stronger every day but it was now seven months since the accident and he was still under the doctor's care. He could walk normally now and his ribs had healed well. He was anxious to get back to work. He saw his mother struggle to get a meal together and wished that he could help her.

A government-funded unemployment system paid out according to need, and applicants were subjected to a means test. Because Willie was young, single and living at home he received no money, as unemployed married men with families were considered more needy. Besides, he wouldn't have taken the money.

"I'll no' rely on dole money," he said when the doctor suggested that there may be some financial aid for which he could apply. "I've a strong arm and I'll work for my money. I'll be back in the pits before long." But the doctor had other ideas. When Willie visited the hospital for his next fortnightly check-up, the doctor sat him down after the examination.

"You know that your injuries were extensive," the doctor said. "And I know you're recovering well, but things do not look so good for you in the future."

Willie finished buttoning his shirt and looked at the doctor. "Have you some news for me?" he asked impatiently.

"With your injuries," the doctor hesitated, "I'd say you'll live no more than another twenty-five years."

Willie sat down on a chair to digest the news. "So you're saying I'll be dead by the time I'm forty-two."

"I'm afraid so," the doctor said. "You're lucky you didn't die in that cave-in, so you can be thankful for another twenty-five years."

Willie stood up and pulled on his cap. "Aye, I should be grateful for another twenty-five years and I'll be grateful for another twenty-five after that."

"Ah, well I wish you well. I'll see you in a fortnight," the doctor said.

Willie was full of bravado as he left the doctor's office, but when he walked outside and the cold, fresh air hit him, his resolve crumbled a little. He thrust his hands deep into his pockets and walked slowly home, taking in what he'd just been told. He looked around him at the grey buildings and brown countryside burned from the Winter snow, the runny-nosed children in thread-bare clothes playing barefoot in the streets and the wizened old men loitering outside the inn. He felt sick to his stomach at the thought of having his life cut short.

'Well if that's all the years I have left, I'd better make the most of them,' he thought. He didn't mention to anyone what the doctor had told him. Proving him wrong became Willie's personal challenge.

Chapter 34 (1945)

MEAT ON THE TABLE

Willie wanted to prove the doctor wrong, more than he had ever wanted anything in his life. He took long walks up to Corsencone every day to build up his leg muscles and to fill his damaged lungs with clean air. He vowed that he would never again smoke a cigarette, to give his lungs every chance of staying clear. It hurt him to see his mother struggle to put food on the table. His father was still employed at the mine but things were not as good as when the two men were bringing in wages. He arrived home from his walk one afternoon to see his mother take a soup bone out of the pot and carefully wrap it in a muslin cloth.

"Margaret, will you take this next door to Mrs Daley for her pot," Mary said to her younger daughter. "There's still some meat on the bone and it will probably do the other families as well."

Willie was horrified. 'Is this what it's come to?' he thought. The next day after his walk, he arrived home with a hen and a dozen eggs in his jersey.

"Here's our tea, mither," Willie said placing the eggs on the table as the hen struggled to escape from inside his jersey.

"Where did you get these?" Mary asked.

"It doesnae matter where I got them – take them. They'll no' be missed."

Mary's face was red with anger. Yes, they were doing it tough but that was no reason for her son to steal from a local farmer.

"I'll no' have stolen goods in my house, Willie McMurdo. Now take them back at once," she said angrily. Willie left the eggs on the table and carried the hen outside. Twenty minutes later he was back, the hen cleaned and plucked and ready for the pot.

Mary reluctantly cooked the fowl and they sat down to boiled hen with gravy and potatoes. "God forgive me that I don't choke on the first bite," Mary said and then looked at Willie who was already tucking in. They may not be willing to take him back on at the mine until he had fully recovered, but he intended to contribute to the household in his own way.

He bought a pair of ferrets and used them to hunt out rabbits and hares which he snared and brought home to his mother for the table. It was not just his own family who benefited from his hunting skills. Many a time he would leave a pair of skinned and gutted rabbits outside a neighbour's house, then knock on the door and hide to see the look of surprise and delight on their faces. He loved to make people happy. The rabbits and hares lived freely in the countryside and they were there for the taking.

While he felt a little better knowing that he was keeping his mother supplied with meat that they could otherwise not afford, he grew tired of never having any money of his own. The war still raged on in Europe and as he was feeling stronger, his wish to join the fighting came to the fore again. He spoke to the doctor but the news was not what he wanted to hear.

"You wouldn't pass the medical at this stage," the doctor said. Willie was disappointed.

"Am I fit to go back to work then? It's been nearly eighteen months and I cannae sit idly by for much longer," Willie said.

"Yes, you can go back to work but take it easy for the first few weeks."

He was glad to be back with his pals at the mine. Many of them had visited him while he'd been convalescing, but he wanted to be among the men every day and earn a living by the sweat of his brow. They were all glad to see him back.

"We've missed yer pranks, Willie," MacDonald said. Willie smiled.

"How's yer heid?" Willie asked the man who had tried to free him from the coal fall.

Oh, it's well mended. Come on, let's go down together and get you started."

George had hoped to take his son down the mine on his first day back at work, but he watched Willie stride off with MacDonald and marvelled at the lad's independence. He took to the work easily and even though he was often breathless and his back ached, he would never show any sign of weakness to the other men. He wanted, and earned, the respect of the men around him.

His first pay in eighteen months felt good in his hand. He hurried home from work at four o'clock, gave his mother a pound note, got cleaned up and was out the door to meet his pals for a game of cards. By eight o'clock he was back in the door with a hundred pounds in his pocket.

"Did I give you a pound, mither?" he asked.

"Aye Willie, you did."

"Then here's another five pounds for you. I've won a fortune," he said as he took the roll of notes from his pocket. Mary was astonished and George sat and shook his head. Willie went to have a wash and change his clothes then sat down at the table as Mary served him his tea.

"Thank you, mither. I'm away now," he said as he pecked her on the cheek and took off out the door again. He returned two hours later, having lost the lot.

"Easy come, easy go," he said as he told George and Mary the following morning. "I'll win again next week," he said confidently.

On May 8, people across Britain rejoiced at Victory in Europe when the allies formally accepted the unconditional surrender of the armed forces of Nazi Germany and the end of Adolf Hitler's Third

Reich, which ended the war in Europe. The people of New Cumnock lit bonfires to celebrate – all but the families of the thirty-seven men lost in the war. As America had entered the war in the Pacific, the war against Japan came to a swift and horrific end on August 15 when bombs were dropped on the Japanese cities of Hiroshima and Nagasaki resulting in massive loss of life. The war was over.

Willie was glad to see his family and neighbours so overjoyed that the hardship of the past six years was coming to an end, but he was disappointed that he didn't get a chance to serve his country.

"Ye've served your country by working in the mines," George said. "We all have. We've kept the home fires burning and kept coal production up."

"Aye, but it's no' the same as being there," Willie said.

"No, it's no' the same, son – and be thankful that you weren't there." George sat down beside his son as they shared a sandwich at a break down the mine. "Ye've felt the pain of punctured lungs." Willie nodded. "I inhaled mustard gas in the first war and had blisters the size of saucers on my arms and legs. I couldnae see from being blinded by the gas and was in hospital for weeks." Willie listened intently as his father had never before opened up to him about the war. "I was in the trenches where men were dying and writhing in agony." George swallowed hard. "And I saw a lad's face blown off – a good, young lad with glory in his eyes who didnae go hame to his mither." Willie looked at the ground as George continued. "I couldnae see yer mither go through the pain that that lad's mither would have. No son, ye've missed out on nothing."

George picked up his piece box and walked away, leaving Willie sitting by himself. MacDonald, who had been within earshot of the conversation, came and sat beside him. "Just take in what yer faither has said, lad. He's no' one to express his emotions."

"Aye," Willie said thoughtfully. "I've a lot more respect for him now. I had no idea."

"The young ones never do," MacDonald said as he patted Willie on the shoulder and went back to his work.

Chapter 35 (1948)

FEEDIN' 'EM, NOT NEEDIN' 'EM

Three years after the war had ended and Britain had emerged victorious, the stress of financing the conflict began to take its toll as the British Government took stock of finances. People throughout the United Kingdom found that they were no better off than during the war, with food, clothing and even furniture still rationed, and a high unemployment rate. Times were still hard. While there was no immediate threat of another war, the British Government's defence forces were depleted as men and women from the armed forces returned to their homes and loved ones. New recruits were needed to join the Regular Army so that, in the unlikely event of another war, the nation would be ready.

Willie saw this as his last chance to join up. As he and his seventeen-year-old sister Margaret and their parents sat having their tea one November night in the fading light of Autumn, Willie chose his words carefully.

"The war is over but there is still much to be done," he said as he placed his knife and fork on his plate and sat back in his chair. "I'm twenty-two and can make my own decisions and I've decided to join the army. I can come to no harm, mither. I won't be sent overseas but I'll be happy to do my duty. I can send you money home, and it will be one less mouth to feed around here."

Mary looked at George who was staring at her for her reaction. She heard the words 'I can come to no harm' and that was all she cared about. "You have my blessing, son," was all she said as she continued eating her tea. Willie looked at his father who just nodded. Margaret smiled as she had been expecting a family quarrel.

Willie reported to the local Ministry of Defence office, as it was now known, and completed the necessary recruitment forms. To his great relief he passed the medical. A few weeks later he arrived home from his work at the pit to find a plain brown envelope on which was printed ‘On His Majesty’s Service’. It contained details of when and where he was to report for basic training, a travel warrant and an advance on wages. Enlistment always happened on a Thursday, so the following Thursday Willie and other new recruits from New Cumnock boarded the train to take them down to England to the Primary Training Centre at Derby near Nottingham.

He had been to Blackpool in England with his pals for a holiday, but leaving Scotland was still a big event in his life. When they reached the railway station at Derby they were greeted by a Non-Commissioned Officer who shouted orders at them to line up, get in the truck and hurry up. When they reached the barracks they were called up in alphabetical order and required to state their surname, initial and height which were noted in a book, then they were handed the Soldiers’ Service Book and Pay Book. They were subjected to another medical and given a raft of injections.

They were then directed to a line of barbers to have their hair closely cropped. As Willie sat down in the chair, the barber smiled.

“Oh, I’m gonna love cuttin’ off this lassie’s blond bob,” said the barber. Willie rolled his eyes then closed them as he felt his hair brush his nose on its way to the floor. He got up from the chair, ran his hand through the short hair that was left on his head and was ordered into a large warehouse. Here he was issued his kit by corporals reading out items from a long list, before pressing them into his outstretched arms. As a final severing of ties with civilian life, the new recruits were given brown paper and string and told to send their civilian clothes back home.

Willie could see that some of the young men had been pulled from farms or apprenticeships and not used to being bullied, but he could take it. Coming from the pits, he was used to the colourful language used by the Corporals, Sergeants and Sergeant Majors as they tried to intimidate the men. They wouldn't intimidate him. He would play along with them, all the while planning ways to make their lives difficult and his own time profitable.

Arms laden with clothing, a mess tin, water bottle, knife, fork, spoon, towel, socks, gas mask, rifle and bayonet, beret, blankets, sheets, pillow cases and boot brushes, Willie followed the Corporal's directions to the barracks. This was to be his home for the next eight to twelve weeks of basic training. He looked around the men but didn't see any familiar faces. He was quick to make friends and tried to take the discipline in his stride. They learned how to make up their beds and store their kit, before it was time for a meal and lights out.

The next morning he was up at 6am, dressed and having breakfast in the canteen by 7am followed by cleaning the barracks hut and platoon area. At 7.45am it was kit layout and hut inspection, 8am platoon muster parade, and a day filled with weapons training, physical training, firing training, lunch at 1.30pm, evening meal 6pm and lights out 11pm. He was used to working shifts in the mines, and then having the rest of his time to himself. He wasn't used to drill instructors constantly shouting basic moves, and he hated taking orders. He was an individual and he needed to learn to act as part of a unit. After five weeks of basic training he had had enough of 'yes sir, no sir'. He was more like his father than he realised.

At a morning bed inspection, Willie was belittled for not having perfect corners on his bed. The Corporal put his face close to Willie's and shouted "not good enough, McMurdo!". Willie didn't flinch and stood perfectly straight. "Fix the corners – now!" Willie turned around and moved the sheets and blanket around a bit but didn't improve upon his corners. He stood to attention again. "You can do better than that," shouted the Corporal. Willie looked him straight in the eye.

"I'm afraid not, sir. That's the best I can do," he said as Rab, one of the other Scottish lads Willie had befriended, sniggered.

"Is that right?" said the Corporal. "Now let me think. You were a coal miner, McMurdo?"

"That's right, sir," Willie said in a mocking tone.

"Then let's see the best you can do with the coal that lines the garden beds outside. I want you to take a bucket of whitewash and paint all the pieces of coal white."

"I'd be happy to, sir," Willie said with a straight face. He wasn't going to let some cockney upstart get the better of him. His mate had a broad grin on his face.

"And you," said the Corporal as he moved closer to Rab, "You can take your knife and fork and cut the parade ground grass. That should take you all day and I'll be around for inspection at 5pm." The Corporal left the room and the men burst into laughter. Rab turned to Willie.

"I thought he was goin' to burst, he was so angry."

"Bring yer knife and fork, Rab. And look at the bright side. We won't have to be on the parade ground or cleaning guns," Willie said.

Willie and Rab spent the day on the pointless tasks of whitewashing pieces of coal and cutting already mown grass. They sang songs and told jokes and the day passed pleasantly. When the Corporal arrived at 5pm, the jobs had been completed and Willie stood there with a smile on his face. The Corporal vowed to crack him, and Willie vowed that he never would.

The army was a man's world and Willie fitted in well. Finally the day of the passing out parade arrived, and after boozy celebrations the men were sent home on brief leave. His family was happy to see him.

"Oh, Willie you look so handsome in your uniform," his mother said and he soon discovered that the local girls liked a man in uniform. He turned up to a dance and wasn't short of a lass to dance with, and he competently twirled them around the dance floor.

He received his posting and was sent to the military base at Blandford in the county of Dorset in southern England. As well as learning to be a driver, he learned how to drink and there were nights out, and forty-eight-hour leave passes, that relieved the men of their money. More than once, on returning to camp drunk, Willie was issued with punishments such as having his leave cancelled or being given extra guard duties. He enjoyed the work and the company of the men, and three square meals a day, but he couldn't bear taking orders from anyone, especially smarmy-faced Corporals who thought they were superior to the rest of the men.

He made friends with the Quartermaster and managed to swap some boxes of chocolate he had procured, for a dozen white towels which he had parcelled up and sent back to Scotland for his sister Mary to cut up and use for napkins for the baby. Mary had married Willie Cravens and was busy raising a young family. She still had to use coupons for clothing, and with four children to clothe, Willie thought he could help her out.

On one of his leave passes, he went into a shop in Blandford and saw two dolls with golden curls, dressed in tartan, and he thought of his sister Mary's twin girls, Moira and Nancy. He walked up to the counter of the shop and the shop assistant smiled.

"Those wee dolls," he said as he pointed to them in the shop window. "I've two nieces in Scotland that I'd like to send them to. Can you arrange that?" he asked.

"You just write down the address and I'll have them posted for you," the shop assistant said.

Willie handed over the money for the dolls. "How much extra will it be for the postage?" he asked.

"You leave that with me," the shop assistant said. "It's not often that we get a soldier in here buying dolls for his nieces. We'll include the postage in the price you've paid for the dolls."

"That's very kind of you, thank you," Willie said and as he left the shop, the dolls were already boxed and being wrapped in brown paper and string. He thought about how the wee girls would get a surprise when they opened the package.

On January 1, 1949 the British Government enforced National Service as a mandatory government program for all young men aged eighteen to twenty-four, to complete eighteen months in the armed forces. This form of conscription met with mixed public opinion but Willie saw it as his ticket of leave from the army. He was given the option of getting out at the eighteen-month mark, instead of two years, and he was happy to leave. He had had enough. After eighteen months living in barracks, joking and swearing with the men and taking the piss out of the Corporal at every opportunity, he put on civilian clothes again, returned his kit to the store, grasped his Certificate of Dismissal then boarded a train for New Cumnock. A social revolution had taken place in the years since the war and he wanted to be part of it. He could feel a change in the air – it was time he decided what he wanted to do with his life.

Chapter 36 (1949)

TAKING UP THE CHALLENGE

It was early November when Willie got off the train at New Cumnock station. He was welcomed home with open arms. His mother had missed him and life at Lochview had been quiet with just George and Mary and young Margaret at home. Their older daughter Mary, her husband Willie and their children - six-year-old William, the four-year-old twins Moira and Nancy, and baby George who was nearly one - were now living at Raws Farm in Kilmarnock.

After having spent the past eighteen months with plenty of food, clothing and bedding, Willie was shocked that some of the shortages that had applied during the war years were still being enforced at home. Life in Scotland was still bleak, with unemployment and homelessness still a major issue. He had a few quid in his pocket, and after giving his mother a couple of pounds he was off to the inn to seek out some of his pals.

As he headed towards the door, wearing the new shirt and trousers he had bought in England, he hesitated.

"Do ye feel like a whisky?" he called to his father. George looked up from the newspaper and took his pipe from his mouth.

"Aye, I do," he said, pleased to be asked by his son, and they walked to the inn together. Willie knew a lot of the men at the inn and they talked and drank for several hours, then he and George wandered home to a meal that Mary had been keeping hot on the range. She wasn't upset that they had stayed too long at the inn. She was glad that father and son could spend some time together.

Within a week of returning home, Willie was seeking employment and was offered a job at the Knockshinnoch Castle Colliery which was operated by New Cumnock Collieries Limited. A new shaft had been sunk in 1942 on the site of an older pit that had been abandoned almost sixty years earlier. The project brought employment to the area and with its policy of advanced mechanisation, it was one of the best equipped and most productive collieries in the Ayrshire coalfield. Around seven hundred men were employed at the mine and around five thousand tons of coal per week were extracted from the two seams known locally as the Main Coal and the Turf Coal. There was even talk that the company would be installing pithead baths for the men to wash before they went home, but that was a plan for the future and one which the women of the village looked forward to greatly.

Willie was glad of the opportunity to learn about the new systems being introduced into the mines, but he was restless and looking for a new challenge. The army had broadened his horizons and he felt that there was more to life than slaving away in a coal mine in New Cumnock. One afternoon after work, he was at the inn chatting to his pals Rab McDickens and Wally Clegg. They sat at a table drinking their pints of ale. Willie leafed through the *Cumnock Chronicle*, then he put the paper down on the table.

"Here's an advertisement for coal miners wanted in Australia," he said excitedly.

"Oh God, the land of kangaroos and snakes," Rab said.

"No, the land of opportunity – and sunshine," Willie said as he looked out the window at the rain pouring down outside. "Passage is just £10 and there's a guaranteed job when you get there." He looked up at Rab and Wally. "It's your round, Wally," he said and as Wally Clegg got up to buy another round of beers, Willie was already hatching a plan. When Clegg returned, the beers were downed and another round ordered.

"What is there here for us?" Willie asked of his pals. "We're still on rations and houses are in short supply." He read again from the newspaper. "Australia wants white British stock to populate its shores and build its burgeoning post-war economy." He looked up at his pals. "Well they wouldnae get much better stock than this," he said thumping his chest with both hands. They all laughed.

"Are you serious, Willie?" asked Rab McDickens.

"Aye, I am. It would cost £120 to go to Australia and here we're being offered the same trip for £10. And there are the same sort of schemes being offered to go to Canada and America. You'd be a fool not to give it a go."

Willie got up to buy another round, then bounced back to the table full of enthusiasm.

"What do ye say – Australia for two years, Canada for two years and America for two years, then we come back hame wi' our pockets full." The more the trio drank, the better the scheme sounded. Then the table fell silent.

"I'm in," said Rab. "Aye, me too," said Clegg.

"Right, are we goin' to the picture house?" Rab asked. They downed their drinks and headed to the picture house to see a film. They settled into their seats with two pies each, to curb the alcohol-infused hunger, and the picture reel began.

'Come to sunny Australia – the land of opportunity,' the newsreel began as pictures of sunny skies and white beaches and happy smiling children filled the screen. 'Plenty of employment for everyone. Australia – brings out the best in you'. Willie nearly choked on his pie.

"That's it," he said to his pals. "It's a sign. I'll find out about it tomorrow. Hoo-hoo! We're goin' to Australia!" he said and sat back to enjoy the rest of his pie and the film.

Chapter 37 (1949)

IT'S ONLY FOR SIX YEARS

Without mentioning his intentions to his family, Willie wrote off to the Department of Immigration, Australia House London, requesting three applications for assisted passage to Australia under the United Kingdom and Australian Government Agreement. By the week before Christmas he had filled in his form, and Rab and Wally had done the same. There was a space on the form to specify which state in Australia he would like to go to. He went to the local library and looked at a map. He noticed 'New South Wales' and thought that, with all the coal mines in Wales, then perhaps New South Wales would be as good a place as any to find a job, so he marked it on the form. With the application came instructions that he should deal through Mackay's Travel Agency in Glasgow as an agent to get the application processed faster. He took his completed application to be witnessed by the local policeman, Sergeant Robert Leslie, who had kicked his backside many times when he was a lad.

"Australia, is it?" asked Sergeant Leslie. He signed the application and handed it back to Willie. "A lad like you will do well there. Good luck to you. I think a lot of the farmers around here would wish you farewell also." Sergeant Leslie smiled. He knew of young Willie's exploits over the years nicking cigarettes at the picture house, or tossing apples over the fence to his pals, or hens and eggs going missing, but he knew there was no malice in the boy. He was ambitious and resourceful and never caused any real harm.

Willie took his application to Mackay's office in Glasgow on January 24, 1950. The form was stamped and he was referred on for a medical which he took six days later. Despite the doctor's concerns some years before about his injuries not healing, Willie passed the medical with flying colours, the doctor pronouncing his lungs healthy, his general health good and his physique excellent. Typhoid and small pox had broken out in Scotland but he got his needles and carried on in his own invincible way. All forms were returned to Mackay's Travel Agency for sending to the Commonwealth of Australia, Department of Immigration in London, but not before the office at Mackay's marked his application 'a good type, ex-service with underground coal mining experience'.

Willie carried on working at the Knockshinnoch Castle Colliery, wondering what his chances were of getting to Australia. The early Spring afternoon of March 2 was dreary, cold and wet and he arrived home soaked to the skin after peddling his pushbike in the rain, coal dust streaming down his face. He bid his mother hello and started to make his way to the bathroom.

"Willie," Mary called after him, "there's a letter here for you. Who do you know in Australia?" she asked as she turned the letter over. Willie stopped, swallowed hard, and took the letter from his mother. He saw a logo of a kangaroo and a large bird that he didn't recognise, and the words 'Commonwealth of Australia'.

"Dear Sir," the typed letter began, "It gives me very great pleasure to advise you that your application for settlement in Australia under the provisions of the Assisted Passage Migration Scheme has been approved. You have been selected for settlement in the State of Queensland and your occupational classification upon arrival in Australia has been noted in our records as Miner."

'Not New South Wales, but Queensland', he thought, as he tried to imagine where on the map he would end up.

"Woo-hoo," he shouted as he hugged his mother, covering her apron in wet coal dust.

"What is it, Willie?" she asked. Then it suddenly dawned on him that he'd have to tell her he was going away. He decided to wait until they were all together for tea before breaking his news.

"Wait till our tea," was all he said. He didn't bother washing, but got on his bicycle and rode to Rab McDickens' house. Wally Clegg was already there. They had all been accepted for assisted passage and would leave from Glasgow.

"We've to send £10 each to the Chief Migration Officer in London," Willie said as he read from the letter.

"Aye, and we've to stay for two years or repay the Government contribution towards the cost of the fare," Rab said. "Two years is a long time. What if we don't like the place?"

"Oh, you're no' gettin' cold feet are ye, Rab?" Willie asked. "This is the adventure of a life time. Think of the money you could make, then you could come home and get a house and maybe open a shop or something." Rab's initial doubts were gone and the three excitedly talked about the forthcoming trip. Willie got back on his bicycle and stopped at the grocer's shop to buy his mother a box of chocolates. As they sat down to their tea that night, Willie was excited and nervous about his news.

"Do you like the chocolates?" Willie asked his mother.

"Aye, but it's a wee bit extravagant, Willie," his mother replied as she fetched the blue and red box of chocolates and put them on the table for the family to enjoy. "What's the occasion?"

Willie pushed his plate away from him and cleared his throat. There was no easy way to say it, other than to say it.

"The letter I received today was to tell me that I've been accepted for assisted passage to Australia," he began. "I'm going to Australia to make my fortune." As the family sat in silence, he thought he may as well continue. "I'm to go for two years, then on to Canada for two years then to America for two years, then hame to Scotland."

His mother sat down heavily in her chair and stared at her son. "That's six years, son," she said softly. "That's a long time to be away from your family – and so far away. Australia! It's down the bottom end of the world!"

Willie looked at his father. "It'll do the lad good," George said. "There's nothing here for him. Knockshinnoch's still producing, but elsewhere the mines are in decline and what other work is there here to do. He'd have to leave New Cumnock soon anyway to find work."

"Aye, but doon the burn, or into Glasgow, no' the other side of the world!" Mary said as she took a handkerchief from the long sleeve of her dress and dabbed at her eyes. "When do you go, Willie?" she asked.

"I've yet to hear, but it's definite and I suppose it will be a few weeks yet," he said, then carried on quickly. "I'll no' be on my own – Rab and Wally are coming wi' me." But that did nothing to allay Mary's fears. "Can you no' be happy for me?" he asked.

"I'm happy for you, Willie," his sister Margaret said, "and so will our Mary be when she finds out. It's a great adventure and you'll see all sorts of things. And you'll send us presents from Australia and letters." Willie was surprised at the support he was receiving from his sister.

"Aye, letters, lots of letters mither, to tell you how I'm doin'."

"I'm happy for you son, even if it doesnae show. My heart is heavy to think of you leaving me but if it's to give you a good future then you have my blessing." Mary took her son's hand. "I'll be so lonely without you, lad. You bring such brightness into all our lives. It's as though you're taking the sun wi' ye."

"No mither," corrected Willie. "I'm going to find the sun and when you're sittin' here on a cold Winter's night, ye'll have my news of the sunshine and beaches to keep ye warm."

Chapter 38 (1950)

LEAVING AULD SCOTLAND BEHIND

Willie had spent the weekend at his elder sister Mary's farm. He had become great friends with her husband Willie Cravens and enjoyed spending time with his nieces and nephews. Mary was going through a hard time with her youngest son George who was not yet two. He had contracted polio and Willie went to the hospital to see the boy before he left for Australia. It tugged at his heart strings to see the little snowy-haired lad lying there, and he hoped that young George's health would have greatly improved by the time he returned to Scotland.

It seemed incongruous that the day he left Scotland was a warm Spring day in April, when it had rained for most of February and March. Willie's mother and father, and sister Margaret, had travelled into Glasgow to see him off. Margaret was seeing a young fellow called George Pirie and Willie wished that he had more time to get to know him. The dock was bustling with long queues of fellow migrants and Willie strained his neck to find his two pals. He had given his mother money to buy him three new shirts with tartan collars, a new pair of trousers and some underwear for the trip. Willie had just £5 in his pocket to leave Scotland, but he hoped that when next he stepped on Scottish soil his pockets would be full of money.

The ship was called the SS Brent and had been a troop carrier known as the SS Letitia during the war. The vessel had been sold in 1946 to the Australian Ministry of Transport and was completely overhauled on the Clyde, before commencing an emigration service between the UK and Australia, with a capacity for 965 emigrants. Willie looked up at the ship and marvelled at its sheer size. As he spotted Wally and Rab, he turned to his mother, kissed her on the forehead and gave her a hug. He shook his father's hand and hugged his sister Margaret.

"God bless you son, and hurry home," was all that Mary could say before she dissolved into tears. George put his arm around her, then Willie turned to board the ship. He was sure that he was doing the right thing and that he would make his parents proud. He stood on the gangway and turned to wave goodbye. He could see his mother's handkerchief lifted in the air and for a moment he had a lump in his throat and wanted to turn back. 'No, it's my life,' he thought. He took a lasting look around the grey dock and shipyards of Glasgow. It took another hour before he made his way along the queue and had his paperwork processed. The three lads were directed to their accommodation – eight men to a cabin - but it was clean and tidy. There was a communal bathroom and toilet, but it was adequate. They stowed their gear in the lockers provided and set out to explore the ship. As the SS Brent pulled away from the dock, and after waving a last farewell to the crowd below, his heartbroken mother among them, Willie and Rab and Wally had made their way to the dining room which was decorated with cane chairs and palm trees to give it a tropical feel. Already they felt as though they were on a holiday. They sat down at a table and read the menu. No rationing here!

"Roast loin and leg of pork, apple sauce, creamed swedes and boiled potatoes, with a soup to start and lemon blancmange to follow," read Rab. "And there's lots of other meat and vegetables and sweets - and coffee – I've never had coffee."

"Well they can stick their blancmange, but if this is what we have to look forward to in Australia we will at least be well fed, lads," Willie said. The three of them laughed as a waitress came to take their order.

The trip to their final destination in Australia would take six weeks and there was nothing to do on the ship but eat and enjoy themselves.

The first port of call was at Malta to pick up more passengers. Willie was happy to watch the passing parade of people as they boarded the ship, and smell the aromas from exotic food being cooked in nearby stalls. In Port Said, a number of boats drew up alongside the ship offering all manner of things for sale to the passengers. The merchants threw a rope up for the passengers to tie to the ship's rail and they affixed a basket on the other end to accept payment and send up the sometimes dodgy goods. The ship made its way slowly through the narrow Suez Canal out into the Red Sea and they were on their way. When they reached Aden, Willie and his pals were able to go ashore for a couple of hours. It was hot and dusty and they got their first case of sunburn but they didn't care. After a life spent either down a mine or in the cold and wet weather of Scotland, the sun felt good on their skin and they lapped it up.

The days went by in glorious abandon as they got to know their fellow passengers, join in card games, attend the dances and shows on board and look forward to the next port of call. They marvelled at the sights and sounds of each new country they visited. Willie's £5 didn't go far and he was glad to win a couple of pounds at cards so that he could buy a few drinks. He made friends easily and was popular with the other guests, especially those whose table the three shared for their meals, as he was always quick with a joke or to help anyone. There was no shortage of fish and meat, fruit and vegetables and desserts. There was a bowl of fruit on each table at night and passengers were encouraged to take an orange for the vitamin C content. Willie often didn't feel like eating the fruit – the taste spoiled his liking for the beer – so he left his orange in front of him.

"If you are not going to eat your orange I shall have it," said Arthur, the Yorkshireman with the brown cardigan, and glasses perched on the end of his nose, who already had two oranges in front of him. As he reached for the orange, Willie looked across at the twin girls sitting opposite him. They reminded him of his sister Mary's lasses. Because Arthur had already taken two oranges, one of the wee girls had missed out. Willie had a strong sense of fairness and this, he felt, just wasn't right. As Arthur's grasping fingers grabbed the orange, Willie stopped him.

No, you won't," he said. "The children need the fruit more than we do." He reached over and then took one of the oranges that Arthur already had in front of him, plus his own, and handed them to the girls. "There you are, girls," Willie said as Arthur sat with his mouth open. Willie glared at him and then got up from the table. "I hate gluttons," he said to Arthur. He had seen so many families go without and he wasn't afraid to speak up when he felt the need. He had inherited his Grandfather Bell's toughness, his Great-Gran Mary Hamilton McMurdo's tenacity and his mother's generosity.

As the ship crossed the equator, the heat and motion of the vessel affected some of the passengers. Some decided to take a pillow and blanket up on deck to sleep, and Willie followed suit. He was glad to get away from the close confines of the men's quarters on the lower decks. He lay on his back, looking up at the stars and wondered what his family in Scotland was doing.

By the end of the fourth week, news got around the ship that they would soon be in Australia.

"Really," Willie said to one of the stewards at breakfast. "I thought the trip would take six weeks."

"Oh, yes it will to where you are going in Sydney, which is the last port of call. That's on the east coast of Australia. We are heading for Freemantle in Western Australia. That will be your first port of call in Australia," the steward said. Willie and his pals had a long discussion about what they expected to see in Australia, as anticipation grew.

The sun was shining brightly, and the sky was a brilliant blue, as the SS Brent pulled into Freemantle Harbour.

"Everything looks so clean and bright," Willie said as he wiped the sweat from the back of his neck with a handkerchief.

"Aye, and hot," said Rab.

"Oh, don't start yer greetin'," Willie cautioned. "We came here to get away from the cold." He reached into his pocket and pulled out a few coins. "I'm more concerned about how we're to buy a meal when we go into the town." The other lads felt around their pockets and were in the same situation. As they made their way down the gangplank into the blazing sun, the wharf was bustling with immigration and customs officials, baggage handlers and delivery personnel, photographers, welcoming parties and hostesses employed by the Harbour Trusts. They were known as the ‘blue’ or ‘red’ ladies (according to the colour of their hats) and were on hand to guide and assist new arrivals.

Amongst the throng, Willie spotted a young man with horn-rimmed glasses, dressed in a long-sleeved shirt and tie, with a clipboard under his arm, walking around greeting the newly-arrived. “I’m from the Buffaloes. Welcome to Australia,” he was saying, but wasn’t getting much of a response from anyone.

“Hold on, lads,” Willie said, “leave this to me.” He walked over to the man to find out his business.

“Welcome to Australia,” said the man. “I’m from the Royal Antediluvian Order of Buffaloes. Would you be members of our benevolent organisation?” Willie had heard of the ‘Buffs’, as they were affectionately known in Scotland, but he wasn’t a member. “Aye, we are,” Willie lied, “and we’re very glad to find a brother to greet us as we first set foot in Australia. What can you do for us, brother?”

“Oh, you’re Scottish – that’s splendid,” said the man in an Edinburgh accent. “You’ll love it here. It’s a great life.” As they stood boiling in the sun and shifting from foot to foot, the man continued. “Now you have a few hours to spend in Freemantle while the ship refuels and restocks so we’d be happy to show you around and you shall be our guests for lunch.” Willie looked at the other two.

“That would be grand,” Willie said and set off with his pals, other passengers that the young man had been able to round up, and the Brother Buffs. The water in Freemantle Harbour was so clear and clean and the people were friendly. They walked past men fishing and catching mussels, and Willie breathed in the smell of the ocean and longed to get a fishing rod in his hands. They boarded a waiting bus and after an hour of sightseeing, they were taken to the Buffalo Lodge where a buffet lunch was laid out before them.

"How much will this cost?" asked Rab.

"For a fellow brother, there is no charge. It is our way of welcoming you to this wonderful country."

Rab looked across at Willie who was smiling.

"And very kind of you it is," Willie said to the man. Rab and Wally never ceased to be amazed at Willie's resourcefulness. By evening they were back on the ship and talking about the capital city of Western Australia called Perth. They marvelled that there was a place in Australia also called Perth, like the city in Scotland. The ship skirted the coastline of Australia, around the bottom end of Victoria. On May 12, 1950, Willie celebrated his 24th birthday on board ship. His mother had baked him a fruit cake and he was under strict instructions not to open it until his birthday. He was excited to celebrate his first birthday in Australian waters and took the cake to the breakfast table to share with the group of people who always sat at his table. They sang 'happy birthday' to him and laughed and enjoyed the cake with their morning cups of tea and coffee. Willie even offered Arthur a second piece, which he greedily accepted.

Four days later, they were in New South Wales and got off the boat at Sydney where they enjoyed the views across the harbour to the expensive-looking houses. Some of the buildings in Sydney had been built by convict labour, but most were new and of all shapes and sizes, unlike the uniformity of the housing Willie had been used to in New Cumnock.

On the dock, Willie presented his papers to the immigration officer who looked them over and then stamped them. "Can you confirm that you are William Bell McMurdo?"

"I certainly can," Willie said.

Handing the papers back to Willie he said "Welcome to Australia, Bill." Willie had never been called 'Bill' before, but he was determined to fit in. If that's what they wanted to call him it was all right with him. "You're to make your way to Central Station by 1pm for the train to Brisbane leaving at 3.55pm. Here are your luggage checks for your heavy baggage. Now hang on to them and here are your cloak room tickets for your hand baggage which you are to hand in at the cloak room at the station."

"Right then, thank you very much," Willie said and went to look for Rab and Wally.

"They call me 'Bill' here," Willie said, enjoying his new moniker, "so that's my name from now on. Now we'd better get something to eat before we get on the train." They each emptied their pockets and had four shillings and six pence between them. They walked along the docks carrying their heavy coats and saw a fruit seller.

"What can I get you, fellas," said the young fruit seller. "Apple, orange, passionfruit, pear, pineapple."

They looked at a strange fruit with a green spiky top and rough yellow skin. "What's that?" Bill asked.

"That's a pineapple, mate," said the fruit seller.

"And how do you eat it?" said Bill.

"How come you blokes have never seen a flamin' pineapple before," the fruit seller laughed. "You take off the spiky top and cut off the skin." Bill looked at the other two.

"Aye, well it's the biggest piece of fruit ye've got so we'll take one."

"That's six pence, please," said the fruit seller handing over the fruit to Bill. "Here, I'll cut it up for you." They each took a large slice of pineapple and made their way to the railway station. The fruit was sweet and cold and they enjoyed it.

By 4pm that day they were on board the train heading north from Sydney for Brisbane, the capital city of Queensland. The trip would take around twenty hours sitting up in a carriage, but they enjoyed looking out the window at the countryside. They passed dry paddocks full of merino sheep and watched the dogs rounding them up. There were huge gum trees of red or white, and wooden houses, some with peeling paint, set against a brilliant blue sky. The puffy white clouds really did have a silver lining as the sun shone through them.

"Look, look, look!" said Rab. "It's a kangaroo – no, two of them!" The lads all looked out the window in amazement as the kangaroos bounded along in the paddocks beside the train tracks.

"We're in Australia now," Bill said. By midday the next day, they arrived at South Brisbane Interstate Station on the outskirts of the city. They collected their luggage and were directed to a waiting bus that would transport them to the State Migration Office and Reception Centre called Yungaba. The two-storey brick building was erected in 1887 and sat alongside the Brisbane River in Main Street, Kangaroo Point. Single quarters were on the upper level while married couples were taken to the ground floor accommodation.

"What does 'Young-gah-bah' mean?" Bill asked the officer at reception.

"It's an aboriginal name meaning 'place of sunshine'," said the officer.

They'd only been in the country a few days and already they'd encountered kangaroos and were staying in an Aboriginal-named establishment. There was so much to learn. The sun was shining in the 'place of sunshine' and they settled in to spend the night. Each of the lads was given £2 in the form of four 10 shilling notes as a loan from the Australian Government to help them until they found a job. The currency in Australia was pounds, shillings and pence just as it was in Scotland, and roughly equivalent in value. Bill noted that the ten shilling note was reddish brown in colour and was marked with a photo of King George VI, and a kangaroo and the large bird that he later learned was called an emu. The kangaroo and the emu were the Australian coat of arms. Two pounds wouldn't go far, but Bill didn't intend to be without a job for too long.

Early the next morning the 'place of sunshine' was drenched with rain.

"Good to see the rain," said the receptionist when she saw Bill.

"I've seen enough of it where I'm from," Bill said with a smile.

"We haven't had rain here for four months," said the receptionist, "and we sure need it."

"Four months," Bill said incredulously. "Look, I'm here to see about work. I said on my immigration form that I wanted to work as a coal miner so where do I go?"

"Oh, you won't get work as a coal miner in Brisbane," said the receptionist. "Let me see, you'll have to go to Ipswich to work in the coal mines." 'Ipswich', he thought, another familiar name.

"Aye, that's all right. How do I get there?"

"You'll need to catch a train to Ipswich. I can give you a map. And you'll need a place to stay so here are the names of some boarding houses in Ipswich."

Bill went back to the single men's quarters where Wally and Rab were just waking up.

"I'm away to a place called Ipswich tomorrow, lads," he announced. "I want to see about a job."

"How far away is that?" asked Rab, rubbing at his eyes.

"The lassie on reception says it's about an hour by train. There's no mines in Brisbane," Bill said.

"I thought we were supposed to be given a job when we came here," said Rab.

"Well there's no job arranged Rab, so ye'll have to fend fer yersel' and get out of bed and start looking," Bill said. "I'm off for some breakfast and a look around Brisbane. Who's coming wi' me?"

"Aye, just give us a minute and we'll be there," said Wally who was now sleepily sitting on the side of the bed.

After breakfast the rain had stopped so they strolled along the tree-lined streets of Kangaroo Point, looking at the electric light poles standing in line and the timber houses with their tin roofs, some with ornate ironwork on wrap-around verandas and others on stilts to protect them from floods and to catch a breeze. They walked across the Story Bridge that spanned the winding Brisbane River to take them into the city centre. They walked past the wharves and Customs House and marvelled at the architecture that had been built mostly by convict labour, similar to some of the buildings they had seen in Sydney. They could see the City Hall clock in the distance, and palm trees lining the streets gave the city a tropical feel. The sky was so blue and the heat rising from the wet ground made them sweat. Even in the last days of Autumn, the weather in Australia was sticky and hot. Brisbane was a bustling city with cars and vans filling the streets as people went about their business. Everything was so new to them, yet there was a certain familiarity. Many of the inner city streets were named after British royalty – Queen, Edward, George, Albert, Adelaide, Alice – and the people looked much the same as anyone they would meet in Edinburgh or Glasgow.

It was a long walk and they were hot and thirsty. The trio happened upon the Australian Hotel on the corner of Albert and Queen Streets. Outside was a sign 'Bulimba Beer is Best' so they ventured in to the public bar.

"What can I get you?" asked the barman. Bill looked around and saw Gold Top Light Bitter pale ale and Bulimba draught. "Well, as your sign says 'Bulimba beer is best' we'll have three glasses of that."

The barman poured the beer. "Are you Irish?" he asked.

"No, we're from Scotland," Bill said proudly.

"Ah, fresh off the boat, eh?" the barman said as he handed over the beers. "That's six pence each."

The lads paid for the beer and gulped down half the glass in one swallow. Bill was pleasantly surprised. The beer was cold and he enjoyed the taste. He drained his glass.

"Another, please," he said and handed over his six pence. They finished their beers and while they wanted to try the food in a café they decided to keep their limited funds and head back to the hostel for lunch. In the afternoon, Bill packed up his belongings ready for the train trip the next day. He found a card game among some of the residents and managed to win a pound, so that would keep him going a bit longer until he could find work.

"Well I'll say goodbye now as you two will be still asleep when I'm away in the morning," Bill said to his fellow travellers when they went back to their room. He shook hands with them both. "I hope you find work soon, as I'm hoping to mysel'."

"Good luck to you, Willie," Rab said.

"Aye, good luck," said Wally. "Once I get used to this heat I'll start looking for a job."

"There's no time like the present," Bill said and got under the bed clothes. He wondered what lay ahead for him in Ipswich.

Chapter 39 (1950)

STRANGER IN A STRANGE LAND

The train trip to Ipswich took just over an hour. It had rained the whole way, but Bill enjoyed looking out the window at the countryside and trying to pronounce the names of the railway stations – Auchenflower, Indooroopilly, Toowong, Booval. He arrived at Ipswich Railway Station and waited to collect his trunk from the porter. The rain was still bucketing down and he had no idea where he was headed. He stood on the platform looking around until all the other passengers were gone. The porter walked up to him.

"Are you right, mate?" he asked.

"I've just arrived and I'm not sure where to go," Bill began. "I suppose I'd better find lodgings. I have a list of addresses here."

"Ah, you're Irish," said the porter with a smile.

"No I'm a Scot," Bill said. "I'm here to work in the mines."

"Ah right. Well let's see," said the porter stroking his chin and looking at the list. "There's a boarding house in Brisbane Street where you'll probably find a room, but it's a few streets away and you won't want to lug that big trunk in the rain."

Bill looked at the heavy trunk that had been his constant companion since stepping on to the boat in Glasgow. It contained all his worldly belongings.

"Tell ya what," said the porter. "I knock off work in half an hour, so why don't you go and get yourself a cup of tea in the refreshments room and I'll put your trunk into the boot of my car and take you to the boarding house."

Bill was impressed that the porter had a car – Australia seemed to be a place where anyone could buy a car or a house.

"That's very kind of you," he said and he sat with a cup of tea and read the local *Queensland Times* newspaper to familiarise himself with his new city. Ipswich employed around 1900 people in local mines and was responsible for producing fifty-eight per cent of the state of Queensland's coal output. With the letter of recommendation he had been given by the National Coal Board in Scotland, which had taken over the Knockshinnoch Castle Collieries from New Cumnock Collieries Limited, he was confident of finding work.

The porter's car pulled up outside a large timber house, similar to those he had seen lining the river in Brisbane. They carried the trunk between the two of them and stood before a dour looking woman in her fifties, called Mrs Foster.

"New chum here wanting a room," said the porter to the woman, then turning to Bill he put out his hand. "Hope you do all right, mate," he said and then he was gone. Bill smiled at Mrs Foster.

"How long will you be wanting accommodation, Mr…," she said.

"McMurdo – Willie, er, Bill McMurdo. I'd like to take it week to week if that's all right."

"The cost is £10 and for that you will get room and board."

Bill didn't have that much money on him but he was sure he'd be able to find a job and meet his financial obligations.

"I'll pay you at the end of the week if that's all right Mrs Foster," Bill said thinking quickly. He looked around. "You have a lovely place here. Surely you don't do all the work yoursel'." He took her by the hands. "With these fair hands you can't be doing hard work." Mrs Foster smiled and removed her hands from Bill's, then bounced her hand on the back of her hair. He could turn on the charm when he wanted to and his good looks always helped.

"That will be fine, Mr McMurdo. Come and I'll show you your room."

He dragged the heavy trunk up two flights of stairs and Mrs Foster opened the door to a tiny bedroom that contained a bed with a sagging mattress and lumpy pillow, and a chest of drawers. 'Ah well, it's a place to lay my head', he thought.

"You've missed lunch but dinner is at 6pm," said Mrs Foster as she closed the door and left Bill to unpack. But unpacking was the furthest thing from his mind, as he had no intention of staying there long. He had a wash and walked to the nearest hotel. It was still raining and he turned up his collar and ran between the shelter of the shops. He found himself in the Hotel Metropole at the top end of the city.

"A pint of Bulimba draught," Bill said to the barman.

"Eight ounce glass or eleven ounce glass here, mate," said the barman.

"Right, then give me the eleven ounce," Bill took a swig of the beer. "Can you tell me where a man would go to find out about getting a job in a coal mine?"

"Are you Welsh?" asked the barman. Bill felt his blood pressure rising but kept his cool. "A lot of Welsh coal miners settled in Ipswich in the early days, you know."

"No, I'm a Scot," Bill said calmly. "I've just arrived and I need a job."

"Hey, Woodsie," the barman called out. "Got a bloke here lookin' to pick some coal."

The man called Woodsie was dressed in a red flannel shirt, black shorts and working boots. He was of medium height, well-built and in his early forties. He walked up to Bill.

"Can you fill wagons?" asked Woodsie.

"Aye, I can – and I'm fast as well," Bill said.

"Hey we've got a new chum here," Woodsie said loudly to the bar.

"Are you one of those Ten Pound Poms?" one of the men called out. Bill had never heard the term before.

"I don't think so," he said. He reached into his pocket and pulled out his letter of recommendation. Woodsie eyed him up and down and read the letter. He put his beer down on the bar.

"Don't take much notice of the ribbing you'll get around here," Woodsie said lowering his voice. "It's all part of the test to see if you can take it."

Bill smiled. "I can take anything you or anyone else wants to dish out. I'm here to work and make some money and you'll find that I'm honest and hard-working."

"You'll be right, son," said Woodsie. "Where are you staying?"

Bill told him. "Oh, old Ma Foster's. Righto. I can get you a job at Rosewood starting in the morning. Have you got work boots?" Bill shook his head. "No worries, we'll get you kitted out and it can come out of your pay. Now be at the railway station at 5.30 in the morning. There'll be a few other blokes lined up as well and they'll show you where to go." Woodsie put out his hand to Bill. "Good on ya mate, you'll do all right here. Come and have a beer with the boys." Bill drained his beer and Woodsie quickly placed another into his hand. His days of drinking at home with his pals were good practice, as he could see that these Aussies could drink.

He arrived back at the boarding house for dinner, hungry as a bear as he hadn't eaten since the watery porridge he'd been given in the migrant hostel that morning. There were four other boarders seated at the table when he walked in and he introduced himself. The evening meal was disappointing, with a small piece of overcooked, dried up steak surrounded by grey peas and brussel sprouts. There was plenty of bread though, so he filled up on that.

"Will you be wanting a packed lunch tomorrow, Bill?" Mrs Foster smiled and asked.

"Well, that would be lovely Mrs Foster. I'm away about 5am. Oh, but I've no piece box." Mrs Foster looked at him. "You know," he continued, "to put my sandwich in."

"Don't you worry, Bill. I'll wrap up your lunch in waxed paper to keep it clean for you," she said as she continued to stare at him. Bill shifted uncomfortably in his chair, flicked back his blond hair and smiled to himself as he drank a cup of tea. He had a job to go to in the morning. He'd been in Australia for only four days, and he was on his way.

Chapter 40 (1950)

MAKING FRIENDS

Rosewood was a small town in the Bremer Valley, about thirty-seven miles west of Brisbane. Instead of walking or cycling the short distance to the pit as he had done at home, it was a twenty minute train trip from the city of Ipswich to the mine. The city was often referred to as 'the cradle of coal mining in Queensland' with a history of mining stretching back to 1848. It was originally called Limestone when Captain Logan found lime deposits on the shore of the Bremer River. He sent convicts to quarry the stone and construct a lime-burning kiln to create cement to be used in the construction of the first buildings in Brisbane. The township of Limestone was surveyed for free settlement in 1842 and was renamed Ipswich after the town of the same name on the Orwell River in Suffolk England.

Bill walked with the other men the short distance from the Rosewood Railway Station to Westvale Colliery and was signed on. He was amazed that most of the mining could be done standing up, not crouching in three feet high spaces as he had had to do in New Cumnock. He worked hard all morning, determined to prove himself to his new workmates. When it came time for a break, he eagerly opened the waxed paper that Mrs Foster had packed for him. Inside he found four slices of thin white bread, each covered in a black substance. He tentatively took a bite and recoiled at the bitter taste in his mouth.

"Here, take a swig of this, Scotty," one of his workmates offered as he handed him a cup of sugary black tea. "Vegemite takes a bit of getting used to," he said as the other men laughed. Bill was hungry so he ate the sandwiches followed by lots of hot, sweet tea. After another few hours of work the men headed up top and he was directed to a communal bathroom. Now this was different from home. Knockshinnoch Castle Colliery had only just introduced pithead baths before he left Scotland. He was pleased that he could wash and change his clothes at the mine, and wouldn't have to go back to Ipswich on the train covered in coal dust. It was his first experience using a shower, as they only had a bath at home and also at the boarding house. He scrubbed away and started singing.

"We've got Harry-bloody-Lauder working with us," said one of the men, then ten bars of soap landed on Bill's bare body. He was angered at first but then realised that it was good-natured ribbing. He would have to get used to the Australian sense of humour – and being called Scotty.

That night at dinner, the fare was no better. Mrs Foster served a watery soup, followed by a small joint of lamb rationed out between six people. 'I've just come from rationing', Bill thought, 'I'm no' having it again.' He suffered Mrs Foster's vegemite sandwiches every day and her watery soup every night. At the end of his first week's work he received his pay. It was thirteen pounds, seven shillings and sixpence – a fortune compared to the wages back home. The first thing he did when he got back to the boarding house was pay Mrs Foster for a week's board. "Would you have a pen and paper and envelope, Mrs Foster?" he asked.

Mrs Foster handed him six pieces of paper and a couple of envelopes and he went to his room. The first letter he wrote was to the State Migration Officer, Mr D W Longland.

'Dear Sir,' he wrote, 'enclosed please find the two pounds that was loaned to me when I arrived in this country. Yours sincerely, William Bell McMurdo.' He sealed up the envelope with the letter and four ten shilling notes inside, then began to write a letter back home.

'Dear Mither and Faither, you will be pleased to know that I have settled well into Australia and I have a job and a place to stay. The cooking's no' up to your standard mither, and it doesnae feel like home, but it is all working out for me. In Australia, you'd never think there had been a world war. There's more meat here than we've seen in Scotland for years and plenty of fresh fruit and vegetables grown in the farming land around Ipswich. And the fashions are different too. The lassies dresses don't have sleeves as it's too hot. All for now, Willie.' He left the letters in his room and went down to the dining room to face his bowl of tomato soup. As soon as the meagre meal was finished, he was out the door. His debts amounted to twelve pounds and he was now debt free. He took the one pound, seven shillings and sixpence to the Hotel Metropole. Some of the men he had met the previous week were there, so he sat with them, had a game of darts and drank a skinful. He was satisfied.

The rain continued into its sixth week with a few dry days in between. It was unusual to have so much rain and while the farmers loved it, most people were tired of it. It was the middle of Winter and still the days were warm, even if the nights could get a bit cold, but it was nothing compared with the rain, sleet and snow of a Scottish Winter. Bill had grown tired of Mrs Foster's unpalatable food and was seeking an alternative. One Friday night he discovered Con's Café in Brisbane Street, just down the road from the boarding house. He had seen the Greek proprietor as he passed by most days, but he'd never ventured in. But this night he was homesick and hungry. He walked into Con's Café and was directed to take a seat.

"How you like this rain?" asked Con who made an imposing presence with his thick wavy greasy black hair and wide grin. "Itsa no good for business. People, they stay at home," he said shaking his head. "Now, whatta you like?" Bill looked at the menu.

"Steak and eggs, please," Bill said.

"Oh, you havva the accent too," Con said. "Where you from? Letta me guess."

Before he could guess, Bill said "Scotland".

"Ah, for you, you like the haggetts, but I have no haggetts only steak, so for you a bigga steak." Bill smiled at the man's attempt to say 'haggis'. Con seemed friendly and he could use a friend. He had his workmates but most of them were married and their spare time was spent working on their houses or doing things their wives wanted to do. It was lonely for a single man and he was so tired of living at the boarding house. Con arrived with a large, juicy steak spilling over the edge of the plate, two eggs and a pile of potato chips. Bill's eyes lit up. He was to have a proper meal at last. He ate hungrily and when he was finished he got up to pay.

"That's the best meal I've had since I came to Australia," Bill said. He gladly handed over the six shillings.

"You come back again. Maybe it no rain. You havva enough of rain in your old country."

"I'll be back." He visited Con's Café at least three times a week for 'a bigga feed' as Con called it.

"You eatta the steak and eggs and still you look hungry," Con said one night. "For you, another plate of steak and eggs – on the house – no charge. You good customer." Bill ate the second plate of food as well. He was working hard and needed fuel but he wasn't getting it at Mrs Foster's. He wrote another letter home to tell the family that he was doing well and was happy, but in truth he longed for his own pals in New Cumnock.

The rain finally stopped, and Bill woke on a Saturday morning to see sunshine streaming into his bedroom. He opened the window and breathed in the sweet smell of gardenias. There were pink and grey birds, which he came to know as galahs, perched on the electricity wires and he watched them for a while as they swooped to the wet grass below to feast on seeds, then fly back up to their perch. The sun on his face made him feel happy, but as the rain cleared and steam started to rise from the ground he could feel the humidity and it made his skin sweat. He washed and dressed and went down to breakfast. He had grown used to the peanut paste that was available to smear on burnt toast so he gobbled it down and was eager to get out into the warm, dry day. He headed for the post office where he bought his overseas stamps. The girl at the post office suggested that buying air mail letters would be a cheaper way to send a letter home so he bought two. He looked around the shops. There were large department stores called Cribb and Footes, T C Beirnes and Bayards and plenty of smaller shops that sold clothes and shoes, a couple of newsagents, several banks and business offices. He looked at them as though seeing them for the first time, as he had always rushed past before, with his collar turned up against the rain. He'd grown tired of the Hotel Metropole so he sought out a new watering hole. In Bell Street he saw a pub called The Caledonian. Again, he was pleased to see the familiar names. Maybe he'd find some Scots in there and have someone to talk to that didn't make fun of his accent. He soon found a Scot, and as they settled down to enjoy a beer together, he told Bill about the history of The Caledonian Hotel.

"They say that Black Neale haunts this place," the Scotsman began. "In 1883 a Mauritian Sea Captain, nicknamed Black Neale, blew into Ipswich with a publican's licence that he had acquired in Sydney. He settled on this place and called it the Red Cow which became famous for its rum. The authorities started to ask questions when the pub's trade in rum seemed to outweigh the duties being paid by Black Neale and they carried out raids to try to expose an illegal distillery, but they never found anything. Until the original wooden building was demolished in 1896 to make way for this brick building, and there in the kitchen fireplace, was the rum distillery. Now they say that Black Neale still roams the corridors of this hotel – but I've no idea how it came to be named The Caledonian," he said and they both laughed. Bill loved a good ghost story.

After a break in the conversation, Bill went up to the bar to buy his new pal a drink. He bumped into a tall fellow in his late twenties, with wavy fair hair and a wide grin.

"Sorry mate," said the young man.

"It's no bother," Bill replied.

"Ah, you're a new chum," said the young man holding out his hand. "I'm Alf Hansell. How ya going?"

"Pleased to meet you Alf," Bill said, glad to make a new friend. "Can I buy you a drink?"

"I'm in a shout over there with two blokes but bring your friend over," Alf said. They spent the morning downing beers and Bill enjoyed hearing about the exploits of Alf and his friends. He was a coal miner too and, like Bill, enjoyed getting into a bit of mischief. Bill could take his fair share of alcohol, but these boys were big drinkers and by mid-afternoon Bill had had enough. He drained his glass and stood up to go.

"See you here next Saturday morning, mate," Alf said as he put a hand on Bill's shoulder. Bill walked out of The Caledonian Hotel with a smile on his face. The week passed and the next Saturday morning he was back at The Caledonian. He saw Alf propping up the bar and walked over to him.

"Hello there," Bill said with a smile. The young man looked at him and gave a half smile.

"Yeah, g'day mate," he said and turned his back on Bill as he chatted to his friends. Bill was disappointed. Alf had been so friendly the week before, but he wasn't bothered. He took his beer from the barman and as he took a sip he saw Alf across the room waving to him. He turned around and the other young man was still standing behind him. He'd only had one sip of beer but already he was seeing double. Alf made his way over to Bill.

"G'day mate, thought I'd find you here again," Alf said. Then looking across Bill at the other man, he called: "Mike, the old man wants his beer."

The other young man turned around and he was the spitting image of Alf. Seeing the look of confusion on Bill's face, Alf explained.

"Bill, this is my twin brother Mike," and the two shook hands. "Come on over and meet the old man." The twins walked with Bill to a table where a tall, thin man with a kindly face sat. "This is our father, Alf Hansell."

"How do you do, Mr Hansell," Bill said shaking hands.

The older man stood up to his full height of six feet two inches. "Just call me Alf, lad," he said. Bill sat down and told them all the story of how he was not long in the country. Old Alf's family had arrived from Yorkshire, England in the 1890s and he was the youngest of his family and the only one born in Australia. As well as the twins, he had four daughters. Alf was also a coal miner.

They met regularly every Saturday morning at The Caledonian Hotel. As Old Alf got to know Bill, he liked him more and more. He seemed to be an honest sort from a good family. As they finished their drinks one Saturday, Bill prepared to say goodbye to them when Old Alf took him by the arm. "You're coming home for lunch with us. It's about time you saw a bit of family life, because I suppose you are missing your folk." Bill was touched at the generosity. He had no idea where they lived but he was glad of the chance to have a home-cooked meal. They all piled on the bus outside The Caledonian Hotel and travelled the five miles to Dinmore, an outer suburb of Ipswich. The Hansell home was a large, well-kept Queenslander with verandas on three sides, and sat on a couple of acres of land. The front door lined up with the back door to take advantage of cooling breezes in stifling summers. There were two large water tanks to catch the rain water, a pear tree, a mango tree, a pond, several outbuildings including a toilet, and a vegetable garden. Old Alf lead the way and as Bill entered the house he could hear women chatting. He was introduced to Mrs Hansell, a roly-poly little woman less than five feet tall, but, as Bill was to learn, she was not to be messed with and she ruled the house with an iron fist. After the twins, the eldest daughter was Peg but she had married and moved with her husband Syd to Toowoomba. Then there was Eileen who was married to Bob, and Nell who was married to Nev. On the day Bill arrived for lunch, Nell was there, along with the youngest daughter Myrt who was quietly helping her mother prepare the lunch. She was slender, with wavy brown hair and deep blue eyes. She smiled at Bill and held his gaze before shyly looking away. He thought she was sweet but quite young. He was twenty-four and she was just seventeen. He shared a hot meal of roast beef, baked potatoes and pumpkin, carrots and peas, followed by home-made apple pie and custard with the Hansell family, and formed firm friendships with Alf and Mike. Old Alf enjoyed his chats with the young Scot and looked forward to their Saturday morning drinks and game of quoits.

Bill started to go parties and dances with Alf and Mike and their mates and as well as The Caledonian Hotel on Saturday mornings, he added the Prince Alfred Hotel at Booval to their stable of watering holes. It was here that he was introduced to Wally Johnson, an older man, who had moved from Scotland to Australia some years before. They got talking and Bill told Wally about the dreadful conditions at the boarding house where he lived.

"Ye've no need to put up wi' that, lad," Wally said. "Ye can come and board wi' us. The wife, Doris, will look after you like one of oor ain."

Bill paid Mrs Foster up until the end of the week. Wally arrived with his car and they carried the large trunk down the stairs and off he went to live with the Johnsons at Booval. He had a decent bed to sleep in, and Doris was a good cook. She offered to do his banking for him and any errands he may need doing. He couldn't believe his luck. Within the space of a few weeks everything had turned around. The sun had started shining, he had met new friends and he had a decent place to live with a family that came from Scotland. Life was good.

Chapter 41 (1950) Scotland

TRAGEDY AT KNOCKSHINNOCH

On Thursday September 7, George had worked the day shift at Knockshinnoch Castle Colliery in New Cumnock. It was where he and Willie had worked together before his lad decided to head off for Australia four months before. George could see in his son the hope and promise that he had once had. He had been a lad who wanted more from life than that of his uncle and grandfather, but his experiences in World War One had left him shaken and bitter. Now he watched his son, so full of energy and enthusiasm, with a mix of admiration and envy. His boy would achieve all the things George may never do. Their personalities were similar – both were stubborn, yet each had a generous streak and would help anyone in trouble. It was their sameness that led to many clashes, but George thought of Willie often.

He was at home with Mary, listening to the radio, when they heard the siren go off at the pit. The afternoon shift at the Knockshinnoch mine had started like any shift, but by around 7.30pm a large volume of liquid peat broke through from the surface into the No. 5 Heading section of the main coal seam in the South Boig district of the mine. The liquid matter burst into the pit, rushing down the steeply inclined heading, filling miles of underground workings and sealing off all escape routes to the surface.

There were 135 men working underground at the time – six working close to the pit bottom managed to escape, reaching the surface by way of the shaft before the inrush sealed their exit. Cut off from the pit bottom were 116 men who found refuge from the encroaching sludge deep within the extensive mine workings. A further thirteen men who were working in the No. 5 Heading at the time of the inrush were unaccounted for. On hearing the siren, people rushed from their houses, especially those whose sons and husbands were on the afternoon shift.

It became a race against time, but the men remained trapped underground for two tense, traumatic days under constant threat from the encroaching liquid peat, rapidly deteriorating air quality and gas. A telephone link to the surface remained intact, allowing the men to provide those on the surface with details of their location. Media from around the world descended on the village of New Cumnock as rescuers, Margaret's fiance George Pirie among them, worked tirelessly to free the trapped men. The men were eventually reached and led through the old disused gas-filled Bank No. 6 mine workings which ran close to Knockshinnoch.

The thirteen men trapped close to No. 5 Heading could not be reached. They were lost.

When the worst of it was over, Mary sat with George, her hands clasped on her lap.

"It could have been you and Willie trapped down there," she said quietly. George nodded his head. "It's the first time since he left that I've been glad he is so far away."

Chapter 42 (1952) Australia

FALLING IN LOVE

Bill had been in Australia for almost two years and he quickly learned the new and improved methods of mining. Working conditions were still harsh and the mining fraternity confronted continual danger and discomfort. He had moved closer to Ipswich to the Haigmoor Colliery at Tivoli, and then to the Aberdare East pit, which was close to where he was boarding with Wally and Doris Johnson. He worked a forty-hour week but with higher pay and better working conditions than in Scotland. He followed opportunities to better himself and had taken on the responsibility of Shot Firer, storing, transporting and using explosives underground. He had a good practical working knowledge of the mine's procedures and was able to conduct risk assessments and advise on shot firing patterns and conduct inspections, particularly for misfires, and test for gas in the mines.

He fitted comfortably into the Australian way of life. There were no miners' rows or pit villages, as there were in Scotland. The miners lived where they wanted to and some had cars, so transportation to the mines was much easier. It was a place where anyone who worked hard could own a house and a car or even a boat.

Ipswich was a bustling city, but it still had the feel of a village about it. In some areas, the baker still delivered bread in a horse and cart or perhaps a van, and Bill had even seen a herd of cattle being steered through the streets of West Ipswich on their way to the sales yards at nearby Churchill. Refrigerators were becoming more common, but the ice man still called at many houses with blocks of ice to put into ice chests. The city was progressive, yet a little old fashioned and welcoming, and he enjoyed the mix of old and new.

Bill enjoyed living with Wally Johnson and his family and they had some happy times together. He learned how to play Snakes and Ladders and other board games with the children, and helped them fix their pushbikes and scooters. He also felt very much part of the Hansell family. He saw Myrt when he went home for a meal with the boys, but they had barely spoken to each other in all the time he had known her. She had recently turned nineteen, and was no longer the young girl he had first met. She was a talented girl who could sing, and play the violin, piano and harmonica. As a four-year-old she had played harmonica on the radio at 4IP studios in Ipswich and became known as 'the baby with the harmonica'.

"Do you think Myrt would go out with me if I asked her?" Bill asked Alf one Saturday morning in The Caledonian Hotel.

"Only one way to find out, mate," Alf said. "Tell you what. There's a party tonight at Dinmore. Myrt's going there to play the violin. Why don't you come along and you can get to talk to her without Mum being there." Bill smiled. He liked Mrs Hansell but she kept a weathered eye on Myrt, and Bill hadn't even had the chance to sit next to her.

That night at the party she was dressed in a red and white floral, just-below-the-knee dress with short, capped sleeves, in the style so popular with young women in the early 1950s. There was a lot of alcohol and questionable activities at the party and while the crowd listened as she played the violin, she didn't seem to belong there. When she had finished playing, Bill walked over to her.

"I enjoyed listening to you play, Myrt," he said. "Would you like to go out with me some time?"

Myrt blushed. She didn't have much of a social life and was glad of a chance to go out, but she was thrilled that it would be with the young man she'd had her eye on for some time. Bill told Alf he'd walk her home, then arranged to pick her up the following Saturday night. He caught the bus from Booval to Dinmore, suffered a stern lecture from Mrs Hansell about getting Myrt back home at a decent hour, then they caught the bus into Ipswich to see a picture show at the Ritz theatre in Bell Street. At interval, they went next door to the Ritz Cafe for supper, then returned to the theatre for the feature film. Bill took her back to Dinmore and then caught the next bus back to Wally's house. It was a lot of travelling about but he was happy to do it. She was every bit as sweet and innocent as he had first thought and he felt instantly protective of her. By April of that year they were 'going together' and by August he had bought a ring.

"Alf, there's something I'd like to talk to you and Mrs Hansell about tonight," Bill said to Old Alf in The Caledonian.

"I thought there might be," Old Alf said. "Come for tea and we'll talk."

That night after the dishes had been cleared, Bill, Myrt and her father and mother sat around the kitchen table. "I've come to ask your permission to marry Myrt," Bill said. Before Old Alf could say a word, Mrs Hansell spoke.

"You'll have to turn a Catholic," she said bluntly. Bill shifted slightly in his chair, not realising that his Presbyterian upbringing would be an issue.

"I won't turn a Catholic but I won't stop Myrt from going to church and the children can be raised in the Catholic faith," he said confidently. Before Mrs Hansell had a chance to argue, Old Alf spoke.

"I think that's fair enough." Myrt was pleased to have the support of her father, and surprised that he had the last word on the matter.

Two years after leaving Scotland, Bill had found a life of freedom and opportunity. Now he had the girl of his dreams to build a family with. Excitedly, he wrote a letter home to his parents.

Chapter 43 (1952) Scotland

DISAPPOINTMENT AND JOY

Mary put the air mail letter into her apron pocket and saved it until George and their daughter Margaret were both home. She cherished the few letters she had received from Willie and when they were all gathered she sat down with a cup of tea to read news from her son. He had been gone for two years and she missed him terribly. 'Two years have passed,' she thought 'only four more to go until he is home.' She carefully opened the letter.

'Dear Mither and Faither, you may be surprised to know that I am not travelling on to Canada and America,' the letter began. Mary looked up excitedly at George and Margaret, then continued reading. 'I am doing well in the pits here and have a lot of friends. Well, my biggest news is that I am getting married.' Mary read more slowly. 'Her name is Myrt and she is a darling girl. She's very musical and comes from a good family who have been very kind to me. I hope you can be happy for me. I plan to make a life for myself and Myrt here in Australia. God bless and keep you, Willie.'

The blood had drained from Mary's face. Did this mean that Willie was never coming home? She folded her arms on the kitchen table and buried her head in them. Margaret rose to comfort her mother and George just walked to the mantle and lit his pipe. They may not have always got on, but even he had missed the vitality that Willie had brought to their home. There was no way that they could afford to go to Australia for the wedding, and Willie wouldn't be coming home.

Mary took to her bed for the next few days and cried herself to sleep most nights. George didn't know what to do for her. He tried to be more help around the house and spent less time at the inn, but she was inconsolable. Her heart was breaking.

Chapter 44 (1953) Australia

STARTING A NEW LIFE

They were married in Sacred Heart Catholic Church at Booval, a suburb of Ipswich, on February 7, 1953 with Alf as Bill's best man and Myrt's sister Nell as matron of honour. After the ceremony and reception, they boarded a bus to take them to Palm Beach at the Gold Coast for a week's honeymoon. They spent glorious days in the sun, on the beach and at the flat, cooking and laughing. Bill revelled in the sunshine and enjoyed swimming in the Pacific Ocean. They ate prawns and crabs and oysters and fresh tropical fruit. The week went by too quickly and soon they were back at Dinmore, ready to live with the Hansells until they could afford their own home. They settled in to the sleepout – a long room on the side of the house, and shared the kitchen and bathroom with Myrt's parents. The house was still quite primitive in lots of respects. There was electricity and running water, but water for a bath had to be heated in the fountain of the wood stove. Washing was done in a copper in the big backyard and then hung on a wooden clothes prop line. The outside toilet was a 'thunder box' with a pan that had to be emptied by a nightcart worker once a week. In the Summer, the smell could be overbearing. There was little privacy in the house as, even though they were married, Mrs Hansell was uncomfortable with Bill and Myrt sharing a room. Some nights she even peeked into their room to see what they were doing. Bill worked hard and saved his money and Myrt helped her mother around the house during the day. She could have continued to work in a shop, but Bill was adamant that no wife of his would work – it was an affront to his masculine sense of pride. By Christmas that year he had grown tired of living in someone else's house. They had saved enough money for a deposit on a house, and he began looking at the real estate pages and circling properties that he felt were suitable. He would then leave the newspaper open for Mrs Hansell to see. She would have been happy if they'd gone on living there forever but Bill had other ideas.

They found a large, colonial house at Bundamba and put down a deposit. The house cost £1010 and they borrowed the rest of the money from the bank to be paid off in instalments, as did most people. They bought a new bedroom suite for £80 and gradually bought more furniture each week after they moved in. It was a spacious home with a big backyard in a street full of friendly people.

In March 1954, Myrt gave Bill the happy news that he was to become a father.

"I'm over the moon," he said. He was nearly twenty-eight years old and ready to become a family man.

Myrt was glad of the company and guidance of the two elderly ladies who lived across the road. Even though she was only a few miles from her parents, she missed them and would need help when the baby came. Bill still had his regular nights out with the boys, drinking and playing cards. Without telling Myrt, he took part in some amateur boxing matches to earn some extra money. He worked hard and played hard, just as he had done in Scotland. He wondered how his mother was feeling.

Chapter 45 (1954) Scotland

A NEW GRANDCHILD

The news of Bill and Myrt's wedding made the *Cumnock Chronicle*. He was 'the local lad who had gone to Australia' and everyone was interested to know how he was getting on. The letters from Australia were few and far between, but Mary walked to the post office every day in the hope that there would be word from her son. In April, three years after Willie had left Scotland, Mary received another letter.

'You will be pleased to know that I have bought my own home,' Mary read. 'It's big and stands on its own piece of ground. We have a vegetable garden and hens. I've also to tell you that I will be a father before the year is out.'

Mary shed a tear. Her boy was to become a father. She carefully folded the letter and placed it in her apron then walked to the large oak box she kept in her bedroom. She took out the white linen and lace trimmed christening gown that Willie had worn, and parcelled it up for the grandchild she may never get to see. She wrote a letter to put inside the parcel.

'Dearest Son and Daughter, we are so pleased to hear that you are doing so well in Australia. Things are much the same here. You faither continues to work in the mines but has had times of ill health. Your sisters are busy raising their families and send you their love. We look forward to hearing news of our grandchild. I miss you with all my heart and pray that you are happy and safe.'

She wiped a tear from her eye, placed the letter into the parcel and tied it up with string. She walked to the post office and placed the parcel on the counter.

"I'm sending Willie's christening robe for my new grandchild in Australia," Mary said proudly.

"Oh, aye, your Willie – how's he doin'?" said the postmistress.

"Grand," said Mary, "he's doin' grand."

Chapter 46 (1954) Australia

A FAMILY MAN

The baby was three weeks overdue, and finally the pains started on a warm Spring morning in October. A friend drove Myrt to the Ipswich Hospital where the baby had to be induced. At 11.15pm on October 9, 1954 Bill and Myrt became the proud parents of a little girl whom they named Carmel Margaret Mary. Her very Catholic name came from Our Lady of Mt Carmel and she was also named after her two grandmothers – Margaret Hansell and Mary Bell. It was a happy coincidence that she also bore the names of her two aunts in Scotland and the names of great-grandmothers stretching back 200 years. She was baptised in the Catholic Church, wearing her father's christening robe.

They would take Carmel on the bus to visit her grandparents or into town and the little blonde-haired, blue-eyed tot caught many an admiring glance. Bill and Myrt settled into family life and the baby blossomed. She was the apple of her father's eye.

Bill had left his dog Raven with his sister Mary on her farm, when he left Scotland, but the dog had long since passed away. He bought a little white dog that he called Sandy and taught him to do tricks. He wished that his mother could see how happy he was, and that she could hold her grandchild in her arms. He missed her gentle touch and he looked forward to the day when he would see her again.

Chapter 47 (1955) Scotland

A STROKE OF BAD LUCK

Mary had begun to feel unwell. The stress of not having seen her son for five years was taking its toll. With every letter that arrived she hoped that it would be news of him coming home. On one of her regular walks to the post office, she stumbled and fell. A neighbour ran to her aid.

"Are you all right, Mary?" the neighbour asked.

"It's my arm, I cannae lift it," Mary said slowly.

Mrs Daley beckoned her husband who was standing close by, and they helped her into the post office. The doctor was called and she was taken home and put to bed.

"You've had a stroke, Mrs McMurdo," the doctor said. "You must have bed rest."

Mary was in bed and Margaret had been called to attend to her by the time George got home from work. He was shocked when told the news and sat by her side.

"Oh, I'm fine," Mary said slowly. "Never you heed about me. Get on and get yer tea."

Over the next few months Mary suffered a series of small strokes and she was bed-ridden. Her only wish was to see her son again. Her heart ached to see him.

Chapter 48 (1956) Australia

ANOTHER ACCIDENT

By February 1956, Myrt was pregnant again and they were happy to add to their little family. But their happiness was overshadowed by the news that Carmel had asthma.

"It's hard to watch a child so young struggling for breath," the doctor said. "She'll need medication. Now tell me, do you live in a high-set house?"

"No, the house is low-set," Myrt said.

"Does water sit under it when it rains," the doctor continued.

"Sometimes – yes."

"It is my strong suggestion that you move to a drier area. It's the damp that is exacerbating her asthma."

Myrt told Bill that evening when he got home from work. "I don't want to move from this lovely house," she said.

Bill had experienced damp in Scotland and he knew how it could affect people's health. There was nothing else for them to do but move house.

"We'll find a nice house, but I think we should wait until the baby is born," he said.

Bill continued to take every opportunity that was offered to him to better his position in the mines and earn more money. He had moved to New Hope Colliery and wasn't afraid of taking on more responsibility. His knowledge of mining was growing. He was working a range of shifts – day, afternoon and night - and bought a motor bike as a cheap form of transportation. He found a new freedom - he could go where he wanted, when he wanted.

Their second daughter was born prematurely on September 1, 1956. They named her Colleen Joy, in deference to her Irish grandmother, and she was taken to a hospital for premature babies where she stayed for some weeks until she could be taken home.

The day of Carmel's second birthday, Bill had stopped at the Racehorse Hotel at Bundamba, as usual after work to have a drink with some friends. Also as usual, he put two large bottles of beer down the front of his shirt, and hopped on his motor bike for the short trip home. He waited his turn at the corner of the street to turn right and as he did the driver of a large black car shot across in front of him. There was a screech of brakes and a crash that brought people running out of their houses. The driver got out of the car and saw the motor bike, dented and crumpled, several feet from the car. Bill was trapped under the car.

"Someone call the ambulance," a passerby said. The fire brigade arrived to lift the car and the ambulancemen gave him first aid, then transported him to Ipswich Hospital. After examination it was discovered that he had a dislocated hip and cuts and scratches. He had survived – and so had the two bottles of beer. The attending police officer went to the hospital to see Bill.

"Those two bottles are at the station when you want to collect them," he said with a smile. "You're a very lucky fellow. You could have been killed."

"You keep them and give them to the lads," Bill said.

Chapter 49 (1956) Scotland

A MOTHER'S LOVE

Margaret cared for her mother in the front room of their home at 20 Lochview, Pathhead, New Cumnock. George would often go to Mary's farm on the weekends as he couldn't bear the sadness at home. Margaret was annoyed with him as she had her own family to care for, but she couldn't see her mother suffer. She watched as Mary's condition grew worse.

"Willie," she would say. "Where's Willie. I want to see my lad." George wished that he could do something but there was nothing he could do. Willie was 12,000 miles away in Australia and he knew that Mary would never see him again. George had grown up with loneliness. It seemed like everyone in his life that he ever loved would go away. And now he was losing Mary – the rock of the family who coped with all his moods and bad temper, who stuck with him through life's ups and downs. She didn't deserve to suffer.

As her condition worsened, Mary was taken to Ballochmyle Hospital in Mauchline. There was a sadness about her that no pill could cure. Her kidneys were failing and she didn't have long to live. George and his daughters, Mary and Margaret, were called to her bedside. She saw them and smiled and loved them dearly. But a part of her was missing. It had been for six years. The smile faded from her face and she surrendered into peace at fifty-eight years of age. She would worry no more about the son she had lost.

Chapter 50 (1956) Australia

TIME RAN OUT

Myrt was kept busy running from the special care hospital for premature babies to feed and visit Colleen, visiting Bill in hospital every day then going to Dinmore each night where she and Carmel were staying with her parents. She would take a bus to her house every morning to check the mail and do a few jobs around the house. This morning there was an air mail letter amongst the post.

She finished reading the letter from her father-in-law in Scotland, wiped the tears from her eyes and put the letter in her purse. She wondered what more could happen to them. She got some clean pyjamas for Bill and caught the next bus to the hospital. As she approached his bed he seemed a lot brighter. His leg and hip were in a full cast and suspended above the bed, but he smiled when he saw her. As she drew closer he could see that she had been crying.

"Is it the girls?" he asked as his first thoughts were for his daughters. Myrt pulled up a chair and sat down beside her husband.

"Bill, I've got something to tell you," and she pulled the letter from her purse. "It's your mother – she's dead." Bill's face went white and she reached out to hold his hand. The tears started to flow and he cried and cried.

"I was going to go home, she wanted me to go home, but I always thought there was time."

Myrt got up and drew the curtain around his bed for some privacy as he sobbed. He was not a man to show his emotions easily, but he had loved his mother dearly, and while he thought of her often, he was busy living his own life and creating his own family. He always thought that he would see her again, and now he'd run out of time. She was gone. It was a hard blow.

He sent money home to help pay for the funeral and a headstone. It was all that he could do. But in his heart he would carry the memory of his beloved mother, and think of her sweet face smiling at him. Through all his cheekiness and pranks as a child, she always forgave him. He carried the guilt of not being there for her, and more than anything he wanted her forgiveness.

Chapter 51 (1959) Scotland

HEADING DOWN UNDER

George was lonely in the house at Lochview. On the weekends he would go to his daughter Mary's house at East Raws Farm in Kilmarnock, and he spent a lot of time at The Waverly Bar in West George Street and taking long walks. He would often take his grandson William to the football to see Kilmarnock play of a Saturday afternoon, then have something to eat and put the lad on a bus home, before heading to the Waverly. There was a hole in his life now that his Mary was gone.

His daughters and grandchildren were a great comfort to him but he had a longing for purpose in his life. He was now sixty-two years of age and could finish up in the pits and get a small pension, but then what would he do? The letters continued to arrive from Australia, telling him about the two little granddaughters he had never seen, and of the lifestyle that his son Willie had grown to love. He finished reading the latest air mail letter and placed it on the mantle with the others, then he took out the newspaper, lit his pipe and sat down in a comfortable chair. He read the news of the day and got up to make a cup of tea and some toast for his evening meal. He took down the letter from the mantle and read it again.

'Our wee lassies are now nearly five and three years old, and they love to play in the big back yard where we have mango, banana, mulberry, orange and lemon trees and a big run for the hens. Our new house is in a suburb called Ebbw Vale, like the town in Wales. It is brand new and I have named it Glen Afton. I have also bought my first car – a Ford Prefect, grey in colour with a running board along the side. I'm glad I learned to drive in the army. I just went to the local police station and got my driver's licence. Myrt has a new electric washing machine which saves her a lot of work with the children's clothes and my pit clothes. There is plenty of work and money to be made if you are prepared to work hard. And the sun shines every day. Even the Winters here are warmer than the Summers in Scotland.'

George stoked the coal in the fireplace and pulled his jacket tightly around him. His bones ached from the cold and he read over and over that 'the sun shines every day'. He wondered if he too might go to Australia to enjoy the sunshine and meet his daughter-in-law and two granddaughters, and see his only son again.

The next day George sent a letter off to Australia House in London, enquiring about passage to Australia. Within the month he had news that he could go to Australia for two years, provided that he could support himself financially. He smiled for the first time in many months and immediately sat down to write to Willie in Australia.

Chapter 52 (1959) Australia

AN UNEXPECTED VISITOR

Bill walked in the door from work. "There's a letter from your father," Myrt said. "He wants to come and stay with us for two years."

Bill kissed her on the cheek and took the letter from her hand.

'Your mither would want me to see you again and to meet your family,' the letter read. 'I've to find a job if I'm to stay for two years but I still know how to work. I would like to come to stay with you.'

Bill put the letter down and took a long swig on a cold beer. "Well, what do you think?" he said to Myrt.

Myrt was excited at the prospect of meeting her father-in-law. "Two years is a long time but I'm sure we'll manage," she said. "We can take the furniture out of the dining room and make it into a bedroom for him."

"Well, I suppose I'd better make enquiries about finding him a job," Bill said. He was excited thinking about seeing his father again, and hearing all the news from Scotland, but he wasn't one to show his feelings so he left the letter on the table and went into the lounge room to read the newspaper. He hoped that his father would be proud of all that he had achieved in Australia. He smiled to himself.

Chapter 53 (1959) Scotland

THE BOAT COMES IN

The furniture from the flat at 20 Lochview, Pathhead, New Cumnock was sold and George packed up his few personal belongings. It was the home that his family had grown up in, and the home where Mary had become so sick. He had mixed feelings about leaving it, but he knew he had to move on if he was to have any life at all. He handed in his notice at the pit and went to Raws Farm to stay with Mary and her family in the few weeks before he was to leave for Australia. There was great excitement at the Waverly as he sat with his pals and talked about his adventure.

On a grey day in early November, George arrived at the docks with his travelling trunk. His daughters, Mary and Margaret, were there to see him off. The Iberia loomed large in front on him. He took off his cloth cap and scratched his head as he looked at the ship that was to take him 12,000 miles across the sea. The last time he had set foot on a ship, he was crammed in with hundreds of other young men to be taken to France to fight a war. The Iberia was a converted troop ship and the memories came flooding back. He had to take a moment to compose himself before he could set foot on the ship, but he gathered up his strength, pulled his cap back on to his head and hugged his daughters goodbye, as the tears welled in their eyes.

"Oh, cheer up now, lass," he said as he hugged Mary. "I'm away to see your brother Willie. I'll no' come to any harm." He walked up the gangplank and turned once more to wave to them, then disappeared into the ship. He was off to find some sunshine and, despite the sometimes difficult nature of his relationship with Willie, he was looking forward to seeing his son and the home and family he had created.

The ship was well laid out with an entertainment room, dining rooms with crisp white linen and shiny silver, and a smoking room. He could play cards, listen to music played on the grand piano and go to the dances, although he mostly sat and watched the passing parade. He passed through all the ports that Willie had nine years before, and enjoyed the freedom and the space. He stared at the ocean and had never seen such deep, blue water. He breathed in the fresh, ocean air and felt happy and wondered about his life in Australia for the next two years. It was a welcome distraction from his sadness.

On a hot December morning, the Iberia berthed in Brisbane. George smiled when he saw that he would be getting off the ship at Hamilton Wharf – Hamilton was one of his own family names. It took two hours for all the passengers to get through customs and to collect their luggage. When he finally emerged from the terminal he was greeted with a bright blue sky and brilliant sunshine streaming down upon him. There were people everywhere and he scanned the crowd for his son. As the crowd thinned out, he heard a voice behind him.

"Are ye lookin' for Willie McMurdo?" He turned and saw the beaming face of the son he had not seen for nine years. George was relieved to see him and they smiled and shook hands. He noticed that Willie had filled out and his skin was slightly darker. He looked strong and fit. Willie introduced his father to Myrt who hugged and welcomed him. George could see that another child was on the way, and not far off from the looks of it. Then he looked down at the two little blonde granddaughters who were staring up at him, and bent down to give each of them a kiss on the cheek.

"Let me take that," said Willie as he took the trunk from his father. He noticed that the old man looked even older than he had remembered. The death of his beloved Mary had taken a toll on him and it showed. They walked to where a sea of cars was parked and Bill unlocked the doors and placed the trunk into the boot of the car.

"Is this your car, Willie?" George asked.

"Aye, it is. You need a car here. Everything is so far away. We've nearly an hour's drive to get to our house from the wharf."

George settled himself into the back seat of the car, between the two wee girls who were still staring and smiling at him. Bill pointed out places of interest on the trip from Brisbane to Ipswich and George listened intently. This country was so different from Scotland. He had left green fields and regular rainfall, and arrived in a country so starved for rain that the fields were brown and the heat came up from the road to create a haze. The car pulled into the driveway of the timber house at Ebbw Vale. It was neat and sat on a large block of land with neighbours all around in their own separate houses. As Bill carried the trunk into the house, Myrt put the kettle on.

"This will be your room," Bill said as he showed George to a bedroom off the kitchen. It was modestly furnished with a single bed, a chest of drawers with a mirror and a wardrobe, but it was adequate for his needs. Bill put the trunk on the bed and George opened it.

"Mary has sent you a fruitcake," he said as he carried the six-week old cake into the kitchen.

"Oh, you don't get fruitcakes like that here," Bill said rubbing his hands in anticipation as he took a knife and cut off a slice to have with his tea. They chatted for hours about life in Scotland as Bill was eager to hear all the news.

There was a subject that they were both avoiding, until George spoke.

"Yer mither was awfully bad at the finish. She missed you so, and you broke her heart," George said.

Bill looked out the door and blinked back tears. They sat in silence for a minute.

"You got the money I sent," Bill said, still staring into the distance as a tear escaped from one eye.

"Aye, I did. She has a nice headstone."

That was all that was said. There was another awkward silence as Bill wiped his hand across his cheek to brush away the tear.

"Ah, you were well out of Knockshinnoch," George said as he shook his head. "We lost a lot of men. Our cousin John was working that day and was trapped, but they got him out. It's a sad place now."

George listened as his son told him about his work in the Australian mines.

"The unions are very strong here too," Bill said. "Just last year we had a stay-in strike. Because of a reduced Coal Board allocation, the company said that the mine would close for a week and then go back with only twenty-seven of the thirty-four men. We were no' having that. We went down below at seven o'clock on the Wednesday morning and camped in a tunnel off the main shaft, about 200 yards from the surface. Other mines went out in support and the Queensland Trades and Labour Council backed us." Bill paused to get a beer out of the fridge for himself and one for his father.

"The women got involved in making meals and sending down bedding – we were set to stay down as long as was needed. Management got the jitters and reduced the number of jobs lost from seven to five and found work for three of the men at Haigmoor. One fellow decided to leave and we put pressure on them to find a job for the other bloke. We were back up on top two days later. Ah, we had a great win." Bill took another swig of his beer.

"The miners here call me Scotty, otherwise everyone calls me Bill."

"Oh, aye," George said, taking it all in. "Well, if ye don't mind, Willie's still good enough for me."

Bill asked about Mary and Margaret and their children, and was especially glad to hear that young George had recovered from the polio that he had been suffering when Bill had left for Australia.

"Your sisters are doing well, but things are still hard, even all this time after the war," George said.

"Well, you won't go without here," Bill said. "There's plenty of work, plenty of food and the people are generally a good lot."

"I've to find a job if I'm to stay here for two years," George said, getting down to business right from the start. "I'm sixty-two years old. What kind of job am I likely to get? I've no wish to go down the pits again."

"I've made a few enquiries and we'll get you registered with the employment office on Monday and they'll find something for you," Bill said. After tea, George went for a walk down the back yard to see the hens and the fruit trees.

"What's this?" George asked, pointing to a small outhouse.

"That's the toilet," Bill said. "It's what they call here 'an outside dunny'. Every week the night cart man comes to take the full pans and bring a new one." Bill could see George turning up his nose.

"Are we back in the miners' rows, having to share an outside ashpit?" George asked.

"Ah well, this one is for our family only – we own this block of land, it's not like renting a miner's cottage. It takes a bit of getting used to. Some suburbs have sewerage connected and we will have one day, but for now it's 'the thunderbox'." George looked bewildered.

"That's another name for the outside toilet," Bill explained. He thought he would tease his father a little more. "And we have snakes and spiders and flies – it's all part of the charm of this country," Bill said and laughed. "Don't worry, you'll be right. Come on, let's have a beer." George noticed that his son had taken to talking like the Australians, although his Scottish accent was still strong. The little girls chased each other around in the cool of the evening that came after a humid and hot Summer's day. They played and laughed and he watched them and smiled. He had made a good decision to come to Australia. He felt happier already.

Chapter 54 (1959) Australia

MAD DOGS AND SCOTSMEN

George had taken a job working for the main roads, out in the burning heat of the day. At first he was glad to be working in the sun all day but, as many a newcomer to the country was to find, he had under-estimated the ferocity of the sun and after an initial sunburn, he had taken to wearing a broad-brimmed hat and long sleeves to protect his Scottish skin. In the heat of an Australian Summer, the tar on the roads would melt and, as the locals would say, you could fry an egg on the footpath it was so hot. He gave Myrt money to buy him some Summer clothes and put away his flannel underwear and heavy coat. He was becoming great friends with Myrt's father Alf and mother Maggie, as Bill now called her. He bought a pushbike and would often call into their home at Dinmore for a whisky or a rum, before heading home to Ebbw Vale for the night. George and Alf were about the same age and both had been coal miners. Alf was losing his eye sight and he looked forward to George's company, as there was little for him to do each day.

In the heat of a Queensland Summer, George experienced his first Christmas in Australia. He found it difficult to eat a hot meal and plum pudding in ninety degree heat but there was plenty of cold beer to wash it down with. He noticed that Willie had taken to the Australian beer and enjoyed it regularly. He had been introduced to his son's friends and workmates, and joined in their long sessions at the pub 'to wash down the coal dust', but George still enjoyed a whisky and he was partial to the local rum. He liked the relaxed lifestyle that Australia provided, and was content most evenings to sit on the back veranda and smoke his pipe and enjoy the cool breezes that often followed the long, hot days.

He liked to watch the kookaburras perch on the wire clothes hoist in the back yard, as they called out to one another with a curious laugh. He watched the men with their noisy lawn mowers cutting grass on large blocks of land every weekend. He saw the local children playing cricket in the street after school, using rubbish bins for wickets, and neighbours washing their cars with the hose and spraying each other. He laughed when, on Sunday mornings, Willie would have his radiogram cranked up to the highest volume, entertaining the street to the strains of Glen Daly, Harry Lauder and Andy Stewart. But he could not abide some of the television programs which mostly hailed from America. When shows like 'I Love Lucy' or '77 Sunset Strip' came on, he would get up from his seat in the lounge room.

"I'm not watching this rubbish," he would declare and take himself outside to suck on his pipe. Bill would look up from his newspaper and stare out the door, but say nothing. It was the old man's way and he knew it. They were both outspoken and that's just the way it was.

He noted that Australians took regular holidays and weekends away to the beach, and he enjoyed the two-hour car ride with his family to Palm Beach, where he went fishing and swimming in the ocean. He loved the sunshine, fresh air and fresh food, although the heat could sometimes be stifling.

George was keen to learn all about Australia so that he could tell everyone when he returned home.

"What are the prices of things like here, compared to Scotland?" Myrt asked George one afternoon as he sat at the kitchen table and watched her make a mulberry pie.

"Well I'd say things are fairly even, but you have a better selection of meat and fruit and vegetables here," George said. "A pound of rump steak back home was costing three shillings and four pence when I left, but I see in the paper that you can get it here for two shillings a pound. You can't complain about the variety of food you can get here."

George was pleased that he would be on hand when Bill and Myrt's third child would be born, and he knew that his wife Mary would have loved to help bring the child into the world, just as she had done with her daughters' babies. But it was different in Australia as most women went into hospital to have their babies. There were some complications and Myrt was admitted to hospital for a few weeks before the birth. Her mother looked after the girls during the day, while George helped Willie to care for them at night. After four weeks of anxious waiting, Willie had a son, born on February 2, 1960 whom they named Bruce William. He was named William after his father, but the long Scottish tradition of naming children using family names was not followed so much in Australia, and Willie was happy to go along with whatever Myrt decided. The baby was christened in the Catholic Church, in the robe that his grandmother had sent from Scotland when Carmel was born. George had no real problem with Catholicism, even though the McMurdos had been christened in the Church of Scotland for many generations. And he wasn't really saddened at the loss of tradition – things were just different in Australia. It was a new time, a new age, and he was pleased to see that Willie was adapting so well in this new country. But he was also pleased that his son was proud of his Scottish heritage and still loved to read and recite Burns, and break into a chorus of 'A Wee Deoch an Doris' when he'd had a few drinks. Willie's accent was still strong, and his patriotism could not be questioned. George believed that Willie had found the best of both worlds.

The baby grew into a chubby toddler. George delighted in playing with his grandchildren, going to the pub with his son and talking to his friends, but he missed having female company. He would often take the train to Brisbane on the weekends to let Willie have time alone with his family, and on one particular visit to a pub where he liked to have lunch, he met a woman much the same age as himself. Her name was Sadie and he enjoyed her company and would often meet her and take her to lunch or to the pictures, but it was not the same. He was trying to fill a space left by Mary, and while Sadie wanted more from the relationship, George was just glad of her company and nothing more. He delighted in getting letters from his daughters Mary and Margaret, and hearing all about their lives, and he missed them greatly. When his two years were up in Australia, George gladly returned to Scotland.

They arrived at Hamilton Wharf, and Bill unloaded the trunk from the car. George hugged Myrt and the three children, who didn't understand where their grandfather was going. He held out his hand to his son.

"We've not always seen eye to eye, but I am pleased that you have made such a good life for yoursel'. Your mither would be proud," George said. "I'll likely not see you again, son. I'm away hame to where I belong, to where I've lived and to where I will die, but I'll look for yer letters and I'll think of you often. I'll take some of this sunshine home in my heart." Looking at the children, he said: "Ye've a fine family and yer doin' well in the mines – ye'll probably get further here than if you'd stayed at hame."

"Tell everyone I'm askin' fer them," Willie said, and that was it. George walked up the gangplank and glanced back once to see them all waving him goodbye. The ship stopped in Aden and he bought two silk scarves for his granddaughters and sent them off to Australia. He couldn't wait to tell everyone at home about his time in the land down under. He was on his way home to Scotland, the place where he belonged.

Chapter 55 (1962) Scotland

A CURE FOR LONELINESS

George had been home in Scotland for six months and staying with his daughter Mary and her family at the farm. He had taken a job at the creamery in the small village of Waterside. While he was glad to be back to familiar places and people, he was still lonely. He had picked up where he left off, going to the Waverly Bar in West George Street Kilmarnock, where he could regularly be found warming a bar stool. The men stayed in the bar while the women usually sat in the privacy of the snug, and drank and laughed. The more adventurous women occasionally drifted into the public bar with the men.

"Fancy buying a girl a drink?" she said as she sat down beside him. 'She's hardly a girl', George thought as he looked at the woman who was at least his age of sixty-four. But he was lonely and in need of company – female company was especially welcome.

"What will ye have?" he asked.

"Oh, a gin and tonic," she said slowly. He ordered the drink and they began to chat. She knocked back drink after drink but she was friendly and seemed to take an interest in him.

"I'm George, by the way," he said holding out his hand.

"Oh darling, I'm Ethel," she said and hugged him around the neck. "Me and the girls drink here all the time. Have ye no' seen me here?"

"Well, I've no' been looking," George said for he had to confess he had not seen her there before. George looked at his watch and knew that his daughter Mary would be keeping his tea warm for him.

"I must away," he said as he drained his whisky glass.

"Oh, so soon?" Ethel said. "Well, you take care George, and I'll see ye here next Saturday." She rose from the bar stool and kissed him on the cheek. George blushed and smiled and hurried out of the bar. He had a new spring in his step and was looking forward to the following Saturday.

Ethel was already in the snug when George arrived. He joined her there for a few drinks and summoned up the courage to ask her out for a meal. From then on they met regularly every Saturday night for six months. Ethel seemed very interested in hearing his stories about Australia and bragged about her globe-trotting beau to her friends. George had his earnings from the creamery and some money he had saved in Australia, and he gladly bought drinks for Ethel and her friends. As the months went by, he had grown fond of her. It wasn't love exactly, but she seemed interested in him and he thought she was fun.

After breakfast one Friday at Mary's house, George made an announcement. "I am to be married tomorrow," he said matter-of-factly. Mary looked at her father.

"Married!" she said in astonishment. "And who are you marrying?" George explained that he had been seeing Ethel for some time, but Mary was not convinced that it was a wise move.

"Ah well, it will get you out from under my feet," she said as she looked him straight in the eye.

George packed up his few belongings the next day, went to the registry office with Ethel and they became man and wife. They set up house together in Kilmarnock in a small flat. He was glad of the company but he hadn't bargained on having to do most of the housework himself. After a while he grew tired of Ethel's demands.

"Where's all yer money from Australia?" she would ask him constantly. "I need a new dress."

George would give her the money for a new dress or a new hat, but they were only ever worn to the Waverly. It was their one source of entertainment.

In his quiet moments, he reflected on his life. His marriage to Mary had been for the most part happy, and any unhappiness, he felt, had been largely due to him and the moods he found himself in. But Mary always knew how to snap him out of it, how to run the household and keep a clean and sober house. He missed her more than ever and longed to be with her again. He missed her singing around the house, and chastising him for coming home full of whisky. But most of all he missed her tender touch and the love they shared. He knew that marriage to someone else was a poor substitute, but he had made his bed and he would lie in it. At least he had company – and someone to drink with.

Chapter 56 (1969) Scotland

AUSTRALIA BOUND

Bill had not taken the news of his father's remarriage well, but they continued to correspond and George was always glad to receive some news of his family in Australia. He regaled his grandchildren in Scotland with stories about their Uncle Willie in Australia. Their differences were largely forgotten, and Willie's reputation had grown to hero status from the stories George would tell about how he had worked hard and made a new life for himself. Mary's youngest son George, now twenty, had started to show an interest in his uncle and Australia.

"Do you think I would do well in Australia?" George asked his grandfather.

"I don't see why not," George said. "It would do ye good, lad, just as it did yer uncle good."

"I'd like to go there for two years and make some money then come back and make my life here in Scotland. Do you think Uncle Willie would let me stay with him?"

"Why don't you write to him and find out," George said, excited that the lad was starting to make plans for his future.

The news back from Australia was positive and young George was soon embarking on the trip that his uncle and grandfather had taken. He was greeted at Hamilton Wharf by his uncle, and the aunt and cousins he had never met. He had expected that the children would all be young, and was surprised that Carmel was now fourteen, Colleen was twelve and Bruce was nine. He was taken back to the house at Ebbw Vale and stayed in the same room that his grandfather has stayed in eight years before.

At first, he enjoyed all the things about Australia that every newcomer enjoyed. He lapped up the sun and trips to the ocean, the cold beer and the seafood. But it wasn't like home. He missed his family. He took a job at the woollen mills and was surprised to learn that his Aunt Myrt was expecting another child. Their third daughter Leesa Maree was born on May 14, 1970 weighing just two pounds and nine ounces, and it was feared that she would not live, but she survived and was able to be brought home when she was three months old.

George saw his uncle as a tough man, and he was right. He worked hard and played hard and remained a man's man. Bill now mostly drank at the Commercial Hotel at Redbank, near to the woollen mills where George worked. He often witnessed his uncle in action as the unofficial bouncer at the pub. Whenever there was a disturbance in the public bar, Bill was called upon to eject the troublemaker. After having already consumed several beers, Bill was ready for a fight and he seemed to enjoy the opportunity to show his physical prowess. Many a man was sent flying down the pub steps on the end of a McMurdo fist. He'd grown up tough and it was his toughness that had seen him pull through accidents and pain. Perhaps he was trying to prove something to himself. After all, a doctor in Scotland had told him that he would live to only forty-two years of age and he was now forty-four. He had a great confidence in himself and his abilities. He could take care of himself and his family. If anyone or anything dared to knock him down, he would come back faster and stronger.

George knew that his uncle's work in the mines was dangerous, and the reality of it was brought home that year when one of Bill's neighbours was trapped in a cave-in at the Rhondda mine in Ipswich. Several others had been rescued, but his neighbour, Charlie, was trapped underground for three days. He was eventually rescued but had to have his right arm amputated.

"He'll never get the renovations on his house finished, now," Bill said to his mates at New Hope Colliery. "I'm going to give him a hand and if anyone wants to join me, I'll be at Charlie's place at 4.30am tomorrow before we start the shift."

The next morning, Bill was on the roof of Charlie's house at the break of dawn, hammering down nails. He looked up and saw three car loads of men, with ladders, saws and shovels, pull up outside of Charlie's house. They worked for two hours before heading off to the pit for their day's work, and came back every morning for a week until the extensions to the house were finished. Bill had been prepared to do all the work himself, but he had a way of inspiring confidence in people to follow him.

It was those leadership qualities that had stood him in good stead as he worked his way up in the mines from Shot Firer, to Deputy and Check Inspector. He was a leader who took his responsibilities seriously, and the men trusted him. He found himself back in the classroom, but this time it was a subject in which he was interested. To gain certification as a Deputy, he was examined on the practical aspects of mining and related safety practices, strata control, ventilation, gas management, gas drainage, spontaneous combustion and emergency response. His experience as a Shot Firer meant he could deal with explosives and related hazards and he was able to handle emergencies. He needed to be able to apply legislative requirements and identify potential hazards. He was a man who could think on his feet and come up with solutions to ensure the safety of his men. He was clear and concise when writing his reports, and management knew that if Bill didn't think it was safe to go underground, the men would not enter the mine until the problem had been fixed. He earned the respect of his men and the mine's management.

Young George was ready to return to Scotland, and in 1971 stepped on a plane to take him home. He had learned lessons that would last him a life time and he was eager to move on to the next stage of his life. He had heard that his grandfather was not happy and he longed to see him.

Chapter 57 (1975) Scotland

LONELY TO THE END

It had not been a happy marriage. In fact, George had made one of the biggest mistakes of his life. He missed Mary and could not replace her with Ethel – the two women could not have been more opposite. Several times he had left her and gone to live with his daughter Mary, but he knew that she had her own family to care for, and he always returned to the flat he shared with Ethel. He was coming to the end of his life and he felt no peace. He was now seventy-seven years old, and slower these days. The long walks that he had liked to take were replaced by short walks, for he no longer had the energy. He could often be found at the New Cumnock Cemetery, opposite the Knockshinnoch Colliery site, visiting the grave of his wife Mary, much to the annoyance of his current wife Ethel. His pipe remained firmly clenched between his teeth as he sat at a table at the Waverly and studied the people. Old men like him, nursing whiskies, and young men trying to outdrink each other. It was the same in Australia and in Scotland, he mused - old people, surrounded by people, yet living a lonely existence. He finished his drink and walked home to his cold, empty flat while Ethel stayed to drink with her friends. He couldn't be bothered making anything to eat and took himself straight to bed. He opened a book that he kept in a drawer by his bed, and took out the photo of Mary that he had hidden there. He kissed her picture and placed it under his pillow, then drifted off to sleep.

George passed away in the night. His last thoughts were of his beloved Mary. He had suffered a heart attack from hardening of the arteries, and the next morning he was taken from the flat at 18 Bankend Place, Kilmarnock and prepared for burial in the plot with Mary. The family knew that that was what he wanted and it seemed like the right thing to do.

After hundreds of years of living, loving and dying in Scotland, the last male McMurdo in the direct paternal line, had been laid to rest on Scottish soil.

Chapter 58 (1978) Australia

THE SIBLINGS REUNITE

Bill's sisters' families in Scotland had grown and moved on to start families of their own. Mary and Margaret often went on holiday together and decided to go to Australia to see their long lost brother and meet his family. They stayed with Bill for eight weeks and soaked up the sun in his backyard. He took them for a week's holiday to Fingal Head, just over the New South Wales border, where he now took the family every year for their Christmas holidays. Palm Beach had become too crowded and he had found a quiet village where he enjoyed fishing and going out on the Tweed River in his boat.

His sisters thought back to their childhood days and remembered that Willie had always been headstrong and gotten what he wanted. He had a good life in Australia and they were pleased for him, but disappointed that he had never returned home. They thought of their mother's heartbreak at losing him, and the sadness of their father's last days when he could have used a son to talk to. But they realised too, that every man must choose his own path and move in his own direction. He called a spade a spade, as was the Australian way, and he was afraid of no man.

They watched him and marvelled at the man he had become – one minute fiery and ready to take someone's head off, the next telling jokes and displaying a generosity that they could not fault. A friend of Willie's had told them of how he helped out in the floods that engulfed Ipswich in 1974. He took his boat and ferried former neighbours and their possessions to safety, and paid for some of them to have new carpets in their homes. The house he had owned at Bundamba had gone under water and an electric light pole had fallen straight down the centre of the house. It was fortuitous that they had moved away from there twenty years before. He would not speak of any of his generous acts, and preferred to cultivate the tough man exterior. He was a complex human being, and he was their brother.

The three of them had been through tough times and it had made them all strong. They were happy for Willie, but they couldn't help wondering what his life might have been like had he stayed in Scotland.

Chapter 59 (1986) Australia

NEVER AGAIN TO GO UNDERGROUND

Bill had suffered another injury in the mines when a large piece of coal fell from the roof and hit him on the leg. He was taken by ambulance to the doctor's surgery and off work for a few weeks. His body had been battered and scarred over the years from coal falls and when he reached his sixtieth birthday, he felt the time had come to say goodbye to the mines.

The management at New Hope Colliery valued his years of experience as a team leader, and his extensive knowledge of mining. He was offered a job 'up on top' in the office, but he had worked 'down below' all his life and he couldn't betray his men by 'sitting with management'. He had grown up in the shadow of Keir Hardie, and solidarity with his men was important to him. He was also approached to join the Mines Rescue Team, but he wanted to enjoy his retirement years away from coal mining, where he could stand in the sun every day and breathe in fresh air. He was ending an era that had started in the early 1800s when his great-great-great-grandfather, George, had left the farmer's life in the tranquil, green fields around Dumfries in Scotland, and gone down a coal mine in search of steady work and regular pay.

They sold the house at Ebbw Vale and bought a house at Fingal Head in New South Wales, opposite the Tweed River. They called the house Lochview. He had ended up in New South Wales, just as he thought he might when he first applied to go to Australia. There was a lagoon down the back of the house and he would put crab pots in and catch huge 'muddies'. He could go surf fishing on the pristine beach or row over to Cook Island and stay a few nights in a hut with some friends. He could walk across the road and wet a line in the river, and come home for a cold beer at the end of a day doing just as he pleased. His family had grown and soon he had grandchildren. He delighted in taking them out in his boat, teaching them to swim, singing them songs and telling them stories about his early life in Scotland. He had a zest for life and living.

Chapter 60 (2012) Australia

THE END OF THE LINE

It was another ordinary day. It had been a long, sizzling Australian Summer and now the last days of Autumn were drawing to a close. After a hot night, Bill rose from his bed at 5.30am to take the dog for a walk. He was fast approaching his eighty-sixth birthday, but was still spry.

"Here, Bonnie, time for a walk. Here, lass," he called and the little white dog jumped up at the sight of him. She reminded him of Sandy, the little white dog he had when he first got married, but that little dog had been taken by a tick. She was a faithful companion and she looked into his eyes as he fastened the leash around her neck. They walked out the back door of the house and started down the steps – dog and master off for a walk. Bonnie pulled at the lead to cross the road which was quiet in the early morning. They enjoyed a long walk along the Tweed River and Bill picked up the newspaper at the local store. They headed back to the house as the sun rose higher in the sky. Bill let Bonnie off the lead and she followed him down the backyard to his shed as he baited up a crab pot with fish fillets and then walked down to the lagoon to throw it in. He left the carcass of the fish on the sink and would dispose of it after breakfast. He tended to his vegetable garden in the early morning sun, and waved to the lads next door, who were off for an early morning surf. Just an ordinary day.

By 5pm that afternoon, Bill was fighting for his life in the Tweed Hospital. He had been in exceptional physical and mental health, especially for a man of eighty-five, and it took a massive stroke to bring him down. He was not expected to last through the night and the family had been told to prepare for the worst. But he had had so many close calls throughout his life, they were certain this was another and they expected him to bounce back. The great communicator had been rendered unable to speak, but he remained lucid and fought on for seventeen days before finally surrendering to the light.

The spark that had touched so many lives was extinguished. The young man who had set off from Scotland with the dream of making his fortune and returning home triumphant, had had a change of course. His fortune was found in the family he had created and the friends he had made. After hundreds of years in an unbroken direct line, this branch of the McMurdo name would carry on, but not in Scotland - in Australia.

Willie had made his life in the lucky country, but a piece of his heart forever remained in Scotland, with his ain folk.

SCOTTISH WORDS

Aboot – About

Afeared – Afraid

Ain – own

Auld - old

Aw – All

Aye – Yes

Bonnie - Beautiful

Box bed – A pine bed built into the wall of a house to save space

Braw – Fine/good

But'n'Ben – Two roomed house (But – livingroom/kitchen

Ben – Bedroom

Cannae – Cannot

Deid – Dead

Dinnae – Don't

Dinnae fash yoursel' – don't get upset

Doesnae – Does not

Doon – Down

Dram – Small measure of whisky

Drap – Drop

Faither – Father

Fash – Trouble/bother

Frae – From

Feet – Measurement: 1 foot = 30cm

Fer – For

Flesher - Butcher

Halfpenny – Half a penny
Hame – Home
Heed – Mind
Heid – Head
Hissel' – Himself
Hoose – House

Inches – Measurement: 1 inch = 2.5cm

Jeely piece – Jam sandwich

Kirkyard - Churchyard

Midden – Dunghill
Mither – Mother
Muir - Moorland

Nae – No
Neeps – Turnips
Never heed – don't bother
No' - Not

Och – Oh
Oor – Our
Oot – Out
Ounce – Unit of weight

Pence - Pennies
Pie-eyed - Drunk
Piece box – Miner's Lunchbox
Pounds – Currency: 20 shillings; weight = 16 ounces (about 500g)

Shilling – Currency: (AUS) 10 cents; (UK) 10p; (US) 10 cents
Shooders – Shoulders
Sook – Suck
Sweeties – Lollies; candy

Tak – Take

Tatties - Potatoes

Telt - Told

Toorie – Tassel on a bonnet

Weans – Children

Wee – Small

Wi' - With

Ye – You

Yer – Your

4341860R00124

Printed in Germany
by Amazon Distribution
GmbH, Leipzig